ChangeAbility

how artists
activists
and
awakeners
navigate
change

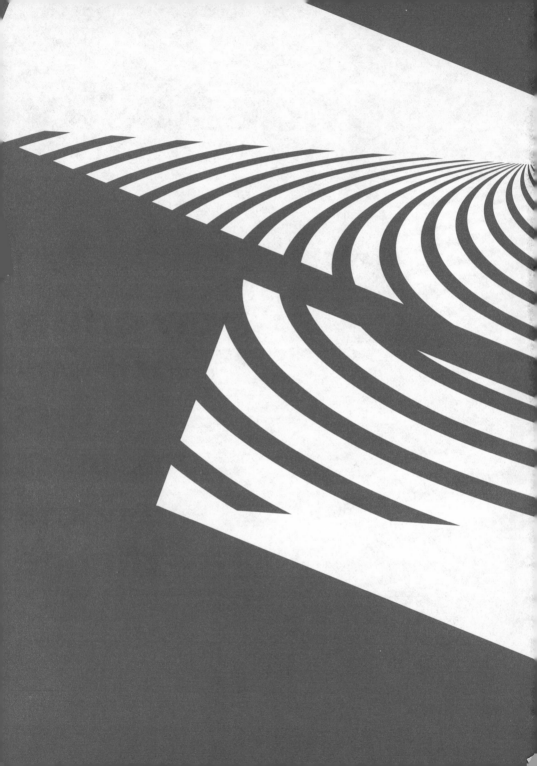

ChangeAbility

how artists
activists
and
awakeners
navigate
change

SHARON WEIL

A Genuine Archer Book | Los Angeles, Calif.

A GENUINE ARCHER BOOK

ARCHER/RARE BIRD

601 West 26th Street · Suite 325 · New York · NY 10001
archerlit.com

Copyright © 2016 by Sharon Weil

FIRST HARDCOVER EDITION

Set in Minion
Printed in the United States

10 9 8 7 6 5 4 3 2 1

Publisher's Cataloging-in-Publication data

Names: Weil, Sharon, author.

Title: Changeability : how artists, activists, and awakeners navigate change / Sharon Weil.

Description: First Hardcover Edition | A Genuine Archer Book | New York [NY], Los Angeles [CA]: Archer, 2016.

Identifiers: ISBN 9781941729137

Subjects: LCSH Change. | Art and social action. | Art and society. | Social change in art. | Artists—Political activity. | Art—Political aspects. | Healing in art. | BISAC ART / General | SOCIAL SCIENCE / General | POLITICAL SCIENCE / Political Process / Political Advocacy.

Classification: LCC NX180.P64 W45 2016 | DDC 701.0309/04—dc23

To the spirit of Change and all the brave souls who embrace it.

And to Emilie Conrad, dear friend and mentor, who taught me
about the movement of change, and how to ride its possibilities.

CONTENTS

PASSING

CREATIVITY

Rebecca Mark
Writer, poet, professor, at Tulane University
Words & Waves

Amy McEachern
Moving, packing, and organizing specialist, Creative Moving
Change, One Box at a Time

Jackie Welch Schlicher
Actress, singer, writer…ceramicist
Creative Translation

Adam Wolpert
Painter, group facilitator, codirector of Intentional Communities Occidental Arts and Ecology Center
The Art of Agreement

EMBODIMENT & MEDITATION

Camille Maurine
Performance artist, author, teacher of Embodied Meditation for Women
Embodiment Secrets for Women

Robert Litman
Movement and breath educator, The Breathable Body
The Breathable Body/Anatomy of Anxiety

Harvey Ruderian
Structural biodynamic bodyworker: Aston Patterning, Rolfing, Dynamic Cranial Sacral
Listening With My Hands

Fred Sugerman
Movement artist and educator
Becoming a Change Artist

NORMAL GUESTS

FOOD & ECOLOGY

Claire Hope Cummings
Environmental lawyer, journalist, and author of
*Uncertain Peril: Genetic Engineering and the
Future of Seeds*
GMO: The Uncertain Peril

Ann Gentry
Founder, Real Food Daily, Los Angeles
You Are What You Eat

Penny Livingston-Stark
Permaculture designer and teacher, cofounder
of Regenerative Design Institute
We Have the Solution

James Stark
Community leader, cofounder, and codirector
of Regenerative Design Institute
*Permaculture & The Ecology of Leadership/
Communities are Ecosystems*

Michael Stocker
Naturalist, bioacoustician, musician, Executive
Director of Ocean Conservation Research
Saving the Sea

REVISIONING MEDICINE

Amber Gray
Body-based psychotherapist
Fear, Trauma, and Restoring Resilience

Deena Metzger
Author, teacher, healer
Revisioning Medicine

John Weeks
Former Executive Director of Academic Con-
sortium for Complementary and Alternative
Health Care (ACCAHC)
Integrating Alternative/Mainstream Medicine

SOCIAL CHANGE

Corinne Bourdeau
Producer and public relations for Social
Change Films
The Passionate Filmmaker

Paul Rogat Loeb
Writer, speaker, activist, awakener
Soul of a Citizen

Beth Rosales
Senior philanthropic advisor
Strategic Giving for Social Change

Jacques Verduin
Restorative justice leader, director Insight-Out
GRIP—Guiding Rage Into Power

Tom Verner & Janet Fredericks
Magician & Artist, Citizen Ambassadors
Magicians Without Borders

SPIRITUALITY

Amanda Foulger
Core shamanic practitioner and teacher
The Spirit of All Things

Rachel Lang
Astrological consultant, intuitive healer
Portals to Inner Change

*Each of these guests, artists, authors,
activists, and awakeners participated in
conversations about seeding change in the
world on the* Passing 4 Normal Podcast.

INTRODUCTION

N 2014, I BECAME EXTREMELY INTERESTED in the topic of change. Life seemed to be moving so quickly. Personally, and globally, the world was expressing dynamic change. Damaging storms, floods, and droughts. Wars, insurgences, and displaced refugees. The chaos of health reforms, the miracle promise of same-sex marriage, and the constant traffic disruption from the Metro transit line being built through my hometown of West Los Angeles. I shared the loss of several dear friends and family members who died. Additionally, a remarkable number of projects and endeavors I had been involved with for years came to their natural conclusion, faded to gray, or fractured in disarray. I was smack center in the vortex of change.

I became occupied with many questions: what is the nature of this changing life, and the nature of our responses to its ever-unfolding movement? I asked myself, "How do we initiate change? Inspire it in others? How do we effectively adapt to the all the many changes that come?" Underneath those questions, was really this one: "How do we find the courage to bring about change, or let ourselves be changed by the forces that shape us? In the face of change, how do we become brave?"

A year earlier, I wrote and published the wild and wacky romantic-mishap adventure *Donny and Ursula Save the World*. This outrageously funny, yet gravely serious, novel about love, sex, and genetically modified seeds (GMOs) is the story of how two highly neurotic and unlikely lovers become even less likely activists and heroes. They save the world from a greedy plot by a nefarious agribusiness giant to own the world's food supply by owning all its seeds. My interest in the courage to change and what it takes to rise to activism came from my fictional characters, Donny and Ursula, who were reluctant activists, at best. The questions in this story were: "When is enough, enough, and we must take action on behalf of what we love?" And, again: "What does it take to be brave?" These characters played out my questions about rising to activism because this was the issue long pressing on my heart.

So, I started talking with people. Fascinating, accomplished, yet everyday people who in their own unique and inventive ways have created or inspired effective grassroots change in the areas of life they care about. I realized that I knew many amazing people within my own circle, or no more than two degrees of separation away. Because of my particular interests and inquiry, these innovators came from social justice movements, permaculture, food, alternative medicine and somatic practices, spirituality, and the arts. I called them "seeders" to match the seed theme in my book, because they were planting so many new and fruitful ideas.

I created a podcast, *Passing 4 Normal: Conversations with Artists, Authors, Activists, and Awakeners about Seeding Change in the World.* In half-hour conversations I was able to share something of the guest's experience and perspective with a larger listening audience. I intentionally programed an eclectic mix of guests to look at the issue of change from many disciplines and perspectives. Unusual couplings add dimension to the whole, and I am fond of counterpoint as a way to find surprising relationships that emerge from placing seeming opposites side by side.

Somatic practitioners, writers, social activists, artists, teachers, permaculture designers, a philanthropic advisor, a vegan restaurant owner, an astrologer, a prison reformer, a bioacoustician, a magician and a mime, a group facilitator, a social change film marketer, a professional home mover, a shamanic healer…each had something remarkable to share, not only about their own work and approach to change, but also about how they find the courage and passion to do so. Often, they are working in the face of seemingly insurmountable odds and devastating disappointment, and yet they continue on. How do they do it?

My hope and intention for the podcast was that by hearing these amazing individuals, listeners would be inspired to make the necessary or desired changes that are in their own hearts and lives. Taking courage from example—*If they did it, so can I!*

In my first season, I featured twenty-four interviews. My second season has informally begun, and my guests continue to amaze, inspire, and encourage me.

Some of the guests are well-known, like Deena Metzger, Claire Hope Cummings, and Paul Rogat Loeb. Others are less public. All of the guests are accomplished experts, highly regarded in their fields, often choosing to place the spotlight on others as part of their strategy for being most effective.

Each time I would add a new guest interview to the lineup, it would change the constellation of the group. Depending upon their area of contribution, whether they were a man or woman, or their more serious or lighthearted tone, each guest's particular worldview changed the shape and the dimension of the entire podcast, week by week.

I like to lead from curiosity. The innocence of genuine inquiry serves me well and opens me to surprises. As an interviewer, by asking an honest question without knowing the answer, I was often delighted by the answer that came. Sometimes the unexpected answer led to more discovery; sometimes it reinforced what I already thought to be true.

Listeners to the podcast have remarked to me how much they've enjoyed this aspect of the recorded conversations, as if they'd been allowed to pull up a chair to a really lively, spontaneous exchange, already in progress. I'd ask questions of the guests and allow their responses to lead me to the next question, creating a path through the conversation together. At the same time, because of what I already did know about the guest and their work, I tried to make sure I drew out certain information and perspectives for the listeners to hear and learn from.

I say this because living in inquiry, speaking from that place, requires me to recognize the changes and shifts that are occurring in the moment, and be able to summon the resources within myself to make changes in response, even in something as simple as a conversation. Therefore, each of the conversations with my guests was the particular play of where our mutual inquiry took us on that day.

Though these accomplished experts come from different disciplines and concerns, I began hearing similarities in what they were prescribing as the necessary elements for navigating change. A certain recipe was emerging for effective activism, personal transformation, and good, balanced health. Without knowing it, many of the guests were speaking to the same elements for affecting change, whether it was to initiate a desired change, or adapt in response to a significant change that had already occurred. So, I wanted to present these insights to you in a book. Here it is.

There are three other activities of my life that bear mentioning here, as they have shaped me, and my thinking, in indelible ways. The first is my immersion as a teacher in the profound fluid movement practice of Continuum. The second are the years I spent working with environmental and social change activists as president of The Lia Fund, a private foundation funding solutions to climate change, holistic health and healing, and community arts, all in support of the recognition of whole systems relationships to the natural world. The third is my lifetime in film and television as a writer, director, producer, editor, and all the necessary ladder-climbing assistant jobs that led to each of those positions.

Continuum, a movement discipline created by Emilie Conrad, and with great contribution to its development by Susan Harper, recognizes that everything is in movement, all of the time. As humans, we are comprised of approximately 75 percent water, and it is our fluid nature, and the movement of the fluids within the body, that allows us to be more mutable than we can ever imagine. As humans, our bodies are in constant fluid flux, stabilized in time and gravity in order to function. It is the nature of the change in fluids themselves—expressed in the fluid movement of the cells and tissues of the body—that is the agent of change, health, and healing in the body. This global perspective of a mutable, resonant, and related world provides me with an expansive view of bio-intelligence and natural design that permeates all my curiosities and conversations.

As a Continuum teacher, I developed an anti-aging program called The Ageless Body®. This program was in recognition that people needed a specialized focus on fitness that addressed changes in joints, vitality, sensuality, and flexibility as we age. One of the primary issues of change in the body as we age is the change that comes from loss of fluid in the tissues, so using the principles of fluid movement and fluid strength in the body, I was able to create exercises and new ways of thinking that could help people regain and maintain strength and vitality as they age—at any age.

Over the course of this teaching, I came to recognize that the changes in aging went far beyond the mere physical. There was also a tremendous amount of loss, grief, stress, diminishment, and an increased need to be able to find flexibility in response to the change—any change, all the change—that comes.

Rather than looking at the program as anti-aging, I began calling it Moving with Change, because that was the true purpose of this flexible strengthening that I was addressing and training. I was teaching how we can move with presence, dexterity, strategy, courage, and strength in response to any and all change. These are vital skills at any age, but become a necessary focus as our tissues and circumstances become tighter and worn down. These are also the vital skills we all need to learn as we face a world that throws us enormous and challenging economic turns, environmental events, and social change at such rapid speed we can barely keep our bearings. Becoming skilled at navigating change is one of the best and most necessary skills a person can acquire!

So, as you can see, I have been thinking about change, and what is needed in order to be responsive to change, for some time now.

In 2006 my sister passed away from breast cancer. Before she passed, she asked that a charitable foundation be created to help fund and further the issues she cared so dearly about: creativity, art, holistic health, nature and the environment, children, justice, and people who did not have access to advantages or the services they needed. She appointed four board members and requested participation from eight advisors, all experienced in the progressive nonprofit world. Along with an immensely experienced philanthropic advisor, we went on a journey together, on behalf of holistic change, that funded many worthy, creative organizations, and forged friendships and learning among the foundation members.

I have tremendous respect for the fund's advisors and for our activist grantees. From 2007–2013, The Lia Fund granted small- and medium-size grants to over one hundred organizations engaged in environmental and social change, the arts, and holistic health. I got to see, up close, the step-by-step and day-by-day courage, moxie, and resourcefulness required to be an activist. I was privileged to witness the passion turned to action, and the well-considered creative strategies set in place by so many dedicated, hardworking people. Through my participation with them all, and through the fund, I joined them.

Several of these people have been interviewed on the podcast, with many more to come in upcoming seasons. There is so much we can learn from each and every one of them, just as there is still so much for me to learn.

In writing this book, many of the skills I have pulled from my bag of tricks were learned from the time I have spent as a film editor, and as a screenwriter. My ability to hold these twenty-five voices from the podcast and to "let the story emerge from the footage" comes from editing documentary films where often I am presented with hours upon hours of footage with no real script. The story is shaped from the material I have been given, and I have to be able to see that story and pull it forward. I also have to keep track of all the material as that story appears, in case there's another story that's the better story. As a screenwriter, I've had to employ the paradox of both a committed surety in my writing and an endless flexibility because scenes, dialogue, characters, action, even the premise can change and change again depending upon whose notes you are satisfying, and the ever-morphing considerations of actual production—like casting, budget, and whether the winter story you have just written has to be filmed in the summer because that's when your star is available, or you have a prep school as your main location and that's when it's available and empty of students. In other words, I've had to be very passionate and then unattached to my work.

I need to tell you, I have not always been so brave or productive. Fresh out of film school, I used to sit by the telephone for a good hour or more rehearsing a cold call to a producer to ask for work. By the time I had talked myself into picking up the phone to dial, it would be lunchtime, so of course I couldn't call because they'd be out. Then I'd have to wait until after two o'clock. Most likely, once I did get through my own wall of fear to make the call, I'd have to leave a message with the assistant, and then wait for when or if they'd call me back. This meant staying near the phone for a least the rest of the day, if not the next. In those days we had no cell phones and no remote access to answering machines. Just cigarettes, coffee, and lots of adrenaline lost.

I've earned my courage by diving through my fears one wave at a time, over and over again. So have my guests. So, I imagine, have you. Or, I imagine, you want to be able to dive through the waves more often without fear of crashing on the rocks.

Change brings newness and, though I wasn't always this way, I have become familiar with the territory of newness. There has been so much of it in these past few years, so many firsts. Going from screenwriter/producer to author/publisher was the exciting journey my novel set me on. I should have known. The word "novel," after all, means "new." And it means "different"— which can also mean new. Hah!

I am not a researcher. I am not a journalist. I'm a gatherer, a gleaner, a synthesizer, a writer. As a writer, my job is to make meaning. My charge is to listen and synthesize what I hear, and then present it back in a form that invites a smooth entry into the subject, character, or story. In this case, the story is about change, and the characters are these wonderful experts I have had the privilege to be in conversation with. I've used excerpts from the podcast interviews to take you, the reader, on a multifaceted journey in and around the topic of change and its many considerations and expressions. For some of the guests, I went back to them with additional questions to hear more about how they navigate and manifest their own ever-changing worlds. This book, by no means, is the *only* conversation to be had about change. What it is, though, is the *particular* conversation I had with these brilliant companions, and it's a fascinating one. These agents of change have incredible insight to offer.

For this book, *ChangeAbility*, the questions posed by my fictional activists, Donny and Ursula, led me to speak with the real ones. Their answers are fresh, thoughtful, inspiring, and instructive. Together, their voices, guided by my inquiry, create an interesting reflection on navigating the one certainty we have in life—it's all going to change! How can we move with change in this changing world and be the change we know we can be?

Let all these voices be an inspiration to you. Let them give you a nudge of courage, some encouragement, a strategy, or an excitement to try something new. Follow their advice and examples, and I promise your next changes will arrive with more grace and ease.

SL
FAST
NAVIGATE
INITIA
EXTERNAL
TERNAL
FE
RESTORE
SPIRE
ADAPT
GRIE
GRI
HEALING
INSPIR
RESISTANCE
NAVIGATE
ANGE NAVIGATE

PART ONE

Navigating Change is the New Stability

CHANGE

SCIENTISTS TELL US OUR WORLD IS in constant flux.
Ever moving, ever changing, nothing remains stationary, constant, or repeatable despite my fixed perceptions and need for stability. The cosmos, our Earth, and the microcosm of the human body are each and together intersecting, variable, creative events. The universe is in chaos, or divine order, depending on whom it is you talk with—but it's in constant motion, nonetheless.

Spiritual traditions and indigenous cultures know that we as humans are all connected to the totality of the natural world, and that connection is our original belonging from which we are never separated. That connection is multidimensional, resonant, impermanent, and constantly unfolding. I don't know about you, but so often I forget to live that way, and need to be reminded.

> "Various cultures see Creation as an ongoing event—not something that happened just once. And we are all part of it."
> —**Amanda Foulger**, shamanic healer

Change is our nature, yet I can become completely unbalanced, uprooted, toppled, grief-stricken, overwhelmed, resistant, or afraid of the changes that move me. Or frustrated, anxious, or thrust into despair by the change that does not come, and thwarted or infuriated by the change I cannot control. Sometimes I'm tickled pink, but that will change too.

"Why would we even talk about change? It's a reflection on our cultural cul-de-sac we're in right now. From the time when we were intimately connected as an integral part of the life system of the planet, we were living change. We were change. We were a verb, not a noun. In that kind of an ecology, it would be humorous to talk about change."

—**James Stark**, permaculturist and community leader

We live in an accelerated time of dynamic, complex change. Advances in technology and communications, coupled with unpredictable climate changes, natural disasters, and population shifts have us living with levels of stress not experienced before in our lifetimes.

Life can seem sudden, random, or to be moving at impossible speed. Just when I think I understand a pattern, it changes. Just when I fall into a comfortable rhythm, something disrupts it. Just when I get used to this version of my smartphone, it's upgraded. An event as simple as the movement of the produce section in my grocery store disorients me each time I go shopping. Or a more significant event like a divorce, a cancer diagnosis, or losing my home in a fire can completely upend my life. Large or small, it's always something, right? And often, it's one change cascading after another, without stop. It seems like all I do is accommodate change, and at times, not very well.

Modern life constantly asks us to respond to the changing circumstances beyond our control. Vast geographies and populations are in desperate need of change, or are changing in unexpected ways. I live in the proclaimed paradise of Southern California where people used to hose down the sidewalks with amply flowing water to clear off fallen leaves, and now we are pulling out our lawns in response to the drought. A friend recently returned from Nepal with photographs of ancient temples that just weeks later were broken to rubble from the devastating earthquake there. Violence, war, and food scarcity have permanently displaced refugees in Sudan and Somalia. The same dangers have compelled Syrian families to flee to Turkey and to Europe. Industrial progress is endangering the health of millions in China from air and water pollution. Oil spills off of Santa Barbara and nuclear reactor waste spills from Fukushima threaten the global oceans. You could watch the news on any number of devices and become numb from all the need. Stress wears us down. Fear shuts us down. It is so difficult, at times, to know what to do.

I honestly don't know anyone who is not in some state of being overwhelmed from trying to integrate the constant barrage of information we receive, and from struggling to accommodate the myriad of changes that shape and reshape our lives. So many people I know are trying to "simplify their lives" as a response to "too much" or "not enough" but even that requires making big changes. Even welcome change is a change.

> "The only person who likes change is a wet baby."
>
> —Mark Twain

I can talk about global change, and environmental change, but there is also personal change. Personal habits I want to transform: consume more vegetables, less sugar; choose more exercise, less driving; drink more water, less alcohol; express my true feelings, less whining and complaining. There is grief to heal and loss to be recovered. Sometimes it feels that change is occurring much too fast, sometimes not nearly fast enough and I am stuck in a rut. Or perhaps, I simply want a different outcome; I don't like this change, I want another one.

> "Change is the only constant; that's the reality of what life is about. It's always changing at any level that you look at. If we could be present with that truth, in most cases, the movement of change would either be easier, or we'd understand somewhere in the back of our mind that everything in the way of that is my own creation of resistance."
>
> —**Robert Litman**, breath and movement educator

So, really, what is challenging is not so much change itself—that is a constant. Every breath is new, every moment unlike the last. What is challenging is to develop the ability to meet change as it comes, be it a change of plans or the loss of a loved one. What is needed is to harness the ability to initiate change in the direction of my desire, like starting a new health regime, or launching a community campaign to save the bird sanctuary of the wetlands against real estate developers. What I experience about change is either the flow of the movement of change or my resistance to it. The resistance, though it comes in many forms, begins with the mistaken belief that I am somehow separate from change, and that I can control it, rather than aligning myself with change as it makes itself apparent, and ride it. It is my illusion of separation that even allows me to have the human construct that divides me from all nature. The construct creates time, comparison, and therefore the concept of change as something that is happening to me, rather than, as James Stark puts it, being in the "ongoing verb of change."

What I experience of change is either the flow of the movement of change or my resistance to it.

Learning to recognize the movement of change gives me the advantage of being able to adapt to new circumstances. Learning to work with change, rather than against it, can facilitate more ease, and less stress in my life. This is the purpose of this book, to help you learn how to facilitate change with more effect and ease in order to have what I call ChangeAbility.

> "Whether change is fearful or whether we thrive in areas of change really has to do with how we frame the phenomena of change, how we look at what life is."
>
> —James Stark

Whether the change is coming from internal motivation or an external call, knowing how to create desired and necessary change greatly affects my health, happiness, and subsistence. Becoming fluid and fluent in receiving and responding to the changes that come is also essential to my well-being in every way. The ability to navigate change is the most essential survival skill we need today. Navigating change is the new stability.

To have ChangeAbility, the ability to effectively navigate change, requires me to be both flexible and responsive, and at the same time focused and harnessed, whether I am initiating something new, inspiring change in others, or adapting to changes that come. In this ever-changing world, the best I can do is become a highly skilled and responsive change-maker and change-rider. If I don't, it is likely that my fears and resistance will cause rigidity and stress that can lead to lack of resourcefulness, illness, and quite possibly despair. How can I develop diverse responses to complex change that allows receptivity, flexibility, mutability, and purpose?

Fortunately for all of us, there are those individuals who are able to successfully harness the ongoing flux of change towards a particular end. They are effecting what they perceive of as necessary change, whether it's to change the world or to change themselves. They have developed strategies that have allowed them to recognize and respond with appropriate action. Innovators, transformers, visionaries, dreamers, activators—I call them seeders, change-makers, brave people, big-hearted fools. This is how I think of the twenty-five people featured in this book. Dedicated people, they might be working local and small or with a larger reach, but their influence is felt in ways that build and expand. Not only do they inspire me, they have strategies they can teach us all about how we might be innovators and transformers, heeding the call of our hearts, too.

When I began the podcast show, *Passing 4 Normal Podcast,* (that eventually led to this book), I was delighted, and a bit nervous, to be able to conduct interviews with many of my personal heroes—people who I regarded as engaged with creating change in the world, or helping others adapt to change in their lives. These guests were working with affecting change in a wide range of fields of interest and expertise. They were working at different levels of outreach and public notoriety. Each was highly regarded in their field and personally accessible to the listening audience.

The guests' interests and expertise fell into categories that held great interest to me: creativity, embodiment and meditation, food and ecology, social change, revisioning medicine, and spirituality. I consider each of the guests to be extremely creative and on the cutting edge of knowledge in their areas. It was fascinating to hear, week to week, just how many ways there are to create something meaningful and inspiring. I heard about the challenges they faced, as well, because the path to change is often slow, and guaranteed to be littered with hurdles and obstacles. I was intrigued to hear about their approaches, their similarities, and their differences, be they an artist, an activist, or what I call an awakener. Honestly, most of them were all three: artist, activist, and awakener; the ways in which they have integrated their talents made them all the more fascinating, and instructive.

Though we all shared the common value of creating change that benefits humanity and the health and healing for the individual and for the planet, I intentionally programed the podcast series to represent a wide range of applications in the exploration of the vast topic of change. How was change working in a program where violent offenders were becoming peacemakers by discovering the roots of their own violence? How does a change in diet change your health? How can a magic show in a refugee camp in Afghanistan bring about the hope that inspires the possibility for something more in life?

I wanted to know how others are doing it. I wanted to know how others play with change, dance with change, bring visions into being, survive deep trauma, create social movements, heal themselves and others, make reparation, remediate the soil, forgive, accept, mobilize others, read the waters...

I wanted to know how artists in particular work with change. So, I spoke with writers, painters, dancers, and an improvisational-actress-turned-potter who now plays with clay as her scene partner. I wanted to know how creative artists use abstraction, and metaphor, and the discovery of story to bring the imaginal world into form. I wanted to know just how much the magic of the creative process is a true courting of the unknown, and how artists come to face it, shape it, and present it to others.

I wanted to know specifically how activists work toward change, how they use their voices to build awareness for their cause, or try, as environmental activist Michael Stocker says, to "throw sticks in the spokes" of detrimental change. I spoke with permaculture experts, environmental activists, social justice activists, and individuals whose intention it is to creatively engage the public in social action. I wanted to know how they have the courage and the fortitude to continue on for seemingly hopeless causes against huge odds. I wanted to know how they deal with their losses as well as their triumphs, how they face danger, and how they bear their grief at the poisoning of the Earth. Mostly, I wanted to know how it is that they are brave.

I wanted to know how to awaken the spark toward art or activism in others, whether it's the spark to believe, the spark to action, or the spark to a deeper understanding, acceptance, or healing. I wanted to hear from these teachers, healers, spiritual leaders, and inspirational soothsayers how they are living examples to others for what is possible.

The podcast was simply meant to be an exploration, to cast a wide net for different perspectives in the name of change...but something else emerged.

In interviewing the guests on my podcast I began to discover common themes that they were all articulating. Over and over again, these highly creative and dedicated people were speaking to similar values and similar actions on behalf of making effective change. Coupled with my previous curiosities and explorations on the subject, I was able to peer through the lens of my experiences, and a theory and a map for change emerged. I was able to identify Seven Principles for Change. Seven interactive principles that are essential for helping us navigate through change. It is these Seven Principles for Change that form the recipe for ChangeAbility, the art of effectively navigating change.

As you know, change is a vast subject, and I can't possibly cover it all. So rather than write broadly, I am writing eclectically based on the conversations I had with these experts and where those conversations led us, and then led me in my thinking. Together, these artists, activists, and awakeners form a rich field of intelligence, as we look, together, on this whole question of ChangeAbility. The variety of their perspectives is of incredible value.

Often, depending upon my own interests and occupations, I seek out or listen to just one perspective. If I'm an environmentalist, I listen to environmentalists. If I am psychologically oriented, I listen to people with a psychological perspective. If I'm a Republican, I watch Fox News on television; if I'm a Democrat, I watch CNN. Even Google will give me search results based on my previous searches, so I might not ever go outside my immediate circle of information. This book is intentionally written as a diverse, interdisciplinary discussion that breaks out of the siloes of normal circles of information. It is a kaleidoscope constellation of the micro and the macro of the movement of change and many of its manifestations: the personal and the social, the human body and the body of the planet, the seen and the unseen forces, hope and despair, the practical and the magical. Throughout these chapters I will be presenting a story about the nature of change and change navigation that turns and turns that kaleidoscope, so that a new picture emerges. Writer and professor Rebecca Mark says, "New stories require new forms." Here's one now.

As a note, each chapter in this book is like a smaller conversation among the particular guest voices who spoke to these ideas. I consider each of these people to be teachers in their own right, whether or not they actually teach as a part of their profession. Each of these people has been deeply immersed in his or her field of practice and inquiry for twenty, thirty, forty years. Though several guests are not of the age to be considered elders, all have a wealth of experience-based wisdom to share, and have lived long enough and made enough mistakes and course corrections to know how the river of change flows, and how to make the most of riding the current. They each have developed a rich and specific vocabulary they use to speak about their issues of participation and concern. It has been a privileged experience for me to be able to absorb their particular language while looking for what it is that spans all language, the elements common to all change.

In writing about ChangeAbility, and putting the issue of change under great consideration, I have needed to put all these ideas to the test, or rather let's say they have tested me. Small changes and big changes have taken place as I write this book. I won't go into details, but I'm happy to report that I have greatly increased my own ChangeAbility over the course of this exploration. I have strengthened my own ability to effectively navigate change with ease. So, it works! That is one of the benefits of being a writer, you write yourself into a new future.

> "If you really think about it, there's no point in doing any writing at all if everything you are writing is not about change, because the point of writing is to access that creative potential in each of us that imagines the world differently, that imagines our immediate circumstance or story differently. We're writing because writing the script, the mark on the paper, actually informs us about prophesies that may be going on in our neuro-system, in our somatic wisdom, in our understanding of the politics of the situation, or even, as many people will find when they are experiencing the really catastrophic

moments in their lives, they will find themselves writing in order to figure out, 'How can I create this mess into this future self?'"

—**Rebecca Mark**, writer, poet, and professor

I am going to end our first chapter here with the image of Spider. Shamanic practitioner Amanda Foulger uses the spirits of animal guides to give us messages of support from the unseen worlds. Native Americans hold Spider or Spiderwoman as the one who weaves the web that holds the world together. Spider has come to me. I am seeing spiders everywhere as I write this book. There are webs all over my yard and on my walks. In a dream, I had the image of a giant spider spread across my back and reaching her legs along the lengths of my arms and legs to help me weave this story, to weave this world together and hold it like a moving constellation, and present it to you. This life we live is a wonder, really.

ChangeAbility is the ability to effectively navigate change

Change + Possibility

Change + Flexibility

Change + Stability

THE SEVEN PRINCIPLES FOR CHANGE

"It is not the strongest of the species that survive, nor the most intelligent, but the ones most responsive to change."

—**Charles Darwin**

AVIGATING CHANGE IS COMPLEX. IT CAN be messy and stressful, and therefore, I can use all the help I can get. The more I can understand the nature of change and the necessities of change, the better I can master ChangeAbility. The more I can locate myself in the particular change that I am in, the more I understand its nature, the more ground I have to stand on, even if that ground is moving as well. When I can locate myself in change I can then see what is needed to help me navigate. I can then decide which tools to reach for to help me move with the movement of change with greater ease and less struggle.

There are Seven Principles for Change. Seven necessary, interactive principles that when spiraled together can facilitate more success, ease, and support for initiating new changes or accommodating the changes that constantly present themselves, large or small. I don't mean to oversimplify, but I do mean to clarify and single out each of these seven principles as a way to slow down the different aspects of change to examine them so you can come to recognize them as they swiftly sweep by you when the shit hits the fan (SHTF) in the swirl and whirl of complex change.

Bring Awareness
Listen Deeply
Find Community
Proceed Incrementally
Align with Nature
Have Hope
Spark Fire

When you think about it, the principles for making change and the principles for accepting change or adapting to change are the same. They all require awareness, responsiveness, support, strategy, a sense of possibility, and a compelling reason why. This is another way of expressing the list of the Seven Principles above. If I am told I have a prediabetic condition and I need to improve my diet to improve my health, the same principles of change are involved as if I am downsized from my job and need to find another one quickly, or if a hurricane floods my home in New Orleans and I need to evacuate and later salvage the house from water damage. Each condition requires the awareness, "I will not remain in my current circumstance," and the intention, "I will survive!" Hopefully also, "I will thrive!"

What I've observed is that in order to create, accept, or adapt to personal, social, or environmental change I will need all of these principles working together, at least *some* of the time. I'll need at least a few of them *all* of the time, and which ones I will need can vary. These seven are the necessary principles common to all change. Whether I perceive the change or not, accept the change or not, or work on behalf of the change or not, I find that when I apply this template of seven to a change situation it holds true. And, if a change I am going through is not moving well, then I can look to these Seven Principles for Change, see what is missing from the picture, and see if enhancing that missing element will create more momentum and support, and a greater ease of ChangeAbility.

THE SEVEN PRINCIPLES FOR CHANGE

Bring Awareness

At the beginning of any journey there is awareness. My awareness begins with inquiry. Awareness can arrive in many forms: sensation, perception, emotion, information, and understanding. In order to know that a change is coming, or needs to arrive, I have to become aware. Sometimes the need is to make others aware. Often, I am aware of the contrast between how things are now compared to how they were before. Becoming aware does not in and of itself imply action, but it is the first step towards any action. Without awareness, I wouldn't even know there was the need for a change, or that one was taking place. With awareness, I perceive the change or perceive the need.

Where am I now? What are my circumstances? Is there a change occurring? Is there a need for a change? What is the nature of the need? What is the problem I need to address? What I am not seeing? What am I not willing to feel? What is my response? What are the possible solutions? How can I help others understand what I see?

Listen Deeply

Change, as with life, does not move in a straight line. It meanders, rushes, pauses and accelerates, weaves and banks. Listening is how I gather information from a source: news, stories, focus-group surveys. By listening, I mean receiving; listening deeply with all my senses gives me information from a deeper source: nature, spirit, feelings of connection, the play of my own breath. Often I can be so busy in my activity that I don't take time to listen to what's going on around me or to my own response. Powering through the river prevents me from reading the current or being carried by it.

Any effort towards change must have enough intention to get going, enough sensitivity to hear the feedback results of the action, and enough flexibility to change course based on the information received in a call-and-response relationship. In order to be effective, be responsive. In order to be responsive, listen. Listen without judgment or predisposition, and be willing to be creative, playful, and take risks. Listening deeply requires curiosity and genuine inquiry, and trusting what I hear.

What am I looking at? What do I need to know? What is needed in this moment? What are the different ways I can "listen"? Can I receive information without assumption or judgement? Am I moving too fast to feel? Am I picking up the signals from my own environment? Are my actions being effective? How then do I need to change course? Can I trust what I perceive?

Find Community

Don't do anything alone! First of all, it's impossible; secondly, it's no fun at all! Our existence is a living matrix of interconnectivity with people, plants, animals, and cosmic forces. So many spiritual traditions tell us separation is an illusion, so don't even try; separation is the root of suffering, and no one truly acts alone. Find Community means find support, in all the ways I can think of. There is safety in numbers. There is power in numbers. There are real and virtual like-minded people everywhere to join with me. Social movements, support groups, mentors and contacts—community can be friends, family, neighbors, organizations, or even the allies of the spirit world. Each can play a role.

If I am not meeting change successfully, I need to ask for more help. I can find more safety and courage when I feel the support of others. I can be more effective when I share my vision and share the work.

What kind of support do I need? Who are my allies? How can I reach out for the support of others? How can others help me bring awareness out, or help me see how best to make this change? How can community protect me from the adverse consequences of unpopular ideas? What are the ways I can grow this movement of change through others? What are the best strategies for connecting the connectors? How can I best resolve conflict when community becomes polarized?

Proceed Incrementally

All change moves incrementally. The best actions are often those that begin small and steady, and continue to grow and ripple out over time. When gathering an action, I start first with whom I know, then whom they know, and then to whom they know. I look out on the horizon for what I can see, first, and then look beyond. I begin by setting small goals that are attainable, bite-size actions I can assimilate.

If change occurs too quickly, even desired change, there can be recoil because I am thrown too far off balance or I'm in too much foreign territory, and I will stop the momentum in order to adjust and reorient. Or, if momentum moves too quickly, it can spin the action like a race car out of control. When I proceed slowly and incrementally, it is easier to see where I am going, identify course corrections, and implement them, recalibrating as I go. I need to be strategic in my plan of action, and, of course, have patience. One day at a time, one brick at a time, one dollar, one signature, one vote.

What are the needed steps I must take? Am I taking on more than I can handle? What is the value in waiting and going slowly? Do I have less stress by proceeding incrementally? Am I more effective? How can I maintain patience? How can I break down a larger effort into smaller steps? How can I make a change doable?

Align with Nature

Nature is change: the seasons, the tides, the weather, day to night. Nature moves in cycles and waves, familiar but never quite the same. Nature has been a successful agent of change and a reflection of change for millions of years. If I look to nature and natural systems for my instruction, I am well informed. Recognizing patterns in nature helps me locate myself and prepare for what's to come. Our world is challenged as our way of life takes place less and less in deep nature. Biorhythms are disrupted by electronic signals and screens, habitats are destroyed, and our food and soil are poisoned with chemicals. To align with nature is to embrace the interconnectedness of all events and phenomenon; to embrace a whole-systems permaculture approach to analysis and solutions. If I can align with nature as my guide, change often moves more intelligently, easily and with less resistance. Go with the flow.

Do I feel part of the world? How can I better facilitate change by better understanding nature and my own nature? How can I embrace impermanence as the way of the world? What can I learn from observing the interdependence of the ecosystem for the thriving of life? Are my own rhythms aligned with the seasons? How can I move like water? Like fire, or wind, or be as fertile as the earth?

Have Hope

Hope is what allows us to dream into being what is not yet formed, but what is possible. Hope carries the questions, "Why not?" and "What else?" Hope springs eternal and flies in the face of facts or the grim reality of the current tragic plight. Hope is the spirit that cannot be crushed. Hope is a fool. Hope is a dream. Hope is an eternal flame that keeps possibility alive. Hope will not take no for an answer. In order to make needed change, I must believe that things can be different; I must be able to imagine new scenarios. Without hope, I wouldn't even try. Hope lifts me to consider new possibilities so I can stay the course of my desire, no matter what.

What do I want? What is possible? What are my wildest dreams? What lifts me? What inspires me to carry on? Can I see my situation differently? What have I given up on? How do I deal with my disappointment? What brings me to despair? Can creativity and imagination help me write a new story about the story I am in?

Spark Fire

Fire. It's the hot flame that kindles both passion and courage. Whether the fire is in the heart, in the belly, or in the loins of desire, I need a compelling reason to take awareness and hope into action. I need an internal activation that surges me to action and keeps the fires burning regardless of setbacks, failure, or the tedium of incremental process. That activation is passion, it is courage, and at its very essence, it is the life force of Eros.

Without this fire that ignites the compelling reason, I might not have the will or desire to move through whatever fears or obstacles come my way. I might simply not care enough to try. What compels me to action is usually love—love of beauty, love of country, love of freedom, love for a people, or love for another. Activists may be incited by anger, but if they fight, they are fighting on behalf of what they love and are trying to preserve. If I have to face my fears, it will be for love. I am sustained in my efforts by a heart that wants the change, knows it can endure what it takes to get there, and fuels the hope for a better day.

What is my passion? Where is my courage? What gets me heated up? What gets me excited? What do I love? What is worth fighting for? What compels me to take awareness and hope into action? What keeps me going? What spark will motivate me to not only want to make a change, but to actually take steps to see the change realized? Where do I take a stand? Where do I refuse to compromise my integrity and the way I want to live in the world?

As I said, these Seven Principles for Change spiral together in various constellations to facilitate my navigation of change. In this following example, all seven come into play. Let's say I need to make a personal change. After my last checkup with my physician, it was determined that I have a prediabetic condition and that I need to attend to my health in a different way to prevent the condition from turning into diabetes. My doctor has already brought me the Bring Awareness of my current health condition. She has also informed me that I will need to lose weight, change my diet to include fewer sugars and carbohydrates, increase my exercise, and stop smoking. The news of all this is shocking, and if I Listen Deeply I would feel my heart racing, and my breath catch in my throat. In other words, I would be frightened. She made my condition sound pretty grim, and the remedy pretty tough.

Let's say I was someone who already had been on several different kinds of diets that ultimately never worked, and it was my smoking cigarettes that curbed my eating. If it weren't for the smoking I'd be even more overweight. But let's say I have a husband and two teenage children. They would Spark Fire and be my compelling reason to make this large change.

I needed help so I reached out to Find Community. I told my friends and they wanted to support me, so they said they would go on a diet with me, and we could be accountable to one another. We made a pact and made accountability rules with one another and did a group check-in once a week, and we each had a "buddy" and checked in every day. I Have Hope that I could do this. I could imagine that this would work.

Fortunately, this all took place in spring and summer when I wanted to be more active anyway. I could Align with Nature by being out more in the natural world—going on walks and hikes. And as I watched the trees bloom and fruit, and the early greens deepen as the season went on, I could mark my own progress as well.

Let's say that at first I was too ambitious and went on a crash diet. I flat out cheated a number of times because I was too hungry between meals and, frankly, just habituated to eating a certain amount of food. So I had to make a course correction and Proceed Incrementally, and chose a slower, more gradual diet, making sure to Listen Deeply in order to make adjustments as I went. The smoking, I decided, I would address after I had lost some of the initial weight. It just seemed like too much to tackle at one time. I found that once I lost some weight and had regular exercise outside I didn't even want to smoke that often, and so when it came time to quit, I was already feeling better, and feeling better about myself. Even though it required a lot of discipline, I was able to pull it off because I kept being fueled by my compelling reason, my family.

Or let's take another example: let's say that I work for a large retail department store and am paid the minimum wage of $7.25 per hour. That wage is inadequate to support my family, so I have to work a second job at night just to have enough money to cover expenses. I don't need to Bring Awareness to myself because I am well aware of my meager finances every time I open my wallet, but I need to Bring Awareness to my employer and my representatives in Congress so that things can change.

Let's say I hear about a demonstration planned in my city to speak out for a wage increase. The demonstration lets me Have Hope that together with other people, with Find Community, the issue will get some attention. My anger at the inequity combined with my excitement will Spark Fire in me and give me the courage to take off work that day and attend. Our action is on the news, but nothing changes. My hopes are dashed. It wasn't a large enough action. However, based on our small demonstration, some other people are encouraged. A national demonstration is being planned to take place in several major cities across the country. Listening deeply, sparking new fire, and recalibrating the action propel our cause to the next level. This time, news spreads on social media, and the issue is taken up in the national debate. Eventually, Congress announces they will introduce a bill in the next session to raise the minimum wage. That could still be a slow process. The message of Proceed Incrementally here is to grow the action and keep up the pressure until the minimum wage is raised. Small steps, including setbacks, can eventually move the action forward towards the goal.

Any change we experience contains at least some, if not all, of the Seven Principles for Change.

In understanding how to work with them and how they apply, we can begin to see more clearly the nature of the change, and therefore how to best respond. A nimble responsiveness will be the greatest contribution to our well-being and the greatest reflection of our ChangeAbility. Our ability to effectively navigate change is best served by mastering these Seven Principles for Change in all their applications and interactions.

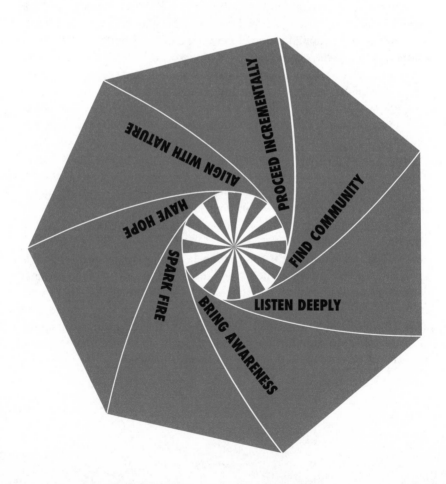

THREE WAYS TO NAVIGATE CHANGE: INITIATE, INSPIRE, ADAPT

"All living things contain a measure of madness that moves them in strange, sometimes inexplicable ways. This madness can be saving; it is part and parcel of the ability to adapt. Without it, no species would survive."

—Yann Martel

I LIKE TO USE THE WORD NAVIGATE when it comes to talking about change because it encompasses the various ways I see people working with change, or working with the effects of change. Depending upon whether you are trying to make a change happen in your life, or are coping with one that already has, what makes someone adept at ChangeAbility is their resilience. In navigating the movement of change we could look at it three ways:

Initiating Change
Inspiring Change
Adapting to Change

Each of these change navigations requires a different approach to applying the Seven Principles for Change, but those principles are present in all three types of navigations.

Bring Awareness/Listen Deeply
Find Community/Proceed Incrementally
Align with Nature/Have Hope/Spark Fire

In order to align with change, and not resist it, I need to understand the type of change I am in, and therefore what the response can be. Let's look at the ways we navigate change.

Initiating Change

"You do nothing, nothing happens. You do something, something happens."

—**Ruth Sweet**, acting coach

When I want to plant a garden, start a new business, or vote for a new candidate, and I take the actions to do so, I am Initiating Change. Even if I want to stop something, like the annoying habit I have of humming at the dinner table, or more seriously, to stop the fracking industry in my state, I am still Initiating Change. I am seeking to make a change from how things are now to how I'd like them to be.

Technological invention, self-help scenarios, and artistic creations belong to the activity of Initiating Change. So does repairing my leaky roof after the rain, writing a critical letter to the editor, and gathering a protest demonstration against the Keystone Pipeline. So does a marriage proposal or working through conflict in a relationship. Whenever I set out to do something new, whenever I set out to effect difference, I am Initiating Change. If I set out to repair a problem, it is still Initiating Change because my intention is to cause a difference from its current state. Whether I start the conversation, bring awareness to the need, plan an action, or carry it through, Intiating Change requires an intention, activation, and a focused effort to help bring the change about.

Taking an educational course, community building, strategic planning, making art, setting New Year's resolutions, moving to different city, starting an exercise program, getting married, going on a needed vacation, resolving a conflict...

Taking anything from an idea to an action, from a notion to a realization: this is Initiating Change. I'm Initiating Change by writing this book. My intention is turned to action through my harnessed daily efforts to put these ideas on the page. My hope is to inspire you to navigate your own changes more easily, but the activity of writing this book is Initiating Change.

We all know, though change can be invigorating, it's not always easy to initiate change. It requires effort, resources, planning, and risk. Let's be clear that the changes I make may not always be popular with those around me. In fact they usually are not. Change creates disruption. It disturbs the status quo. Whenever I step into something new, I shift the way things were. Sometimes welcome, sometimes not. Initiated change can be met with excitement and joy, but more often change is met with resistance and suspicion. We humans are conservative creatures of habit and we like it that way. So, in spite of this, or because of this, Initiating Change requires a certain kind of galvanizing of energy, direction, and attention that either narrows the field of open possibility to a specific channel, or opens it wide to the innovation of the creative process. In either case, the effort needs enough spark, energy, and momentum to move through the solidified structures of habit and the hold of existing forms.

Of the guests on my podcast, several are especially involved in Initiating Change. In speaking with these brilliant, motivated individuals, their thoughts, creations, and efforts illustrate several different examples of how Initiating Change can manifest.

Jacques Verduin, somatic psychologist, restorative justice leader, and mindfulness mediation educator, is the director of Insight-Out. He has developed initiatives for prisoners and challenged youth that create personal and systemic change to transform violence and suffering into opportunities for learning and healing. Through his effective Guiding Rage into Power (GRIP) program in San Quentin Prison, violent offenders take a hard look at the emotions, sensations, and impulses that led to their crimes. Insight, education, meditation, and choice are the tools these men use to change their hearts, minds, and behavior to become dedicated peacemakers. Jacques not only works with change in the individual, but also initiates change in the penal system in California and in countries throughout the world. The GRIP program has graduated many peacemakers, a number of whom have received parole from a system that rarely awards parole to this level of serious offender. Several are now training at-risk youth to turn the course of their lives.

> **Jacques Verduin**: One hundred and eighty-two graduates over three and a half years. These are all life-sentenced guys, a couple of three-strikers too. Thirty-four are out. Nobody came back. Zero percent recidivism. The average for California recidivism is 64 percent. Sixty grand per year, per prisoner, times thirty-four, is two million dollars we saved, and growing every year because that's what it costs to house a prisoner. If the humanitarian idea's not good enough, just follow the mighty buck.
>
> I think that there's so much more that we could do, other than punishing people, that would be cheaper, safer, and more of a ennobling expression of who we are as human beings together. For me, finding that edge in its deepest way in places like San Quentin State Prison has always been the most challenging and yet rewarding place to learn those lessons.

Ann Gentry, founder and owner of the popular Los Angeles vegan restaurants Real Food Daily, initiates changes in customer health and awareness by providing delicious, healthy, plant-based gourmet meals at her four locations. At the center of the vegetarian, healthy food movement for many years, Ann has been a constant advocate for how diet can change health in the most positive ways. The way she initiates change is by providing diners direct experience with vegan food through her restaurants, cookbooks, and cooking shows. The results, people can see for themselves.

> **Ann Gentry**: One of the biggest ways we can make change is to educate ourselves about food. We put high-octane gas in our cars, or charge our EV overnight off the grid. Why not put high-quality food into our bodies? It's best to source enrgentic foods that fuel and create endurance and longevity. We are all on our own personal food journey. We must ask the fundamental question, is the food I choose to eat serving me or not? From there, we can begin to see how our food choices impact our health and life, for better or worse. Choosing foods that are nutritionally sound will create deep change in your well-being.

For most activists in the environmental movement, Initiating Change can mean trying to prevent irreversible, destructive practices that destroy habitat and pollute our soil, air, and water. They are trying to preserve the vitality of the wilderness, the integrity of ecosystems, and the traditional practices of the communities of people who rely on their relation to them. **Michael Stocker** is a naturalist, musician, and bioacoustician—an expert on sound and how sound occurs in nature. His technical skills and passions have led him to be an outspoken advocate for marine life (whales, dolphins, porpoises, seals, sea lions, fish, and marine invertebrates) impacted by noise pollution in the ocean. As founding director of Ocean Conservation Research (OCR), Michael is using his conversancy in bioacoustics to explore the impacts of noise on ocean animals in order to inform ocean policy and practice toward decreasing the human bioacoustic impacts on marine habitats. This includes pushing back against the use of military sonar, seismic air gun surveys for seafloor oil and gas exploration, and the noise made by large ships.

Michael Stocker: I've always been of a mind that if you develop a thorough and informed understanding about something, that the most expeditious, efficient, best solution will come out of that. A lot of the environmentalists were being dismissed because they didn't understand the science, and didn't understand the numbers... What I do is inform the public. I don't have an appetite for that type of political conflict. What I typically do is go to public hearings or write pieces that clarify what the issues are, unweighted by ideology.

When you think about any of these things, oil and gas exploration on the eastern seaboard, there's very little about it that is appealing. If you really look at it in terms of our long-term survival on the planet, in terms of how the money gets aggregated, in terms of how the costs are externalized to the environment, nothing looks good about it. The only thing that looks good about it is that some people get some jobs for a while and there's a bunch of money made. In the balance of harms, it looks lousy. My role has been to basically clarify what these harms are.

Yet another way to engage with Initiating Change is through creativity—the way the artist courts the unseen and brings it into form. Each time the writer faces the blank page—or the artist the blank canvas—there exists the trembling possibility of anything or nothing to appear. But the writer moves her pen, and the painter chooses his color and begins, and something magical moves in and makes itself known. The artist's well-honed craft and skill shape that magic arrival into artistic form according to her style, temperament, philosophy, curiosity, his interest in tradition or novelty, and his or her own ability to meet themselves in the constant process of change.

Jackie Welch Schlicher lives in creative play, no matter what the playground. Long known as an accomplished performing artist, actress, singer, writer, director, and voice-over talent, she now works as a potter with clay. On stage, Jackie is a performer known for her sharp depth, and dry comedic improv skills. She says that the clay is her new improvisation scene partner. Play, improvisation, and transforming the unexpected are key elements in all the different expressions of her art. Artists of all types search and pray to "find the zone" where they feel they are no longer actively initiating the work, but are somehow carried by the process itself.

Jackie Welch Schlicher: It's funny. I find that when I'm making something, and again I'm, as I say, a puppy potter, pretty young at this, I find that if I haven't thrown anything on my potter's wheel for several days, it takes a while for me to get back into that zone. I lose a lot of stuff and things collapse on me, but I have to go again and again. At some point it always flips where I could just put a lump of clay on and I can just go. I can pull the walls up and shape it and do this and do that. It's like I've dusted off all the things I need to dust off to get that clearing so that I'm there, present, tuned in. My body knows what it's doing. I'm not rushing or taking my time, I'm loving what I'm doing and there's no doubt.

Inspiring Change

"Be the change you want to see in the world."

—Mahatma Gandhi

Some people with adept ChangeAbility create change by inspiring others. The effect of inspiration is that it lifts me to the realm of possibility, and it reminds me that what's possible for another could also be possible for me. I'm inspired by the things that appeal to me: by people doing interesting and courageous things, by novel and clever invention, and by the beauty and wonder that animates my heart. The Canadian Rockies fill me with awe and I think, *maybe I could climb them.* Or a landscape painting by Cezanne thrills me to think that maybe I could paint like that. Or in watching my friend run the marathon, I am inspired that, maybe, with enough training, I could do that, too. The joy she had while running was the greatest inspiration of all.

I am tremendously inspired by the bravery of others, and how they hold up hope. Not only do they hold up hope, but they can articulate how they found the courage, so I can learn that courage, too. Change-makers who inspire are all teachers of one sort or another. They teach with the stories of their experiences and ideas conveyed through writing and charismatic speeches. They teach by instructing people how to reframe the way they are currently thinking or functioning. Mostly, they inspire others through their own example of how they live their lives.

Great leaders such as Mahatma Gandhi and Martin Luther King Jr. inspired their followers to take highly risky, non-violent action in response to their oppression. Not without devastating setbacks and consequences, one man helped India become an independent nation from the British Empire, the other helped African Americans gain their civil rights in the United States. To this day, so many social movements have been inspired by these leaders, their strategies, their persistence, and their patience. These men are often quoted for their guidance, even in this book!

Inspirational spiritual speaker Marianne Williamson has inspired hundreds of thousands of women with her Sister Giant initiative, and millions of people with her message of love over fear. As a political speaker, President Obama lifts the American people to their best hope and heart in his national addresses. The Bioneers conference that I attend in San Rafael, California, is an inspiration goldmine, gathering the most creative, innovative, compassionate minds in the environmental movement together each year to cross-pollinate and generate new hope and new ideas that attendees can move forward into all corners of the world.

Inspiring Change gives hope that positive change can occur. It is often instructive as to how. Inspiring Change requires a vision, and people who can see what has not yet come, but could. We so often need a model of someone else who has the courage and the strategy to gather the forces of change, and the dedication and perseverance to see it come true. We need to hear the stories of what they went through, and what they have overcome in order to inspire our own overcoming. Some of the podcast guests are especially involved in Inspiring Change, and are very good at it. They provide varied examples of the ways that inspiration facilitates change.

Corinne Bourdeau, president and founder of 360 Degree Communications, knows how to engage the public through media. As a producer and marketing director, she creates the marketing campaigns for social change films that seek to open hearts, build awareness, and inspire actions on pressing issues of our day. Bringing her innovative expertise to the campaigns for such films as *Fuel, Bottle Shock, GMO OMG,* as well as the Academy Award winners, *The Cove* and *Boyhood,* Corinne brings attention and audiences to these well-crafted documentaries and narrative films so the word can be spread and something can be done. She knows film is a most effective tool for inspiring change that leads to action, large and small, even if the response comes slowly.

> **Corrine Bourdeau:** Change can be a lot of things, but we have to know that we can actually move the needle, and that we can make change. If somebody sees a film, they go see *Food, Inc.* or they see *GMO OMG,* and they go home and they plant a garden in their backyard...there's change. I have people come up to me all the time: "Oh my gosh! I saw XYZ movie, and because of that I did this..." It's amazing, and sometimes it will be years and years later.

Paul Rogat Loeb inspires change through conveying moving stories of political hope. A tireless writer, speaker, and activist, Paul speaks to the public about social engagement, asking what makes some people choose lives of social commitment while others abstain. His book *Soul of a Citizen* is both an examination on why some people are part of social engagement while others are not, and a primer on how to do so. His book, *The Impossible Will Take A Little While,* is an anthology of stories of the achievements of activists in history who faced enormous obstacles. Stories and interviews of activists and artists such as Václav Havel, Ariel Dorfman, Nelson Mandela, Maya Angelou, Tony Kurshner, and Howard Zinn speak of struggle and hope. The actions and reflections of these courageous leaders are presented to inspire hope and courage in the readers, as well.

> **Paul Loeb**: I think people feel a couple of things. They feel there's an issue that calls them—something is wrong, something could be better. Oftentimes they personalize it, that is, something's affecting this person, this community, environmental area, this river. I think coupled with that is a required sense of possibility that says that what they can do matters. Probably most of the reason people don't act more for change is, in fact, because they don't think their

actions matter. So, basically the sense of "can my actions make a difference" is really central. When people don't have it, I call it the hinge of powerlessness. It even makes them feel like there's just nothing I can do so therefore it's not worth it, why break my heart? All the projects I do, that's a core part—just trying to address that and overcome it.

Camille Maurine is a meditation mentor, dancer, performance artist, teacher, and writer. Along with her husband, Dr. Lorin Roche, she is the coauthor of several books, including *Mediation Secrets for Women: Discovering Your Passion, Pleasure, and Inner Peace.* Camille offers trainings in feminine spiritual empowerment and embodiment, and travels the world offering workshops and retreats. She inspires by instruction and example, showing women what it is to live a sensual, integrated, fierce, loving life. She refers to all the work she does as creating contexts where people can discover and fully express the essence of their most authentic self, which spans a spectrum from restful serenity to wild passion.

Camille Maurine: I inspire by creating a context of exploration, discovery, and freedom, and infusing that, I would say, with love, curiosity, and knowing. The knowing, which I now have so deeply rooted in my bones, that whatever arises in such a context is always in the service of evolution, transformation, and ultimately the embodiment and expression of love.

Embracing the fullness and the intensity of being that alive and feeling so deeply allows us to shed our old adaptive patterns of control, and re-describe ourselves and redefine what we think is required of us to survive, adapt, and experiment with new expressions. It happens naturally when women realize that they don't have to change themselves in any way. The transformation comes about through going deeper into their own embodied experience and feeling, therefore, at home in their own essential nature.

When we do that with great tenderness, love, and permission, a lot of those restrictive patterns just simply melt away. You don't have to force anything at all. It's rather that context of appreciation, and building on the gifts that are everywhere around us through nature, through our interactions with others, through recognizing the generosity of life, and feeling that gush of what in the yoga world is called Shakti; the gush of that feminine force of creation and surge of life and love that we actually are. The context and embrace of it all is what seems to make the difference.

Adapting to Change

"Shit happens."

—**Anonymous** (or Just About Everyone)

Since change is always occurring, we are in constant need of accommodating change, or Adapting to Change. Whether the change is to our liking or not, life is a continual adjustment to new circumstances. Appropriate responsiveness is the highly developed trait for stress-free survival and "thrival." Responsiveness and adaptive resilience are at the core of ChangeAbility.

Even as am I writing this chapter, my teenage daughter's airline flight from oversees was canceled once, rescheduled, and now this flight has been delayed, causing her to miss her flight connection and have to spend the night in Newark. My other daughter had to change her travel plans home because of a second job interview in New York where she now lives. My mother went to the emergency room and was then admitted to the hospital. My day's writing was interrupted over and over again as I called the airlines all day from the hospital room to reroute their flights.

My computer and phone are in perpetual need of upgrade or password changes, and frequently must be replaced. I am forever struggling to adapt to the new way the screens appear and the buttons work. The technology of data storage has long rendered my floppy disks and CD drive unusable, so the archives of old information are no longer even accessible. And for someone like me who has been in the film business for a very long time, my archived VHS cassettes are unplayable, not to mention the three-quarter-inch tapes that can never again be viewed without transfer to a newer media—if there are any old-schoolers around who still have the equipment to make the transfer.

Whether the change is coming from the inside, like a change in health or a change of heart, or it's coming from the outside, like a change in the weather, or a change in schedule, the need for flexibility and fluidity has never been greater. So is the need for a good attitude, and a Plan B.

Sometimes the Adapting to Change is more prolonged and more severe, like adjusting to the changes in life that come from the death of a partner, or moving to a new city for a new job. Those large event changes have so many smaller component changes contained within the larger change. Like with a move: let's say I get a job promotion and have to move across the country. I need to find a new place to live, buy new furniture, and learn my way around town, as well as replace what is not replaceable: my favorite doctor, my child's perfect school, my best friend. Even more so, the adjustments to the death of a partner touch upon every aspect of the life once shared, and now traversed alone.

Some of my podcast guests are especially involved in helping guide others in adapting to changes that are affecting their lives and their health.

Robert Litman, founder of The Breathable Body, is a movement and breath educator. He guides clients and students in the use of movement, breath, and sound as tools for personal growth, restoring healthy breathing rhythms, structural alignment, and efficient body mechanics. Combining his vast science and somatic education experience as a Continuum Movement teacher, Buteyko Breathing Technique instructor, and a certified Duggan-French Approach-Somatic Pattern Recognition practitioner, Robert tells us that all movement begins with breath; therefore all change begins with breath. The way we pay attention to our breath, and the way in which we breathe affects all the other functions of our bodies, our health, and even our emotions. He facilitates adaptation by encouraging clients to become aware of the quality of their breathing and to make simple but remarkable changes that affect their health and well-being. Robert says that when change is moving too quickly, we hold our breath as if to stop the momentum. When under stress, this holding can become a habitual pattern that robs the body of its essential nourishment, and causes any number of health problems such as anxiety, heart disease, digestive disorders, and sleep disorders. How can we use the change of breath within to adapt to any and all changes that come from the outside?

> **Robert Litman**: You can go three minutes without breath, three days without water, and three weeks without food. Without this nourishment, you cannot survive.
>
> Really, the act of breathing should be one of great pleasure. Moving towards nourishment and pleasure is a radical act. We talk so much about external stress, but when the body is not nourished, that's an internal stress. When the body is internally stressed, it's less available to manage external stress. Changing the way you breathe will change and affect every aspect of your life.

Amy McEachern, owner of Creative Moving and Organizing, is a professional organizer and house mover. For over twenty-two years she's been helping people plan and execute the move from one home to another, often in a new city. The reasons people move are many, and most often the move is part of significant change in other parts of their lives. Amy is part puzzle-solver, part counselor, part comedienne, as she accompanies people through the many decisions, confusions, stagnations, and emotions that they can experience in making the physical move that crystallizes the personal moves in their lives.

> **Amy McEachern**: When people are moving, most of the change has already happened because people don't move for no reason. Something big has already occurred in their lives that now has caused the move, and so the move is really just the result of something that's changed inside. When I say inside, I mean it can be an outside thing like marriage, divorce, career change, or death of a spouse. We've seen it all. People are in constant flux and oftentimes that means they've got to change locations and when they do, really where they're moving is inside and we're just kind of dragging their stuff behind them. We're just catching up their stuff with them.

Rachel Lang is an intuitive healer and an astrologer. She uses astrology to provide a matrix of understanding for people in transition. Understanding a larger framework for the dynamics of their current situation is one of the helpful ways a person can stabilize themselves in a time of great flux and change. For Rachel, by conveying the influences from the particular configurations and from the complements and oppositions of planetary forces on the individual and the collective, she can provide her clients with insight as to their current circumstance and its cause, as well as the possibilities of new outcomes aided by these forces. As an intuitive healer, she offers her way of "seeing deeply" to help others create new visions for what is possible for their lives.

> **Rachel Lang**: Astrology is a symbolic language that helps us understand ourselves. It shows us how we are connected to the cosmos, how we're connected to nature, to the earth, in ways that are perhaps unexplainable through what we can sense energetically. The value of knowing what's happening at any time, astrologically, is that it allows you to get a kind of preview of coming attractions in your life. If you have a snapshot or an idea of energies being opened or closed, then you have a sense of how you might move in your life in harmony with those influences.

There are some people who have this need to know what's going to happen in the future, and what I say to them is the future is part destiny and part blank canvas. You might have a hint, like there's a base layout of colors there, but you fill in the details. If you want to know what the future holds, look at what's happening in your life right now and you can see what you're creating. If you don't like what you're creating, change it. Change the way you're thinking. Change your attitude. Change your feeling, and adopt a new framework.

In the discussion of these three navigations of change—Initiating, Inspiring, and Adapting—we come up to the beliefs people hold about destiny and free will. How much of the course of my life is predetermined and set in stone, and how much of it is up to me to decide and create? Many of the wisdom-carriers I listen to say that it lies somewhere in between, that there are many elements that shape and determine the direction of our lives, but that we can and do change through our choices, actions, and resistances.

Likewise, there is a range of beliefs about what our response to change ought to be. Some people can be strident and directed, "controlling" some might say, believing change will only happen if they "make things happen" through their intentional efforts and actions. While others like to yield to the course that presents itself and "go with the flow." The art of life, and certainly the art of ChangeAbility, is to be able to move with both, knowing when effort or yield is called for. There are times when the best strategy for adapting to change is to initiate a new action, while at other times the best strategy might be to accept the change and let it move as it will. (Please don't bring up "let it go," because I still don't know how to do that!) Inspiration for change could lead me in either way. Let's say I wanted to build physical strength after an injury to my leg. I could be inspired by my friend to train for the marathon as the way to make a comeback, or I could be inspired to take pleasure in supporting my friend's run, and go for more gentle walks in the park with my dog until I am more healed.

Whether I am Initiating, Inspiring, or Adapting to change, my awareness of the type of change I am in will provide clarity for the ways in which I can and need to respond in order to navigate. ChangeAbility is about becoming aware and responsive, and knowing which type of action or yield is called for at any given time.

ChangeAbility = Change + Awareness + Responsiveness

CHANGE DIRECTIONS:
INTERNAL/EXTERNAL—FAST/SLOW

"People wish to be settled. It is only as far as they are unsettled that there is any hope for them."

—Ralph Waldo Emerson

A S HUMANS, WE VIEW EXISTENCE THROUGH two basic constructs, one is space; the other is time. These constructs also become the larger contexts for the experience of the movement of life, and a means by which we locate ourselves. In terms of space, where am I? In terms of time, where am I now? Where was I before? Where will I be next Tuesday?

Adam Wolpert works daily with change, reflecting his lifelong engagement with nature and human nature. He is a fine arts painter, cofounder of Occidental Arts and Ecology Center, and an adept group facilitator and organizational consultant. Adam observes that there are many different types of change that we must navigate.

Adam Wolpert: As we know, there's slow change like the rising ocean, and there's shocking, sudden change, like a fire or the death of a president of a company—something dramatic. Then there's internally driven or externally imposed change, and all sorts of other kinds of change. Every different kind of change, just like every different painting, requires a new set of techniques and approaches.

Regarding the concept of space, if I envision the world with myself as the central reference, I perceive a difference between my internal landscape and the external one. There are personal changes that come from the inside, and there are social changes that occur outside of me. There are spiritual transformations inside, and corporate acquisitions outside, changes in my personal health inside, and environmental upheavals outside of me. Change can come from the inside through emotions, sensations, thoughts, and convictions. Change can come from the outside from the weather, the workplace, home, family, or bacteria. Some changes involve specific locales; others are more generalized and non-localized.

The area inside my skin—my organs, blood and nerve impulses—are what I consider internal to me. Yet, when I talk about what is inside of me, I am often referring to my direct feelings, my thoughts, and the meaning I am making of my experiences. So, when I am changing my mind, or making a decision to find a new group of friends, or am driven to speak out against the use of pesticides on crops, my change is internal; it's motivated from the inside by thoughts and the sensations of emotion and impulse. If I have heart surgery, or have an upset stomach after eating too much pizza, that is also change on the inside, but more literal.

Using myself as my primary reference, anything outside of my body, or outside my thoughts, feelings, and awareness I consider to be a part of the outside world. I'm constantly uncertain whether or not I can affect it, let alone control it—though it doesn't stop me from trying. If my old neighbor moves out and new neighbors with a barking dog move in, if a rock falls from the sky and hits me on the head, or if the state of Ohio votes Republican in 2016, these are external changes I must accommodate. If I am forced to change my opinion in favor of the majority to keep peace in the company I work for, if I find a new job because I just got fired, or if my car runs out of gas on the freeway, that change is external.

Spiritual philosophies say there is no inside or outside, that all is one consciousness, one matrix of being. Eastern religions, physicists, indigenous peoples, psychedelic journeyers, and seekers of higher consciousness agree. So do I. Meditation and body awareness practices remind me, through sensation, that I am expansive without boundary, that there is no real inside or outside to my existence. I am one with the universe and one with change. However, even with this awareness, I participate in the cultural agreement about time and space. I still manage to live a life that relies on time and space to get my daughter to school for the morning bell, meet my deadline on this book, find my house every day, and pay California state taxes because that's the state and space where I reside. I look in the mirror, see my reflection, and recognize that image looking back as me, even though my thoughts, feelings, and metabolic processes have changed and changed again since I last took a look.

Space: Internal Change/External Change

"We are fluid beings stabilized in time to function here on planet Earth."
—**Emilie Conrad**, founder of Continuum

The best way I know to understand the internal landscape of change is to be able to track my sensations. It is how I can experience what is changing in the places I can't see. Much of what I personally know about change comes from what I know about the body through movement. Because of my training in the fluid movement discipline of Continuum, I am versed in a vocabulary of sensation; I share this skill and perception with many of the podcast guests who are somatic, embodiment practitioners: Amber Gray, Robert Litman, Camille Maurine, Harvey Ruderian, Fred Sugerman, and Jacques Verduin. Sensation has been my best and most reliable guide. The felt sense of touch, as well as the sensory information of taste, sight, smell, and sound are my primary references for knowing what I am experiencing.

How do I even know I am sitting in my chair? If I become quiet, I can feel the weight of my buttocks as they rest across the top of the seat. I can feel the bottoms of my feet pressing into the floor for support. I can feel the edge of the desk press against my abdomen as I lean in towards the computer to write.

How do I know what I know about my internal experience? Through feeling the sensation of response to my own thoughts, emotions, and the events outside of me in the external world. I ask myself, "How am I breathing right now? What am I aware of in my body?" I can feel my eyebrows pull together and my abdomen tighten slightly as I try to find just the right words to phrase this. Sensations are felt all the time, every day, in response to moving through the world, and if I am aware of them, they provide feedback to me about where I feel safe, threatened, pleased, interested, annoyed, engaged or disengaged. What are the sensations of anticipation when I am stuck in traffic and late for work? How comfortable can I be with the sensation of disorientation as I stand on my head in a yoga class? How does it feel in my chest when I am attracted to the handsome man across the room? Or when I have an argument with my ex? We have hundreds of these sensory responses every day, and many or most fly by with out our conscious reception. They still greatly impact the choices we make, we just don't know why we've made the choices. The more I get to know and tolerate the full spectrum of internal sensation, the fuller and more authentic my response to the world can be.

Emilie Conrad made many brilliant contributions to the understanding of movement as the primary resource for experiencing our existence. She said, "Movement is something we are, not something we do." According to her, we are movement, just as we are change. Therefore, what we consider to be internal and what we consider to be external source from the same place and behave the same.

"The way we move in our body is the way we move in our lives."
—Emilie Conrad

Fred Sugerman is a movement artist. Trained as a dancer and an actor, he works with the intersection between healing arts and performing arts, using movement to help others make personal discoveries that promote health and healing. Fred's laboratory is his own body; he has a mastery of tracking the sensations of movement and change within himself. He then teaches others to gain awareness of the changeable nature of their bodies and lives through deep listening in movement and dance practice. This intimate knowledge of self allows for more authentic choices in how to live in the outside world.

Fred Sugerman: I use my body as a way of studying what change means. Because bodies are living, breathing, cellular, biological systems, we are always in the state of flux and always in the state of change. We, as humans, have this thought that we get stagnant, or that we're not moving, or that we're not evolving, or that we're not going forward. In fact, I've come to believe that we're no different than the wind or the currents in the ocean.

When I am internally responding to a change that is coming from the outside, I can consider that to be an internal change. The motivation to change or the impulse to change comes from my response to a changed circumstance, or one that I see needs changing. Many of the guests who are in the healing professions, psychology, spirituality, or the arts represent a view that change begins within that will then manifest in or impact the outer world. Change the inside first. This is their view.

What influence does internal change have on the external world? Podcast guest **James Stark** is the cofounder of Regenerative Design Institute at Commonweal Garden. Permaculture is a design science rooted in the observation of natural systems and applies solutions for food, water, medicine, shelter, and community based on the stability and resiliency of a healthy ecosystem. In the setting of a model, operating permaculture farm and school, James co-teaches the Ecology of Leadership program, about how to cultivate the "inner garden," as part of the larger ecology of being. Aligning with the observations and principles of the natural world, he asks students to look inside and "compost their old beliefs" so that more authentic response and change can occur in their lives. To him, this is what is required in order to tackle the larger, complex problems we face: climate change, economic disparity, the loss of our connection to nature, and how individuals and large populations can resolve their difference and live together for a greater good.

James Stark: The Ecology of Leadership program is where we get an opportunity to really look inside and bring curiosity. We take the same curiosity and excitement you bring to gardening on the outside. Why we call it "inner gardening" is because often there's a tendency that we don't want to look inside because we've been in the emotional landfilling business, and we stuff everything down, and we try to block it out. "Oh, I don't want to go there."

To generate any kind of change in the external world without addressing what's in the emotional body of eight billion people is challenging. Because of the loss of all our cultural healing practices in village life, because we don't have the rites of passage to help us move out of grief and wounds, we're carrying sadness and pain. Without dealing with that underground sea that we float upon, it's pretty challenging. Then we expect all these miracles to happen out there in the external world. It just doesn't happen that way. Shame, anger, and resentment, my experience is that the more we release and compost that stuff that's in the emotional body, then it just opens up tons of possibility in riding the dragon of change and being able to be the artful warrior. You can go through without resistance, because you're not carrying all that stuff in your system.

Other podcast guests are working with ChangeAbility for social change, political change, policy change, and environmental change—change that we consider to be external change. They are working from the outside for the outside: Corinne Bourdeau, Claire Hope Cummings, Penny Livingston-Stark, Paul Loeb, Beth Rosales, Michael Stocker, and John Weeks.

External changes, by their very nature, tend to involve more people and more elements than just me. Somehow it seems easier, or more within my control, to effect internal or personal change—not that personal change is easy. Sometimes external change involves large numbers of people, or animals, or habitats. The same resistances that appear in internal change appear in external change, only magnified by the numbers. There are so many factors that complicate social change and policy change, often rocking back and forth between progress and setback. The challenges of building awareness, of public opinion, political agendas, disagreements, economic impacts, entrenched traditional structures, and fear of change complexify the issues and convolute the movement of change. Challenge to change on behalf of the environment is that environmental change can mean many things to different people, depending upon their values. So again, awareness, economic agendas, beliefs, and direct relationship with the land itself play a large part in whether the change is for stewardship or destruction.

For the past thirty-five years **Beth Rosales**, senior philanthropic advisor, has been effecting social change by focusing charitable funds to social justice nonprofit groups seeking to improve the lives of others who have little access to services. Beth has advised foundations and individuals about how and where to direct their charitable giving for the most strategic impact that aligns with their social values of creating a more just and equal life among class, gender, and race. She has worked in various capacities for progressive foundations including Vanguard Public Foundation, Funding Exchange, Tides, the Women's Foundation of California, Marguerite Casey Foundation, and The Lia Fund. In advising charitable giving, Beth has a large perspective on all the elements of social change, and what is needed for grassroots social change to move forward.

Beth Rosales: Philanthropy cannot create social change, but rather we support people who are trying to make change.

There have been many, many changes in our social structures. The civil rights movement was generally supported by philanthropy—it was institutions and it was people giving money for a certain cause.

There are roles that philanthropy can play outside of financial support, as conveners bringing people together. I think historically, that really had been the role of philanthropy, whether it was Carnegie-Mellon in the earlier days when the family decided to fund libraries, then they brought other families that they knew to fund public schools, etcetera. In many ways we can connect not only groups to other funders, other grant makers, or other institutions, we can be connectors. And then if all else fails, we can be a voice. Many of our grantees may not have the aggregate voice, so we can have a voice that that helps to lift all.

When it come to differentiating between the internal and the external, nothing is ever simple—at least, not in my world. There are very few changes that are strictly internal or external. The inside and outside effect one another in an interdependence of motivation for change that moves in both directions. The external impacts the internal: my mood is depressed by the cloudy weather outside. The early death of a dear friend causes me to question the priorities of my life. The polluted air outside exacerbates my asthma and I consider moving to another city, even though I love it here. And the internal impacts the external: my heartbreak over a relationship breakup compels me to write a sad song. My ill-health robs me of my energy and focus so I have to leave my job and curb my social activities. My distress over so many displaced refugees from the Middle East causes me to donate money to refugee assistance organizations, or to travel and volunteer.

Rachel Lang articulates the complex relationship between the internal and external changes that she sees in her astrology clients.

Rachel Lang: There are some astrological signs that change easier and faster than others. Fixed signs, for example, tend to dig their heels in the ground and they like everything in their environment to stay the same. So, I think that we can talk about change in two ways. One: external events happening in our lives. Two: internal changes that we might not see immediately, playing out in circumstances in our lives. I think that the internal changes can sometimes lead to external changes, and because we fear external changes when they affect and influence some of the people that we love or they influence our immediate circumstances or environments, some people can get resistant to internal change.

What I always tell my clients when they're getting ready to go through a huge transit that signifies external change in their lives is, "you don't have to drop any bombs. You don't have to make any kind of major moves. Just be open. Just go through the internal changes that you're going through, feel into them, and the wisdom that is who you are will help you to discern what external shifts and changes in your environment need to happen." Just saying, "You don't have to make any external changes" gives people permission to go into the internal changes that are already happening, because they're going to happen anyway whether you're moving into them gracefully or you're resisting them.

Time: Slow Change/Fast Change

"Time is too slow for those who wait, too swift for those who fear, too long for those who grieve, too short for those who rejoice, but for those who love, time is eternity."

—Henry Van Dyke

When I look at change in terms of time, I see that the movement of change takes place on a continuum, like a wave. Change moves incrementally on that wave between point A and point B, between then and now. Or it moves between now and the next now. Within the construct of time, I contrast and compare to determine the interval. It's how I derive a baseline in the present or in the past to notice that change has occurred at all: *here in Los Angeles it used to get dark at 5:00 p.m. in February, now in June, it stays light until 8:00 p.m. Back when I was in school I used to play football, now I only watch it on TV. I used to have hair on my head, now I'm bald.* Long or short, it's through these comparisons that we notice and measure the movement of change.

Depending upon the interval of time between one moment and the next, change can appear suddenly, or so long in coming as if to be stuck and never move. A car accident, a heart attack, or the wining lottery ticket can alter life in an instant. The wave of change, then, feels like a sharp and abrupt turn. On the other hand, the long struggle against Apartheid in South Africa, or the rights for same-sex marriage in the United States, at times, seemed like nothing would ever change. And then eventually, it did. Depending upon the personal rhythm to which I am habituated, all change can feel too abrupt and evoke a response of overwhelm, or feel too slow and evoke a response of frustration at the pace of change.

While writing this book in late June, I lived through a most amazing week of change that was the outcome of a very slow and long process that included many failed attempts and reversals, but resulted in significant social change. Three Supreme Court rulings in one week: approval for equal housing, the Affordable Care Act, and marriage equality. Slow change.

Just one week prior, nine African American churchgoers were shot and killed, one shot and injured, while worshiping in the Emanuel African

Methodist Episcopal Church in Charleston, South Carolina. In a short moment, a spray of bullets destroyed the victims' lives, along with the lives of their families, and friends, and all who mourned this detestable act of hatred and violence. Fast change.

As a result of this sudden horror, the long-standing practice, since the days of the Civil War, of flying the Confederate flag was broken, and the flag was permanently taken down from the State Capitol building of South Carolina. The flag was declared to be a symbol of institutionalized racial hatred still carried from the inhuman practice of slavery, and many other public institutions and private citizens retired the flag to a piece of history. A fast change affected an entrenched slow change, e.g., a tradition.

Environmental change, or environmental destruction, can take millennia or moments, as can the movement of Mother Nature, herself.

Because change is a constantly moving wave, even what appears as sudden change has a history; that change evolved from somewhere.

The events of environmental change we experience can either appear to have taken a very long time, or an instant. However, all momentary outcomes are the results of constant evolutionary change. The separation of the continents we know today from the larger landmass of Pangaea took millions of years, and the continents are still moving, today. The earthquake this year in Nepal arrived in an instant and without warning, but the pressures had been building for some time. Climate change is an evolutionary process, exacerbated by human practices and disruptions, but even sudden outcomes are part of evolutionary change.

One of the biggest problems in our culture is the problem of speed. Brought about by the rushing pace of activity, the pulsing speed of technology, and the ease of communication, I'm not only *allowed*, I am *required* to be available on all my devices 24/7. And because of it, I barely have time to respond to *some* information, let alone *all*. I drive in my car, pack as many activities as I can into a day, hurry through dinner, and barely have time to stop. The problem with speed is that I whiz by the details. I whiz by my own sensations and therefore can't even locate myself in space or in time. When I drive fast in the car I miss the nuance of color in the trees, or I might even miss my exit. When I rush through dinner I don't savor the flavor of the food, or the pleasure of the company of my dinner companions. More detail is available when I am moving slowly and not whizzing by. When I slow down, my awareness can be more attuned to both my inner landscape and the one outside.

> "When we really focus our attention and bring our awareness to a very small detail of the dynamic, it's a little safer and it slows the process down. When you're looking for detail, the organism obliges by opening up and slowing down, so you can see the detail a little bit more. Then with that slowing down, you're able to move more slowly with taking out pieces that are being shown to you. True awareness. It helps your ego to feel safe to go slow, because more detail is available."
>
> —Robert Litman

I'm going to side step for a moment. Whether change occurs quickly or slowly, change by its nature is disorienting. Any time I innovate or embark on something new, my status quo is disrupted. Even in pleasant circumstances, this can be uncomfortable. Starting a new love relationship or traveling to the place I've been dreaming about for years is still a disruption. If I am not able to tolerate disruption, I may try and keep things the same. I might retreat into old patterns with my new lover, or I might go eat at McDonald's in Paris because the familiar feels safe. I form habits to create less disruption, more reliability, and more safety, especially when I find change to be moving too fast.

> "Anything new comes with a price. Do I allow something new to penetrate my version of reality or do I push it away? The familiar calms me down and the unfamiliar is disruptive. Depending upon where my psyche is able to go…habit creates less stress. I have to feel supported somewhere, which would be in something familiar."
>
> —Emilie Conrad

All change is a disruption—sudden change even more so.

Amber Gray is a psychotherapist, movement therapist, and public health professional working with survivors of organized violence, torture, war, ritual abuse, domestic violence, and community violence. Amber's important work has sent her all over the world to Haiti, the Middle East, and places of extreme conflict and natural disasters. As a clinician for individuals, and as a trainer for organizations responding to disasters and complex humanitarian emergencies, she works with survivors of extreme interpersonal and social trauma using somatic movement, mindfulness, and creative arts–based therapies, seeking to restore dignity, humor, and beauty. Amber talks about trauma in relation to time.

> **Amber Gray**: The experience of trauma is that it's an uninvited change. No matter what the context or the situation, it's uninvited. Trauma by definition is too much too fast, no transition time, not enough processing. We can consider it an uninvited change.

On the other hand, when change is occurring too slowly, it feels as if nothing is happening at all. We can lose heart or fall into despair.

Tom Verner is a psychologist turned magician. Tom and his wife, fine artist **Janet Fredericks**, founded Magicians Without Borders and perform magic in refugee camps in some of the most war-torn, forgotten places in the world. These are camps created by the urgent need to provide for people heavily impacted and displaced by the inescapable change of war and poverty. They've performed in camps in India, Ethiopia, South Sudan, former Yugoslavia, Iran, El Salvador, Uganda, Ghana, Liberia, and Sierra Leone. After many years of living in the camps, refugees can feel that nothing about their dire circumstances will ever change. Tom and Janet's mission is to entertain, educate, and empower. They bring hope and humanity in the form of magic and wonder, acting as citizen ambassadors of the heart.

> **Tom Verner**: I think we imagined that refugee camps were places where people went for six months or a year, maybe. Then, the war blows over, comes to an end, and they go back home. The people we perform for have been in camps for twenty years. Twenty years. All over the world. People are in camps.

> **Janet Fredericks**: Sometimes these people can't go back to their countries because they've lost their citizenship. They're no longer recognized as Sudanese.

Tom Verner: They've been gone too long, or their village has been completely destroyed. They have nowhere to go. They also have no legal status often in the country that's wonderful to host them. They can't get a job or they…

Janet Fredericks: They can't go home.

Disruption and Orientation

Whether internal/external or slow/fast, space and time are the constructs I use to locate myself inside change, and change is disruptive and disorienting, no matter if its welcome or not. Sudden and unexpected change is even more disruptive and disorienting, often accompanied by shock. Shock is a natural body response to sudden and traumatic change. It is meant to protect the body from extreme and dangerous disruption. Physical injury, terrible news, natural disaster, or the death of a loved one brings along with it physical shock. Even if I've been given a surprise birthday party by my friends, or I win the *Reader's Digest* Grand Prize Sweepstakes, the sudden change can be shocking.

> ### Fast or slow, internal or external, it's always good for me to take the time I need to rest, integrate, and readjust from change.

One way or another I am going to need this kind of adjustment time. Whether it's in preparation on the front end, or in integration after the change has occurred, rest and readjustment are an essential part of good ChangeAbility, and we'll be looking at it in more depth later in the chapters on Healing, Listen Deeply, and Proceed Incrementally. A large contributor to my feeling overwhelmed in response to change and especially complex change is that I have not given myself time to reorient and readjust, or the circumstance has change coming at me so hard and so fast I can't have time to adjust. This is especially true as interdependent waves of change after change come in quick succession, as they often seem to do in periods of major life change. Depending upon the tolerance I have for disruption, the time I need to reorient could take a long time, especially if there is physical shock involved. There will be times when I feel I don't have enough energy or resource to initiate a change after something has happened to me, because I have not recovered from the disruption, and "I don't have it together" or I feel "scattered" or "rattled" or any of these phrases that imply I am not experiencing my wholeness.

Some people's range for disruption and restoration is wide. We consider them fluid, easy-going, flexible, adaptable. Other's range is narrow; they are easily thrown by the disruption of change and do not adjust well. We consider them to be cautious, rigid and set in their ways. They become what we call, "controlling" because they can't tolerate the sensations of disruption of change and so reach for the safety of the familiar and cling to it. We all do it, just in different degrees. To reach for the safety of the familiar internally, I develop schedules and habits: I eat a peanut butter sandwich for lunch every day, I only wear black, I go to bed by 10:00 p.m. Externally, I try to control my environment and the people in it: the thermostat must be set at sixty-seven degrees, I won't fly on airplanes, I only listen to soft rock and no one else can touch the radio dial in the car. Developing an ease with ChangeAbility means that I develop a dexterity for accommodating the varying rhythms of change: fast and slow, in and out. This requires that I give myself enough time, space, and resources to integrate and adjust to what is new, and what has gone.

Locating myself in space and time helps me understand the nature of the change I'm in.

Is this an internal change, or an external one? How is my internal landscape affecting the outward expressions of my life? How are the external changes triggering my internal responses and asking for internal change in response? Is the speed at which this change is occurring too fast? Can I tolerate the movement or do I need to slow the rate of the change down, or slow down my response to the change? What am I missing? Is it moving too slowly? How can I use slower speed to penetrate and increase my awareness of the change? What can I appreciate or savor? How can I keep renewing my hope and my resolve in the face of such slow change?

By understanding how I am located in change I can more readily understand whether I need to adjust to the change, initiate something new, or perhaps open to new possibilities that have not yet occurred to me, or open those possibilities for others. To become flexible and dexterous with ChangeAbility, I need to locate myself in change.

ChangeAbility =

Change + location in space

Change + location in time

WHAT STOPS CHANGE?
RESISTANCE, PROCRASTINATION, AND FEAR

"Everything I've ever let go of has claw marks on it."
—David Foster Wallace

A S SOON AS I BEGIN TO talk about change, I have to talk about fear. Change will always plunge me into the unknown. It's part of the nature of change. The truth is, no matter how much I plan or predict, calculate or control, I DON'T KNOW what is going to happen in the next moment. I don't know how life is going to turn. I don't know if things will get better or worse, or if they'll just drag on day after day in the same monotony. I don't know how long this golden moment will last, or if this pain will ever end. I don't know whether social structures will hold, or how they will evolve. If you live in earthquake country as I do, I don't even know whether physical structures will hold or how they will evolve. So, if I derive my sense of stability from needing to know, or thinking I know exactly how my life is going to move, then that stability will be toppled over and over again. If my stability comes from needing my life to remain the same and not move, then I will constantly be surprised and upended. If the unknown threatens my survival needs for food, shelter, water, safety, love, and belonging then you can bet I will be afraid.

Whether acknowledged or not, whether it appears as caution or panic, fear can easily show up whenever I disrupt the existing circumstance and move into the unknown. *What will happen now?* Fear, in all its forms, can be a normal response. Caution can be a healthy and helpful response, even when I desire the change, and have worked hard to bring the change about, like getting married or having a baby. Caution slows down my response and action, giving me more time to consider.

Change, by its nature, is unsettling. The less capacity I have for accommodating the disruptions that come from change, the more fear I will have as these changes come up.

The more constant or complex the change, the more disruption I will feel, and the more possibility I will try to quell the disruption with a fear response. That's why I want to become adept at navigating change, so I can move with the flow of change without fear or impediment.

The purpose of this book is to explore how to have a greater flexibility in meeting change so that my first response is not fear. Instead, I can meet change with more acceptance and ease, and not resistance. Complex changes are coming at us faster and faster in every realm of our lives, with little recovery time. What took months before to cross the country in a covered wagon now takes hours in an airplane, or seconds in a Skype call. The bank branch where I go is a branch where all the tellers move up to managers, then officers, and are out within eight months. I can't get attached to those friendly faces, because soon they are gone. My parents' generation expected to keep one career for life. My generation came to understand we might evolve one or two careers and then another activity after retirement. These people working at the bank aren't even in the same job, let alone the same location, for a year. And I'm sure each of those career moves and considerations are met with both excitement and fear, because it's all unknown.

When the unknown moves so quickly, there's little time to recover and restabilize. In response to all the quick change, I must become a quick-change artist, able to find stable ground even when that ground is moving. As I said earlier: navigating change is the new stability. I have to learn to stabilize within the movement of change and not lock down in fear. What impedes change is my lack of comfort with its movement. However, it will be my ability to align with that movement that will maximize my ChangeAbility and minimize my stress. To become even more adept at moving with change it helps to understand what stops change or snags it all up, and to recognize how I cause or participate with these stops and snags.

> "Change is like a boat on the sea of fear. We navigate, and we don't know what's going to happen. There's trepidation. There's this level of courageousness that's required...the courage to face the fear."
> —James Stark

Attachment

What delays personal change is attachment. I desperately hold on and don't want to let go of ideas, or of my sense of self. I don't want to let go of outcomes, or of other people. In other words, I fear that I will lose what I now have, the way things are, or the way I want them to be. I can even have attachment to the way things used to be, wishing they could "go back to the way they were" but they can't. Not ever, exactly. Sometimes I'm attached to the thing itself and sometimes I'm just attached to what is known, just because it is known. The known aspect of it provides me with the safety of the familiar, even if I don't really care for what it is. How does the idiom go, "The devil you know... is better than the devil you don't know"? This is the reason why someone gets hired from within the company over someone much more qualified who is new and untried. Or the rationale for couples to remain together even when they are unhappy. I'm not saying it's bad. I'm just saying we find safety in what is known, even if it's uncomfortable, because what is not known has the potential to be even more scary or unsatisfying, depending upon the size of your imagination. Mine can be rather large.

What impedes social change is certainly attachment, but also politics, power plays, dueling values, differing agendas, lack of awareness, bad communication, and greed, to name a few. But, underneath it all is fear— fear of change, fear of large change involving lots of people, and fear of the unknown outcome of large actions taken. Rationales have been voiced, "If we let the gays marry they'll destroy the institution of marriage"... "If we label GMOs then consumers won't buy our food produced with them and we'll lose business"... "If we don't drill for oil in the Arctic we'll be dependent upon foreign oil and we won't have enough to drive our cars." Fear has also been a major motivating factor for activists working in the environmental movement and other resistance movement, and rightly so. "If we don't stop the Keystone Pipeline, we'll destroy our planet"… "If we don't stop proposed anti-abortion legislation, women will not have freedom of choice over their own bodies and health, and we'll return to dangerous, illegal procedures endangering women's lives." Fear can certainly scare me to "make a change or else…" or, more likely, to "not happen, no matter what." If I have too many attachments to how that change has to take place, and how that result has to look, I will limit my ability to navigate both the intention and result that change brings. I will limit my ability to adapt, and limit my ability to make course corrections in response to change. Any time fear is present in the form of attachment, or any time I have attachment to my fears, I will struggle with my ChangeAbility. I will be locking down the movement of change with resistance.

Resistance

Fear accompanies change, and resistance is fear's henchman. Resistance doesn't really stop the movement of change, but it certainly drags it down. Resistance drags on the movement of change, like how air resistance puts a drag on an airplane's speed, adding extra hours to my flight time. I said before: we are either feeling the flow of the movement of change or our resistance to it. Once I set a new intention for change, or am presented with a new circumstance I must accommodate, resistance can show up in many forms, be it procrastination, inhibition, negativity, stubbornness, or runaway imagined outcomes that don't turn out well. I can be so accustomed to my resistance that I barely notice it, but resistance in its many expressions is the body-mind expression of fear of the unknown.

According to **Robert Litman**, the function of resistance is to slow things down when they are going too quickly to be absorbed or integrated. Resistance has it own physiological process in the human body, and is a necessary mechanism for regulation. Robert speaks to the physiology of resistance. As I mentioned in the previous chapter, according to Emilie Conrad, we move in our lives how we move in our bodies, so resistance isn't just being mule-minded, stubborn, it's a physiological response to wanting or needing to be less open, less permeable, and less subjected to what is on the outside, coming towards us.

Robert Litman: My favorite way of thinking about myself as a biological organism is in my ability to regulate the permeability of the membranes. My nervous system and my fluid body can galvanize itself: can pull the skin in, close the pores down, tighten the blood vessels, tighten the muscles, and constrict the fascia. So, therefore, nothing can move through the tissues. Resonant vibrations, vitamins, nutrients, and breath nutrients have a harder time getting through something that's thicker and more dense. That's resistance, a physiological resistance, which is accompanied by the thought, "I'm not going to let this in, I don't like it, I don't want it." Then, you're just not accepting the reality as it is, now you've got a language resistance up against it as well that's interpreted in the body in the only way the body can do that—it creates density.

I can create density at will. Absolutely do it at will. "I don't want to take that thought in right now. It's too threatening. I'm going to move into a different direction." I can do that ongoingly and say, "I just won't look there. I'm just going to stay dumb about that. I'm sorry, I can't look at that, it's too threatening to my existence."

Resistance really limits the change. The opposite of resistance is flow; it's movement. What is engaged with flow is pleasure, so there's a resistance to the pleasure of letting life take you where it wants to take you.

According to Robert, the extreme state of resistance is being "frozen," unable to move. We can take that literally, or it can also describe the many ways and feelings we can have of being "stuck" and unable to entertain change, or to be able to move forward and initiate change.

Robert Litman: Your inner resources come from an extreme articulation of sensing. The more I'm able to sense, the safer I feel, especially if I can sense my own internal experience. Without the feedback that comes from sensation, without the emotional intelligence which resistance limits because it's limiting the movement of fluid, I won't feel safe. If you take a look at the idea of being frozen, that would be the extreme opposite of change. I'm frozen; I can't make a move, right? If we look at the ecology of frozen, we see the ice caps… It separates the underlying fluid ocean from the landmass on top. Being frozen can also be an invitation into, "Let's go down deeper and see what's really moving underneath while I'm protecting myself in this freeze." Freeze is serving me to keep everything away and everything out. I need this time for myself until I understand what's going on and I can allow myself to thaw a little bit.

> "Resistance is faster than a speeding bullet, more powerful than a locomotive, and harder to kick than crack cocaine."
> —**Steven Pressfield**, *The War of Art*

To take another view of resistance, one of my favorite books on the topic is *The War of Art* by Steven Pressfield. I highly recommend you read the book and keep it close at hand by your bedside or worktable. Written by a writer, for writers, Steven Pressfield's book exposes resistance as a force that shows up whenever we set an intention to create a work of art, start a project, or better our lot. To Pressfield, resistance is a force that takes on many insidious forms meant to trick us from the satisfaction of successful completion. Successful completion would mean successful change, and successful change is resistance's sworn enemy and prime target.

> "How many of us have become drunks and drug addicts, developed tumors and neuroses, succumbed to painkillers, gossip, and compulsive cell phone use simply because we don't do that thing that our hearts, our inner genius, is calling us to? Resistance defeats us."
> —**Steven Pressfield**

Whenever I'm in the heat of a writing project, like this one right now, I find I need to read parts of the book every day to remind myself of all the forms my resistance is taking, and to become refueled in my determination not to succumb. Resistance will call up all my demons of self-doubt and distraction, even the necessary distractions, like when my children need to be fed, or my mother is sick and needs my care and attention. But I find that if I can call resistance by name, it seems to go away, at least until it can shape-shift into another form, and return on another day. Just be warned: it gets worse as you go along.

Here's a story about my guest, Rachel Lang, when she was in the throes of completing her master's thesis in theology. A part-time student with a full-time occupation as an astrologer and intuitive healer, she had been struggling for some time with the time demand of completing this program. In the beginning of her final semester Rachel announced to me that she was quitting; she said she had gotten what she needed out of the program and was, in her mind, done. The time spent at school was really hindering her healing practice, which was rapidly growing and needed more of her time and attention. Resistance was in her ear, and it had her.

But then, a few days later, she decided to go ahead and finish since she was so close. However she had done it, she had beaten resistance. Now she was in the wrestle to actually finish the written thesis that would lead to the actual completion of the degree. I sensed she was having troubles bringing it to a close, and it turned out to be true.

Having struggled with completion many times myself, I knew the territory too well. I told her, "When it shows up, you have to call it by name. I've stood there in my office and as distractions and compelling emergencies came up I'd shout out, 'I know you! You're resistance. You are, and you are, and you are, too!'" Rachel told me she'd do just that.

So, what does resistance do? It steals Rachel's cat! She's a day from writing The End and she tells me her cat has disappeared. It's the one thing that would surely get her attention, and pull her off course. Instead of getting upset, I told her, "That's resistance! Don't worry. It's devious and pervasive, but not evil." I told her, "Keep writing. The cat will be back. As soon as you call resistance by name, it will return your cat and have to find another way to grab your attention." Her cat came back the next morning, and she graduated magna cum laude.

> "Procrastination is the most common manifestation of Resistance because it's easiest to rationalize. We don't tell ourselves, 'I'm never going to write my symphony.' Instead we say, 'I am going to write my symphony; I'm just going to start tomorrow.'"
> —**Steven Pressfield**

Procrastination is a common form of resistance to change. I tell myself I procrastinate because I'm lazy or, "I just don't want to." But, taken to its extreme, procrastination is still fear of change. Perhaps the humor in comparing my petty delays with the magnitude of my most extreme fear will jolly me into motivation to just "do it." I don't think I need to say much more about procrastination. I'm sure you know it well.

> "The fates lead him who will; him who won't they drag."
> —**Seneca**

Denial is another of the mechanisms used by resistance in order to stop change. Denial is trying to stop change by ignoring it. It's a form of rationalization, which is the way in which we justify our fear and resistance. However, change cannot be stopped. It's possible to not face the change, but it cannot be stopped. It can be redirected at times, but not stopped. Many a crisis, even personal illness, has been brought about because of fear, resistance, and denial. Health conditions worsen because I didn't seek early treatment, my relationship is ending because I didn't read the signals of his dissatisfaction and address them before they became indelible, my leaky roof caved in during the last heavy rain because I ignored the watermarks on the ceiling. Denial can give us the false sense that the status quo is unchanged and therefore all right. I said false sense. Ignorance is not bliss.

Procrastination and denial knock us out of rightful response timing. They take us out of the proper alignment with nature that would ease and assist the necessary changes. The climate change deniers are not stopping the effects of global warming; they are keeping timely solutions from being implemented. Forestalling immigration reform is not reducing the number of illegal immigrants living in this country, nor is it making their lives any easier. Ignoring the lump on my breast will not make it go away. Such is human nature. We like to wait until it's in our face. Here in Los Angeles, we are in a declared drought, yet the golf course down the road is still watering their lush lawns every morning. What? The drought is not happening in their yard? It's not their problem because water still flows from their sprinklers? If they don't take actions voluntarily, actions will be taken for them.

Let change change you.

"Acceptance" is a word that is used and overused in our current vocabulary as a sure road to inner peace. Almost as much as "letting go," which I already told you I don't know how to do very well. Being able to Listen Deeply allows me to perceive what is, and receive it. I can acknowledge, *yes, this is true. This is what is going on. This is what I need to do.* I don't have to like the changed circumstances in order to accept them, just to acknowledge what they are. Acceptance seems the opposite of control. To accept means to receive; control means to direct. It comes down to this: to accept is to allow movement to flow. To control is an attempt to hold the movement back, or redirect it.

So, again, what stops change? It's the same thing that stops movement: fear.

Fear

Emilie Conrad would often dramatically say, "All fear is the fear of death." Deaths large and small—in one form or another. All fear is the fear of endings: the ending of the moment, of the relationship, of the way of life, or of me. According to her, our existence is in a constant exchange of dissolution and resurrection, of breaking down and rebuilding, either toward greater health and coherency, or toward greater disintegration, depending upon your conscious participation with the process of the exchange. The trajectory of any fear, if you take it all the way out, is always the fear of annihilation, destruction, and death. The break-up of a relationship—*I'll be alone, I will die*. My hip replacement—*I won't be able to walk, I will die*. Even my fear to read my book in front of a large audience—*I'll make a mistake, I'll be embarrassed and die from shame*. All those fears are some form of the fear of death.

> "We're all going to die, so there's nothing to fear because we're not going to get to stay…so why not just have the wildest, most wonderful, spectacular life that you can possibly have?"
>
> —James Stark

The response in the body to fear, real or imagined, is to literally lock down the tissues, creating a sort of frozen armor, as Robert Litman mentioned. In that moment of assessment before the primitive brain determines fight or flight, it can get locked on hold, creating enormous, prolonged stress that can have detrimental effects on all the systems of the body. This doesn't mean that the movement of change is not still occurring or that the context of change is not still actively in place, it just means that now I have to work that much harder, in spite of my locked-down stress, to navigate the change. This causes even more stress. I'm dragging myself across the finish line against a strong wind, rather than using that wind to sail across.

Robert Litman says that our fears are amplified when we cannot sense what is in our environment.

> **Robert Litman**: Like all mammals, we're sensing creatures. If we lose our ability to sense what's around us, then we get frightened. We're anxious, because our nervous system says, "I don't know what's safe or not. I can't feel it." When I can't feel that, then I get isolated. I have to protect myself, because I don't know what's safe anymore.
>
> Or, we shut down our sensing abilities and hold back, because sometimes in our history, sensing what was happening could've been very painful. We shut down, or our ability to sense is shut down, in certain areas. Movement gets started, but things are frozen. If you've been isolated and you're not comfortable with movement, you start being afraid of the movement. You stop breathing to stop the movement of change. I think, "I know I'm connecting this to the fear. Therefore if I don't move, I won't be fearful."
>
> That doesn't really do it for you because what's really true is your body is still freaked out because it can't feel its environment. The nervous system doesn't like that at all. It becomes such a closed system, it becomes imploded on itself and begins to loop around itself. It loses its sanity, because sanity of the mind has nowhere to go if it doesn't know what it senses. If the body doesn't have the sensibility, then the mind is saying, "What am I going to do here? I have no information. There's nothing coming in from the environment."

Even Small Fears are Fears

"What's the worst thing that can happen to me?" I ask myself when I feel the desire to meet change, and yet I don't move. Embarrassment, hurt feelings, shame, and disappointment do not really equal a true death, and yet my fear of rejection can prevent me from taking any number of steps on my own behalf if the territory is new and perceived of as a risk. It can simply be the fear of making a mistake that can stop me from reaching out. Believe me, I have experienced plenty of each, and have struggled over the years with my resistance to expose myself to even more. The freeze of fear doesn't have to be in response to meeting a bear in the woods, it can be a response to a much smaller fear, like speaking in front of a group, making a cold call for a job, being the first one to say "I love you," or being unable to make a choice between majors in college for fear of making a mistake that seems to have a large life consequence. **James Stark** says that it's fear that slows change down:

James Stark: The fear seems to be generated out of some kind of mistrust that we're not going to be safe. We've got some sort of mental framework that if we don't do this right, we're going to really screw up, and then I'm homeless. I think that "homelessness" is like a mantra or it's a symbol of what happens if you don't make the right change. There's fear. We make up stories, "Oh my God, it could go wrong."

It takes us into the whole Rumi world about right and wrong, and transcending right and wrong, because the framework of that dualistic thing really makes change very laborious and time consuming, and slows the whole process down. If we're not seeing everything as right or wrong, or good or bad, then change can be, "Ah, I'm going to change. What is going to happen? This happened and that happened…interesting."

James, who works with groups that explore conscious aging, stresses the importance of valuing the wisdom of Elders, and for people of a certain advanced age to step into their own Elderhood to give back to younger people who can benefit from their wisdom.

James Stark: I think it's the role of an Elder to guide the vision of what the possibility is to have a human life and to not fear the change. Change is the most amazing gift that you have. You only fully appreciate it as you get to be an Elder and realize, "Oh, I didn't die sixteen million times when I thought I was going to die."

Anxiety

I know that most of the fears that prevent me from taking steps are imagined. The outcomes are imagined, but I have a really good imagination! Why not use this good imagination towards fabulous, positive scenarios rather than the scary ones? I don't know. Somehow, I think that if I imagine the worst, I am somehow preparing for myself for it. Lawyers make a good living doing this every day. However, what I am actually doing is creating the bad outcome with my mind, and putting my body through the imagined scenario as if it were real—so, not a good practice.

Imagined fears cause anxiety. This overwhelming sense of apprehension and fear is often marked by physiological signs of sweating, racing pulse, or shortness of breath. When I'm uncertain of the nature of the threat, or about my capacity to cope with it, it can help tremendously for me to have the confidence of experience of having successfully navigated that change before, and to have the strategies to be able to navigate yet more. But my anxiety can come from a different source.

Robert Litman approaches anxiety to be the result of a holding pattern in the breath. When, for whatever reason, the body shuts down breathing, that body is literally starving for air, and is triggered into a fight-or-flight syndrome that produces what we consider to be emotional expressions of worry and panic, as well as the physiological expressions mentioned above. Holding the breath can be the body's adaptive response to change that is occurring too quickly, and the body's attempt to slow the momentum down. Over a long period of time, the adaptive strategy creates its own habitual problems, which can lead to other physical disorders affecting digestion, sleep patterns, and the health of the heart. This is one of the reasons why the best approach to change is to Proceed Incrementally—slow and steady—in a rhythm and amount that can be tolerated and absorbed by the system and the psyche.

> **Robert Litman:** When people get into an anxious state, they begin to think about their problems over and over again as if they are looping. Their thought comes to, "If I can solve this problem, then I will be able to get out of my anxiety." The truth is, it is not the problem they're thinking about that's going to be the solution: it's changing their breathing pattern that will stop them from having these exacerbating thoughts.

We stop breathing to stop the movement of anxiety, or to stop the movement of fear.

Rachel Lang believes that the uncomfortable sensations of anxiety can be reframed to be experienced as excitement.

> **Rachel Lang:** One of the things that I notice in my practice is right as someone's getting ready to go through a Uranus transit—Uranus is the planet of change, of new beginnings, surprises, unexpected experiences—people start feeling change. Sometimes it registers as anxiety in their bodies, but anxiety and excitement stand so close together in terms of how your physical body responds.

The butterflies that you feel in your stomach, you might interpret as heart palpitations.

What I tell my clients when they're getting ready to go through a Uranus transit or a transit that signifies huge change, is that anxiety and excitement are a polarity. When they start to feel anxious, realize that it's just excitement in disguise. I think we can work with our bodily sensations to make space in our lives for moving into change in a way that we're staying on the enthusiastic, excited, things-are-moving-forward, pole of that emotion.

Context

What happens when I am ready to make a change, or actually do make a change, but the larger context around me does not change? Or when the larger context doesn't change at the same rate or at the same time? The larger context for my personal life could be the people in my life: my tribe, my peers, my family, my marriage, my colleagues at work. The larger social context could be institutional contexts like corporations or governments, or like in Jacques Verduin's case, the prison system, in John Week's case, the health care industry, or in my case, the film business or publishing industry. In the largest sense, the context surrounding change would be the culture in which I live. Each of these contexts have rules and customs that are the guidelines for belonging and surviving, whether those rules are spoken or unspoken. Often what stops change, or keeps change from taking hold over the long run is that I, as an individual, have changed, but my outward circumstance has not. There is a tension between what has changed and what has not changed—or what has not shifted enough to accommodate my change. It could be as simple as: I went off to college but my parents still treat me like a child when I return home. Or that women do equal work in the workforce, but, in large part, still earn less than their male counterparts. It's the whole question of whether change can take place "within the system" or if I need to go out of the system and create a new system to accommodate the new change.

Let's say, a group of people within a company has new idea for a way to manufacture an electric bicycle, but the company makes skateboards. Can the group work within the company, or do they need to find another? Will the context allow these people's new idea to come to fruition and profit, or will the context hold their idea back and they will they need to find another context to produce their product? Or let's say you want to eat more healthily with fresh fruits and vegetables and fewer processed foods, but you live in an impoverished community that is considered a "food desert"—meaning there are few grocery stores and little access to good quality food at low prices. Most of what is on the shelves are foods processed with chemicals, and there is a limited choice of brands. In that context, you cannot make your change. This is why groups like People's Grocery and Oakland Food Connection were created in Oakland, California, to create community gardens and bring fresh produce to low income community members, so they could improve their health through their food choices. The larger context needed to change in order to provide for individual change.

When it comes to changing habits and addictions, it can be very challenging if I am recovering from alcoholism and all my friends still like to drink as much as, say, I used to. They are not going to stop partying just because of me, and I might feel isolated from the group because I won't join in. This is why many people in recovery often need to change their social context, because their previous context reinforced their old behaviors, and they need a new context to support the new change.

Challenge to marriage is often a tension between changing individuals and an unchanging context. My marriage partner and I are always changing, yes, but we are changing at different times, at different rates, and perhaps in different directions. Invariably there will be times of sudden change or significant change. Let's say I found a new spiritual teacher and insist on chanting all night when my partner is trying to go to sleep, or my partner is going through a mid-life crisis and just exchanged the family Toyota for a Ferrari we can't afford, or one of us falls seriously ill. The context of marriage or the desire to remain in the context of the marriage could cause one of the members to decide to stop the chanting or trade back the car. Conversely, the context of the agreements of the marriage could keep me from making the individual change. Let's say I was the breadwinner and was the one who fell ill, but didn't admit to my illness because I had to keep my job in order to support the family. Or, let's say the challenge is that of a changing context of the marriage—meaning the agreement or the shape of the marriage itself— which asks the individuals to change. This could happen through an infidelity or the questioning of commitment, or I could get a job in another city and my partner can't leave. It's always a dance between context and content, between the need for the calm of safety and the excitement of the new.

I think one of the sorrows of old age is when I have to realize that the personal health challenges I am experiencing mean that I will have to change the context of how I live. If I am diminished and now need close personal care all the time and the way I live is not set up for that, I may have to go live with my children or live in assisted living. If I won't be able to drive myself around, that will greatly limit my freedom. There is a tension between my personal changes and the current context in which I live. I have to change my context because my own personal context has changed, and this may be very difficult to accept. I may find that my choices are limited and not desirable. I might hide or deny my health changes until it can no longer be denied, and then the change will need to be sudden and more of an extreme contrast. As a note: I certainly hope we figure out a better solution for caring for the elderly than the options we have now.

As I said before, social change moves slowly because of so many complicating factors and because of so many people involved. Oftentimes, the larger and more firmly established contexts are the slowest to change. Tradition is all about preserving the larger context, over time, through ritual and repetition. *We've always done it this way; therefore, this is the way we do it.* Some people cherish tradition, while others find it stands in the way of responsive innovation.

John Weeks has been tirelessly working to change the enormous and slow changing context of health care, with good results. As former executive director of the Academic Consortium for Complementary and Alternative Health Care, John's mission has been to integrate disciplines of complementary and alternative medicine into mainstream medical training, practice, and policy. According to John, the "medical delivery industry" in this country spends $3 trillion a year. That's an enormous context. He and his organization worked with shared values among the stakeholders to not only incorporate alterative and complementary medicine into their practice and policy, but to evolve the entire industry towards the true support of health, and not the just managing disease.

John Weeks: In entering into what may appear to be a monolith, if you're a bridge builder, if you're a connector, you've got to find places. You walk inside of what may look like a huge unchangeable entity and you discover that inside of it, there are people who may have nothing to do with integrative health and medicine, but they're actually promoting a value set inside of that large entity that's pushing its own kind of change. We realized that they can actually power up what I'm doing, and I can perhaps power up what they're trying to do, if the connection is made.

First, it's breaking through the fear that this thing is so large, breaking it down and realizing it's not a thing. It is, itself, an organism with a whole lot of different players who are beginning to articulate that it's not a "health care system" because it's neither about "health" nor is it a "system," but you can talk about a "medical delivery industry," which is a closer description of what we have. That's a large thing, but it's not a monolith because inside of that industry are people who know the difference between industry, and disease, and health. That's different. That can be a very, very positive thing. We all benefit from that. Then you can have, potentially, a system for creating health: saludogenesis.

Lack of Personal Engagement

Claire Hope Cummings has had a life-long participation with social action and social change, first as an activist beginning with the Free Speech Movement in the 1960s, then as an environmental lawyer, and later as an outspoken print and radio journalist, author, and speaker. Her concerns for how our food is grown and how food and farming connect us with each other and the places where we live compelled her to seek out the research and the stories behind the technologies of agriculture and agribusiness. Author of the seminal book, *Uncertain Peril: Genetic Engineering and the Future of Seeds*, Claire has been at the center of the movement to expose the dangers of GMO technology and industry, and agribusiness' control of seeds. As an environmental activist she is acutely aware of the desperate need for changes to environmental policy and stewardship, and of the need to change the destructive practices of agribusiness and extracting fossil fuels. But, according to Claire, what is lacking is a greater personal engagement and commitment.

> **Claire Hope Cummings**: I adore Wendell Berry. I think he sorted it all out in the seventies, and if we would just do what was said back then, we'd be better off. I don't think this situation has improved at all—acting indirectly rather than making a personal commitment to change your life. And I don't mean just recycling. I mean, really, it goes back to this idea that your life has to be about something other than your own life. You can't expect the world to become a better place for you, if you don't [participate]. And it's not something you can dabble in.

The constant drumbeat of personal change, like you have to recycle, and you have to drive a Prius, and you have to not eat meat, and all these other "solutions" are another way that people get to feel like they're making a difference. But, what was I just reading about? Oh, they have another genetically engineered rice, one that emits less methane. When you grow rice it gives off methane, a powerful grenhouse gas. So they want to use GM technology to change the plants to reduce methane as a solution to climate change, right? Hello! Meanwhile we are massively drilling in the Arctic and carrying on with the fossil fuel economy. These techno-fixes will not solve complex and systemic problems. Getting personally involved in social change and getting political will make a difference, however.

All these big environmental organizations, all these laws we passed, all these academic institutions we have functioning, and yet nothing is really getting done. There is no way to overstate how bad our environmental catastrophe is. I challenge people, or I would through you, I challenge people to ask themselves what they're doing. What are they seriously doing? I can answer that question for myself, but I think so much of this "do-gooding by proxy" and that you can just "sort of" act responsibly as a hobby—is not getting the job done. We can all spend a little more time and effort helping nature survive.

Lack of Creativity

To review, what stops the movement of change is fear, anxiety, resistance, constrained contexts, or in some cases, reluctance. We all have experienced that stop. Sometimes we've succumbed to it, and at other time we've overcome the hold that fear and resistance can have. Or more accurately, we've softened the fear and resistance to have less of a hold so that we could experience the desired movement of change more readily. Passion and courage, Spark Fire, can call up the fires that can burn through my fear and resistance to change. Conviction, commitment, and discipline help to harness and utilize the momentum created by the fire.

Artists, activists, and awakeners each have their own ways for how they deal with their own reluctances and how they encourage change to move forward. They have their own ways to recognize when change has come, and to accept that a needed and effective response is called for. They use their skill and their creativity to find workable solutions. ChangeAbility dances with creativity and flow. Creativity does not exist in an atmosphere of fear, or it certainly does not thrive there. Creativity is the play of invention. It needs to be free and open for new possibilities to occur. Creativity is dragged back by resistance and held hostage by fear.

"The creative impulse arises when the system is at rest—not if you're in fight or flight or you're in survival circuitry. Survival circuitry is meant for you to be focused and on alert, so there can't really be a creative impulse in that moment. Letting the system rest allows the system to be open, receiving information to feed the creative impulse."
—**Robert Litman**

Moving Through Fear

If what stops change is anything that impedes its flow—like fear and all its expressions of anxiety, resistance, procrastination, denial, and reluctance—then whatever can increase flow will assist with the movement of change. Ways to move change or move with change include all the ways I can move my body: exercise, dance, swimming, yoga, sports, walking, running, sexual play. They include the way I move my voice: the play of breath, singing, talking, shouting, chanting, cheering, crying. They include the ways I move my perceptions: seeing, hearing, tasting, touching, smelling—in addition to the movement of my thoughts, and the movement of how I make meaning of all the information from my senses.

The more movement I create in my body, in my awareness, and in my life, the more easily change can move around me and through me. The more I can accept the fact that change is moving all the time, and that the change I am experiencing right now is just the change of this moment—and that this moment will change into the next and the next—the less need I will have to clutch in fear. I will not need to employ fear or resistance as a way to slow down or to stop the movement of change. I can make other choices. When I can recognize my clutching response to the movement of change, I can begin to identify the level of my fear, and whether my fears are founded. I can navigate change by taking care of myself in my fears, and learn to slow down my response to the movement of change, incrementally, or to gather momentum through sparking fire, passion, or courage, as needed. My ChangeAbility will have greater ease and calm when I can respect my fears and reluctances, but not be driven by them.

ChangeAbility = Change + Flow

HEALING:
A PATHWAY TO LASTING CHANGE

I F YOU SEE THE WORK OF navigating change as that of restoring or correcting, solving, or improving existing ills, then all my guests are healers. Whether as artists freeing imagination, activists correcting social injustice and repairing environmental destruction, or awakeners seeking to restore wholeness and harmony, each one is working to remedy some part of life that has fractured or come apart and needs to be restored. They go about their work in various ways as teachers, psychologists, movement educators, bodyworkers, spiritual counselors, Elders, group facilitators, film publicists, writers, painters, permaculture designers, health advocates, organizers of social movements, organizers of homes, and people who play for their profession. They work at the intersections of activism/healing, art/healing, or spirit/healing. It's these intersections that give each of these guests so much dimension and make them so fascinating to me.

I consider myself a healing artist, not only for the restorative benefits of the fluid movement work I teach, but because, in truth, all my writing is meant to bring insight to social issues and human dynamics, even the outrageous romantic comedies—or especially so. My message is always about the animating power of Passion, the clarifying power of Truth, and ultimately, the restorative power of Love.

I wanted to include this chapter on healing in the book because so many of my guests address healing, directly.

Healing facilitates lasting change; change facilitates healing.

I know, I know, healing is about as vast and mysterious a subject as change, but healing and change are partners in facilitating one another. Because so many of my guests speak so eloquently on the subject of healing, I wanted you to consider their considerations on healing as the essential context for lasting change. Our discussion on healing is based on what arose from their interviews, and is by no means a comprehensive discussion of all aspects of healing. Again, I remind you, I am not a doctor, nor a psychotherapist, nor a hands-on bodyworker—but some of my guests are. In presenting this topic of healing to you, I am framing a particular view of healing that my guests and I embrace, that of restoring wholeness and connection within the body, and connection to a larger body—be it community, or the larger body of our Earth.

> "On the girl's brown legs there were many small white scars. I was thinking, *Do those scars cover the whole of you, like the stars and the moons on your dress?* I thought that would be pretty too, and I ask you right here please to agree with me that a scar is never ugly. That is what the scar makers want us to think. But you and I, we must make an agreement to defy them. We must see all scars as beauty. Okay? This will be our secret. Because take it from me, a scar does not form on the dying. A scar means, *I survived*."
>
> —**Chris Cleave**, *Little Bee*

Healing is essential for lasting change. What my guests and I mean when we speak of healing is a transformation, not just a quick fix—a change from an inhibited or impaired state to one of greater health, integration, and connection. What was damaged must be soothed, repaired, restored, and given new pathways in which to grow and flourish. In order for change to be thorough, old patterns need to be dissolved, and new, more coherent and refined constructs formed. In creating coherency in new forms, what has become fragmented or separated, injured or diseased must be made whole again, or perhaps made whole for the first time; whether it's opening my heart to a new love after a divorce, healing my knee after surgery, repairing my home after a flood, or restoring the forest after years of clear cutting. The flow of the movement of change will be impeded wherever healing has not occurred.

These new constructs must be well supported in order to sustain the transformation to a new, healthier, holistic way of being. In order to get underneath patterns created by injury in the body, injury in the psyche, injury in the community, or injury to the surface of the earth, I need to discover what might be holding those patterns in place, and why. I need to Bring Awareness and Listen Deeply to make these discoveries. Sometimes these injuries make themselves apparent, as in the case of a broken leg, or not so apparent, as in the case of suppressed personal trauma.

Healing is change towards restoration, a return to the essence of original being, yet because change is always occurring, I can never exactly return to the same place that I came from. Life will never be as it was even a minute ago, let alone a year or more. But, healing can transform me to a greater sense of well-being wherever I am in time or in space, whether it's an internal or external healing, immediate restoration, or a healing that takes place over time. The outcome of the healing may not have me looking the same as I did before, or feeling the same way, but something about me has been moved toward health and wholeness once again.

Healing requires all the Seven Principles for Change that I have spoken about. Healing requires courage, hope, patience, skilled allies, warm encouragement, incremental movement that does not overreach or overwhelm, increasing awareness—sometimes painfully—a heightened sense of deep listening, trust, refreshment, moving in proper timing, and being able to change the course when necessary.

Amber Gray, Robert Litman, Camille Maurine, Harvey Ruderian, Fred Sugerman, and Jacques Verduin work directly with breath, sensation, tissues of the body, and energetic fields to facilitate restorative change.

Rebecca Mark, Deena Metzger, Jackie Welch Schlicher, Adam Wolpert, as well as Camille Maurine and Fred Sugerman, play with movement, words, images, imagination, and the arts to observe changes that authentically want to emerge without inhibition, and then they show others how to shape and reshape them.

Ann Gentry is hands-on with healthy food. Amy McEachern is hands-on with storage boxes and a tape gun.

Amanda Foulger, Rachel Lang, James Stark, Tom Verner, and Janet Fredericks, as well as Deena Metzger, address healing through spiritual transformation and lifting of the spirits towards possibility and hope for the best possible change.

Social activists Corinne Bourdeau, Paul Rogat Loeb, Beth Rosales, John Weeks, and also Jacques Verduin are working with systems and systems change. They're not trying to restore the systems to what they were, but rather to progress the systems in order to restore human value, integrity, dignity, equality, and overall health.

Environmental activists Claire Hope Cummings, Penny Livingston-Stark, Michael Stocker, and also Deena Metzger and James Stark, work to restore the land, the oceans, and the earth to healthy ecological symbiotic relationships, and as importantly, to heal people's relationship to nature.

In considering healing as a pathway to change I ask: am I listening enough, and allowing the appropriate response? Do I need to look at the situation differently? Do I have enough support and community with me or do I think I must act alone? Do I have skilled allies? Have I grieved for what is lost? Have I given up hope? What can be restored? Am I having fun? Joy? Play? What will refresh me towards courage? What inspires this change? What keeps me going through difficult times? Am I going too fast? Am I aligned with nature? Am I forcing the timing for change? Am I trying to skip steps out of impatience? Are my goals too far reaching, too fast? What is the balance between hope and reasonable goals? Am I in the proper environment for healing to take place? Am I asking for what I need? Can I receive this healing? Can I rest in the atmosphere of love?

Restoration

"Healing is a process through which a system returns to its essential, vital dynamic. All the different parts and levels and aspects come into what I have to call its appropriate indigenous or intrinsic relationship."
—**Deena Metzger,** author, teacher, healer

Restoration could be considered another navigation for change in addition to Initiating Change, Inspiring Change, and Adapting to Change. It is another essential and necessary strategy for navigating change.

Initiating Change/Inspiring Change
Adapting to Change + Restoration

Since change is always occurring and the circumstances of my life are always changing, I can never return to things just as they were. That moment is forever gone. But I can bring back health, or trust, or return the stability of physical or social structures even if they don't exactly resemble what they originally were: Like the way the salamander loses its tail to a predator cat in order to escape, but grows a new tail not quite like the first. Or how I've gotten back with a boyfriend after a separation, but the trust between us remained cautious. Or how our company reorganized after the death of the founder, evolving the founding principles to suit the current need. With new insight and awareness, innovations and strategies, and the environment of compassion and care, Restoration can improve upon what was originally there: the lizard has a stronger tail and is more alert to predators, the trust between my boyfriend and I is stronger because we each worked to become more trustworthy of the other and to cherish the trust, and our company had the opportunity to assess what was not working in the past, and reorganize based on our strengths, renewed commitment, and new goals.

As a clinical psychotherapist, **Amber Gray** uses a body-mind-mindfulness restorative process to address the complexity of the human experience. In her work with survivors of extreme trauma from human rights abuses, organized violence, domestic violence, torture, war, combat related trauma, ritual abuse, and community violence she helps them reconnect to a sense of relative safety in order to reconnect to the outer world. Amber also trains teams working in emergency disaster relief. A somatic-based practitioner, she says, "Whether we describe experience cognitively, emotionally, physically, or spiritually—our bodies serve as the primary reference point for our present-moment experience."

Amber Gray: I'm really glad that you use the word "restore" because that's a word that I'm very particular about. The uninvited change that occurs has an impact on a person's life. That will usually be why they seek change. They seek to come back to some sense of equilibrium, or balance, or reconnection.

I never use the term "trauma recovery." I cringe at that because there is always something that will not be recovered. The thing about traumatic experience, and especially interpersonal trauma, is the world will never be the same again. I will never be the same again. It's not possible. It's a life-changing event and it's a life-changing response.

Restoration, to me, is the word that aptly describes the next level of change that's possible. The primary purpose of the work that I do is restoring a sense of belonging and meaning. I think the large picture is, where do I belong? My sense of how I relate to the world, how I stand on this Earth, how I am grounded and connected in my relationships. The work is about restoring enough connection, internal connections and external connections. Whether it's internal connection at the level of connecting the physical sensations to the memories, to the feeling of the memory, to the emotion of the memory, to the beliefs associated with the memory, or how do I get the courage to get up and go out the door? How do I manage two hours, then four hours, then six hours, then maybe eight hours of my workday? How do I go back and ride a public bus again? A lot of people who come from war zones are scared to ride public transportation.

Harvey Ruderian uses his hands to release the body from its many constraints. A master structural bodyworker, he assists clients to come into balance, releasing deep-set holding patterns caused by injury, stress, illness, emotion, beliefs, and simply the daily ways we move in our bodies as we live our lives. One of the early Rolfers and Aston Patterning practitioners, cranial-sacral and biodynamic cranial-sacral therapists, and visceral manipulation practitioners, Harvey trained with and has taught with somatic masters and pioneers: Ida Rolf, Judith Aston, John Upledger, Hugh Milne, and Jean Pierre-Barral. He has also integrated the psychological principles of the Human Potential movement into his work. Harvey holds an expansive view of the body, the process of healing presence, and of all the possibilities of how consciousness takes form.

Harvey Ruderian: Change, in holistic healing, in biodynamic bodywork, really incorporates change as evolution. Evolution, in a sense, has its own extraordinary mysterious wisdom and intelligence. Certainly, you can try to augment or encourage, but in a sense, you're trying to bring the body back to a homeostasis.

The change, itself, is really a recapturing or a re-spiriting that which already is manifesting, and manifesting, and manifesting. In a sense, flowering. But, it gets so interfered with here on the planet, in this particular dimension where there's gravity, that we get overwhelmed and we get overloaded. We get knocked off kilter so much that we're going in a way that isn't necessarily the most efficient. Yes, we're trying to change that, but what we're really trying to do is reignite or reestablish the body's ability to recapture what was overwhelmed at some point, either by a trauma, an injury, a bacteria, or an emotional impact.

The way I encourage change is through listening with my hands very directly to a "wave" as we call it, "the cranial wave." In biology we call it "motility," a natural motion that's inherent in all tissues all the way down to the cells. You look at a cell, it's always moving. But, when you put all those cells together in the body, the entire body has a particular harmonic. Several harmonics. The one that we call a "primary respiratory system" or a "primary harmonic" has a wave that's like an inspiration. It breathes. It expands. Just like the scientists say the universe expands, right? And then it contracts.

There are long expansions that go over many, many, many, many years, and then contract. Like right now the universe is expanding, right? It's still expanding from the Big Bang, but they talk about a time when it might turn around and come back and contract again, so this is the really long tide, and the human body has these different expansion waves that expand. There's one that does it about eight to ten times a minute, expands all the way out from the midline, and it comes back in again.

Deena Metzger is a novelist, poet, essayist, teacher, and above all, she is a healer. She is a modern medicine woman who has developed therapies for ways in which we can use the origination of Story and the understanding of the story we are in to address physical, spiritual, and emotional disease, as well as community, political, and environmental disintegration. Deena conducts training groups on the spiritual, creative, political, and ethical aspects of healing and peacemaking, drawing deeply on alliance with spirit, indigenous teachings, and the many wisdom traditions. She has dedicated her life to healing the individual, the community, and the earth, seeking a sacred language we can use to speak to these times we are in.

Deena Metzger: What I'm beginning to understand about healing is that it exists within a context, so that as you try to heal an individual system—let's say an individual or a body—you're trying to heal the world, the community that it's living in. So the heart needs to be in a healthy body, and a healthy body is more than a physical body. And then that body also needs to be within a community, or a family, or an environment that is healthy. It's not about equal parts; it's about what are the particular needs of each one of the elements in that system that needs to be functioning in a sustained kind of relationship to the others? So, health is a system of dynamic relationships.

Trauma

"I have come to the conclusion that human beings are born with an innate capacity to triumph over trauma. I believe not only that trauma is curable, but that the healing process can be a catalyst for profound awakening—a portal opening to emotional and genuine spiritual transformation."

—**Peter A. Levine, PhD**, *Waking the Tiger: Healing Trauma*

When an event or series of events impacts me, frightens me, injures me, or alters me, I literally become locked in the fear and terror of the moment the event occurred. Major stress, physical injury, a car accident, sexual assault, physical abuse, war, terrorism, torture, witnessing something difficult; any number of events can induce trauma. The activation of my physiological response to danger becomes frozen in time, and often buried from my awareness. Unless I am able to resolve the trauma in some way, the trauma can show itself in many kinds of physical and emotional symptoms. Post-Traumatic Stress Disorder (PTSD), now more readily diagnosed in war veterans and victims of war, victims of prolonged assault, and survivors of natural disasters, is a delayed manifestation of traumatic stress response.

Healing from trauma is possible, with the proper assistance, though it is often an emotionally or physically painful process of reliving past traumatic events and symptoms. Unless I can heal from trauma to some degree, the trauma will shape my response to the world around me, and limit my desire or ability to move with the flow of change. Unhealed trauma will impede my ChangeAbility and quite likely have me avoiding change, altogether.

Psychologist Peter A. Levine, specializes in the understanding and the treatment of trauma and Post-Traumatic Stress Syndrome. He developed Somatic Experiencing® (SE), a body-based approach to completing the initiated biological survival responses that were unable to complete at the time of trauma. His work has been a highly effective, central approach to healing and restoration after trauma. He is the author of many influential books, including the bestseller, *Waking the Tiger: Healing Trauma*.

"In response to threat and injury, animals, including humans, execute biologically based, non-conscious action patterns that prepare them to meet the threat and defend themselves. The very structure of trauma, including activation, dissociation, and freezing are based on the evolution of survival behaviors. When threatened or injured, all animals draw from a 'library' of possible responses. We orient, dodge, duck, stiffen, brace, retract, fight, flee, freeze, collapse, etcetera. All of these coordinated responses are somatically based— they are things that the body does to protect and defend itself. It is when these orienting and defending responses are overwhelmed that we see trauma.

"The bodies of traumatized people portray 'snapshots' of their attempts to defend themselves in the face of threat and injury. Trauma is a highly activated incomplete biological response to threat, frozen in time. For example, when we prepare to fight or to flee, muscles throughout our entire body are tensed in specific patterns of high energy readiness. When we are unable to complete the appropriate actions, we fail to discharge the tremendous energy generated by our survival preparations. This energy becomes fixed in specific patterns of neuromuscular readiness. The person then stays in a state of acute and then chronic arousal and dysfunction in the central nervous system. Traumatized people are not suffering from a disease in the normal sense of the word—they have become stuck in an aroused state. It is difficult if not impossible to function normally under these circumstances."

—**Peter A. Levine**

What role does healing trauma play in navigating change? Past trauma can keep me from initiating change or being able to adapt to it. If I am locked in trauma I can't respond fully, or respond from a full spectrum of choice. Perhaps I can't respond effectively because my repertoire of response is limited by the interruption and my need for protection as a result of the traumatic experience. My response timing could be off if I have been triggered and become cautious, and therefore delay my necessary response, or have none.

Just as the body develops new pathways to compensate for the limitations caused by an injury in order to function, our psyche develops new pathways of avoidance or compensation around personal trauma.

So often there are personal, emotional traumas buried beneath habits and addictions. Cigarettes, alcohol, drugs, overeating, gambling, violence, or sexual compulsion can be habits and addictions I develop to compensate for pain I cannot afford to re-experience. I have known several friends, in trying to overcome their addiction to alcohol, who had to uncover their adolescent history as victims of sexual abuse. Their pain around the wounding from the early abuse, they admit, caused them to want to numb the pain through drinking alcohol, and then the physical addiction set in. But in order to not return to alcohol, it was necessary to heal the early trauma that lay underneath.

Amber Gray speaks about trauma as a body-based experience.

Amber Gray: Trauma is a body-based experience. Being traumatized is living in a body that includes the entire continuum of human experience from sensation and physicality to the most transpersonal experiences. It's living in a body that is locked down in fear or terror. I've observed a difference in how that lock down occurs depending upon whether what a person experienced in the moment of exposure was a disaster or a human rights abuse. There is also a continuum between fear and terror.

When the body remains locked down, it has not been able to move from the physiological, neurological, hormonal, and physical changes that occurred in that moment. What's challenging with trauma, which doesn't really refer to the experience, but to the impact that it has long-term on the human body, is that, as I said, we don't move on from fear. For whatever reason, whether it's the intensity, the number of exposures, the lack of support after, maybe there's also huge loss of community or support, or the inaccessibility to the right kind of support. A person, or people, remain locked down in the state of fear, and it begins to color their perception of the world and affect the way that they feel, and move, and breathe.

The human response to fear and terror is necessary. It's what enables us to survive these situations. That really has to do with the biology and the physiology. The physiological state has to shift in order to create the space for emotional, psychological states to shift. We cannot shift out of these states of fear without shifting physiologically. We cannot shift the way we feel, perceive, move, or think if we don't experience a physiological state shift.

Amber speaks about the effects of different types of traumatic events, interpersonal events and non-interpersonal events.

Amber Gray: In general, what I have observed is that interpersonal type traumas tend to have, what I call, a deeper impact or imprint than non-interpersonal—people who suffered motor vehicle accidents and disasters and things like that. The interpersonal nature of the exposure definitely seems to create a qualitatively different experience because it undermines the sense of trust that is fundamental to being human, to our humanity.

A lot of it has to do with secrecy. What I have found is that human rights abuses are more difficult—the interpersonal traumas that are shrouded in secrecy, which relate to shame. In domestic violence, people can develop a lot of shame. There can be a lot of judgment. The nature of political torture is to shame. It's not interrogation. It's not an even enhanced interrogation. Torture is intended to undermine the threads of humanity. It's intended to send a message to communities, to families. It's done to exert power and control. It intentionally silences, both in the manner of what torture will actually do to a person so that they can't remember, and also the physiological and biological shifts that occur, the hormonal shifts especially, during the exposure to trauma, change our ability to remember. It's now well-documented that traumatic memory is implicit. It's encoded as sensation and sensory motor information and image, and it's fragmented. It's not chronological. That definitely affects the way a person presents and the way that they continue to move through the world.

Harvey Ruderian also works with a body-based approach to resolving trauma in an individual, be it from physical injury, or other layers of personal trauma. He talks about the experience of "overwhelm," and how the body still records what it cannot metabolize somewhere in the system and the unconscious mind.

Harvey Ruderian: Sometimes things come at us and overwhelm our ability to metabolize. We survive but we can't metabolize; you can't stay totally present at that moment because you're in too much pain. Sometimes, we just haven't developed our nervous system. It could be as simple as speaking in front of a group. When I first started teaching, oh, my gosh. I used to sit there, "Please, everybody, excuse the fact that you see my heart is like a cartoon." [*boom, boom, boom*] My heart was pounding, and then pretty soon it just gets to where you get up there and you'll be able to get the energy from the crowd, and just look out there and say, "Wow, I got it. I got what you'd like me to do up here," and then be relaxed and clear because you practiced. And in practicing, just like with the muscle, it gets stronger. Your nervous system gets stronger.

But a lot of life is to learn that we're here practicing. We're practicing how to let go of the fear of many things, the fear of death. And so, I think things come at us and they hit us a little too hard. And they overwhelm our ability to stay totally present. So, for that moment that we're hit, we go unconscious. It can be a millisecond. But that moment of impact, the strongest impacts of the injury, of the overwhelm…it could just be a surprise. It could even be something that, actually, you're really happy about. You can't take that much in. Too much applause, you might say. And when you go into that place where we step out of our conscious, things get recorded in the unconscious 'cause that's where you are for a millisecond, or ten, or thirty. All that's held in a part of our mind—the recall, the unconscious, and it's hard to access.

In addressing personal trauma **Jacques Verduin**'s GRIP program invites inmate participants to "sit in the fire" of their own personal emotional pain, and to witness the pain of others as a way to come to terms with their crimes, their impulses, and their unconscious strategies of avoiding the deep-seated trauma that contributed to the them. The result is a true emotional healing that then leads the way for transforming their violence into lives of making peace. One of the tools they use to Bring Awareness is mindful meditation, the practice of which helps build a capacity for self-awareness and reflection: experiencing and tolerating painful emotion for the purpose of healing and transformation.

Jacques Verduin: We developed this meditation out of a need to address that so many of these crimes came out of people not knowing how to deal with overwhelming emotions, on how to tolerate difficult sensations that lead to strong emotions. It was really important to address that in a way that would ritualize it, but would also empower it, and bring some dignity back.

We developed this exercise where men learn how to sit and reflect and go to what we call "original pain," a collection of traumas that all of us in different ways as human beings gather—often starting at a young age—and don't know what to do with. Frequently, that leads to medicating it instead of processing it. We say, there are four strategies:

You can run, you can hide, you can fight, or you can learn how to face something.

You go in, through, and out. You burn clean and leave ashes, versus reacting to that pain and creating yet more pain—something we call "secondary pain."

Hurt people hurt people.
Healed people heal people.

Contexts and Holding Patterns

In the previous chapter, I discussed the importance of context in relation to change and ChangeAbility. In order for change to move, the context surrounding the change needs to have enough room for the play of change to occur, and the context cannot be so tight as to limit or choke-off emerging change. A context can be a supportive environment for change to take place like Rebecca Mark's Words and Waves workshops where participants in a small group, using Continuum movement coupled with gesture and writing, unearth unexpected discoveries from their imaginations, oftentimes unlocking stories that were well-hidden even from their own awareness. Or a context can be a constraint on the change that is trying to move, like the confining purpose and design of the controls in San Quentin prison. In effect, what Jacques Verduin is doing with the GRIP program in the prison is setting up a supportive, healing context within the larger constraining context of the prison. Graduates from the program are demonstrating the incredible value of the results created within the healing context, so much so that prison officials are starting to pay attention and determine how programs like GRIP can change the way prisons incarcerate and retrain inmates. The graduates from the program who have been paroled have not returned to prison, a marked contrast to the high 64 percent recidivism rate in the state of California. Many of these paroled graduates are training others on the outside in the ways of guiding rage into power to become peacemakers.

When we see habitual constraints in the body, we call them holding patterns. They can be acute, short-term holding patterns coming from the patterns of how I use my body in every day life, like how I hunch over the computer for long hours and I get the same neck pain and headache again and again. The holding patterns could come from how I might compensate with a limp to keep weight off my injured knee, and over time, that compensation causes pain and pulling in my opposite hip. Or holding patterns can be longer lasting and more deeply set: patterns from birth trauma, or early childhood, emotional trauma, or ancestral patterns of learned behavior, genetics, traditions, or beliefs.

As Emilie Conrad said earlier, "How we move in our body is how we move in our life." This can also apply to larger "bodies" and systems. There are holding patterns of thought—stubborn ideas that won't change, and narrow the way I perceive the world or act towards others. There are holding patterns of belief; some might consider institutionalized religion to be a holding pattern of belief, and religious ritual a means to reinforce the pattern.

Unchanging tradition, both cultural and personal could be seen as a holding pattern, in that we do the same thing every year, on purpose. Say, our family goes to the beach for a week every summer. All family members are present, we have a barbeque the first and the last night, we play Scrabble and cards, and the kids have boogie board contests. There can be something delightful about observing traditions, something friendly and familiar, something to look forward to. The habit of the familiar calms my system, and protects against the disruption of something new. But the tight holding pattern or even the well-repeated family tradition becomes a context where innovation cannot enter. We always play Scrabble; to play Cards Against Humanity would break the tradition. To go to the mountains instead of the beach would also break the tradition. If I, as a family member, felt very strongly about keeping out new changes, there would be little room for change or introducing something new into this pattern of tradition.

My thoughts and feelings form a very important context. Even the stories I tell mysef about myself are contexts for what I believe is possible. These stories effect not only my attitudes about myself and others, but effect my behavior in what could become a self-fulfilling prophecy. What I say to myself when I look in the mirror really matters. If I tell myself I am always sick, it could actually effect the way I take care of my health. Or, as a single woman, if I tell myself I'll never meet a good man, I might not even go out and try. If I tell myself it's a Saturday night in busy Santa Monica but I am going to find a parking space, I'll keep at it until I do. I can change my healing outcome by changing the story I tell myself.

The same holds true about the context of the people I surround myself with. If I surround myself with supportive, loving, compassionate friends, I will have a greater sense of well-being, overall, and any healing that needs to take place can move with more ease and support than say if I were surrounded by critical, petty, narrow-minded people. This seems pretty obvious, but it's amazing how much of my immediate environment I may not consider to be my context, or certainly my context for health and well-being, when it most certainly is.

When holding patterns exist for a long time without change or innovation, they become closed systems, looping the same limited information over and over again without refreshment. What was the familiarity of tradition, or the repetitive habit can become tired, boring, and stale. I lose interest. The nature of any closed system is that without the circulation of new information, the closed system will become inflexible to change and eventually in its looping, go into decline. This is true whether it's in the tissues of the body, like if I don't rehabilitate my knee after surgery it becomes stiff and atrophied; or in the tissues of a relationship, like if my husband and I have the same routines over and over again, get bored but don't do anything to change, we get set in that pattern of boredom and eventually grow further apart. The same is true for closed systems of old institutions like the Postal Service or the DMV that will become obsolete if they don't innovate with the times. A closed system is what we commonly see in the aging process when a person's body becomes more limited, and their lives become smaller, and they become more set in their ways and routines. When we say that someone is "closed-minded," it is that they don't allow for the circulation of new ideas, and we lose interest in hearing their old ones loop over and over again.

> "This work is about changing, but in another sense it's about disengaging. It's about decompressing—taking out that deep, deep, deep holding pattern."
>
> —Harvey Ruderian

Through his structural bodywork and biodynamic cranial-sacral bodywork, **Harvey Ruderian**, unwinds, decompresses, and releases the holding patterns that constrain the body, the emotions, and the energy fields around the body, over time. He describes holding patterns and the compensations we create in order to function around those unmoving places.

Harvey Ruderian: Anything that's disturbed is going to cause a contraction. Then as it contracts, it goes into a sort of stillness. It's a holding pattern that's no longer allowing the movement, so you walk around that holding pattern. If you've got a shoulder that's not working too well and your arms don't swing because that shoulder's holding, as the rest of your body moves, it's going to move around that shoulder, and in so doing it's going to cause a series of compensations. Right? Even when you try to compensate for the compensation, for the holding pattern, you're now creating another holding pattern in order to stay balanced. I consider whenever somebody walks into my office that they're balanced, they're just not in the optimum homeostasis because they have holding patterns that are causing them to have strategically, and sometimes brilliantly, found ways to negotiate. Those holding patterns we oftentimes call "functional." They're a function of a primary holding pattern.

We have different kinds of holding patterns. Oftentimes in the work, there is a more original, what we call the "primary holding pattern." But after a while the compensations become their own real structural holding patterns, too. You can't hold on to something for so long—it cuts off circulation, it starts to dehydrate, its tissues glue together. They create adhesions. We get accustomed to walking around something, moving around it in a certain way.

You want to use what's working to free up what's holding. Whether you do it with your hands on a person or you take a person through what's available… so many of those compensations are compensatory holding patterns that aren't necessary if a person had a little guidance. They're just compensating in order to continue to function, now in a kind of aberrated way…because oftentimes when you had an injury you actually protected that injury for a long time. By the time it heals, by time that broken leg healed, you got all kinds of bad habits of walking… even if you don't notice it. And then that exaggerates and exaggerates.

As a practitioner, Harvey listens deeply with his highly trained hands and with all his felt sense of presence for what he can feel coming from the client. He works with what he refers to as "the tides" of the inner body—different energetic waves lengths that run through the nervous system and the fluid system within the body, and in the energetic fields surrounding the body. Restoration to health and homeostasis, and the clearing of deeper trauma comes from Harvey meeting the waves, encouraging their flow, and resolving any disruptions in the movement of the waves that come through the tissues and the fluid system.

Deena Metzger acknowledges the effect of context on the healing process, and holds witness to the positive power of healing that takes place in the supportive community context of the healing groups she offers. She also witnesses that there are contexts that prevent healing. When I asked Deena what could be holding us back from healing, and keeping us from shifting into greater possibilities for personal health, she spoke about the context of our society at large.

Deena Metzger: What is keeping us from being able to shift our personal health is that we're living in a profoundly ill society, and that the ways of healing have actually become ways of poison. So in this time in history, we have to pull ourselves out of the systems that are killing us, and find what the body originally needed and wanted, and what the true medicines were, or what they might be. They're not in the directions that we're going. We now treat most of our illnesses with poisons, and we poison the earth, which is going to kill us down the line, or our neighbors, or our children. So we're in madness, and what's keeping us from being healthy is that we're crazy, really. We have to get sane.

Safety

In order for healing to take place, I need to have a context of safety and trust. At the most basic level, I need to be able to relax my breath, and settle my nervous system. I need to have support. I need to find the ground I can safely stand upon so that I can step out and move to new territory. If there is risk involved, I need an even greater sense of safety. I can find safety through relying on my ability to feel the world around me and trust the perceptual information I receive. As Robert Litman said earlier, I need to be able to have a felt sense of my environment, otherwise, without that sensory information, I will feel isolated, shut down, and afraid. I can find safety in others, through the support of community, by aligning with nature, and through listening deeply to wise ones around me. I can find safety in spiritual connection, in religion and religious teachings. I can find safety in the lessons of my experience, and the experience of others, to tell me what's up ahead.

When things are moving very fast, or things are so new as to be unrecognizable—I want to feel safe. I want to be able to stabilize while all the other parts are moving. I want to be able to ground myself in whatever feels safe that I can rely upon and trust.

Amber Gray believes a sense of safety is paramount to being able to trust.

Amber Gray: I often say that we can't experience trust if we don't have safety. The roots of safety are in the body, in our experience of the body in the here and now. If we don't experience trust we can't be in relationship. Relationship is the essence of why we're here.

What can I rely on or trust for a sense of safety when all else is changing or challenged—like in a natural disaster? **Robert Litman** says we can rely on our breath. He says first we need to feel the quality of our breath, whether it's fast or slow, deep or shallow. By calming our breath, we can calm our entire system, using breath as the primary source. When I calm my breath, I can calm my nervous system and all the systems of the body it effects. In that calmness I can find safety and therefore trust.

> **Robert Litman**: What fear does to the breath, in terms of fight or flight, is it speeds it up. It's almost like a panting rhythm where it's just very quick. The effect when your body is in fear is the same as when you're in fight or flight—the shutdown of digestion, the shutdown of the immune system, and an elevation of those activities that you would need for your survival. You either get away from what's attacking you, or you are able to fight and kill what's attacking you. That probably doesn't last more than five minutes. A constant state of it is not what's meant for our system, to be on alert all the time. There's just too many stress hormones in the body, and those can be really debilitating. The visceral body, the belly, the stomach, they have their own nervous system. When you're on fight or flight, they're much tighter; when things are safe or you feel in love, your whole stomach and intestines, all of that, begins to relax and you feel much softer inside of yourself.

Grief and Loss

> "Grief is the intelligence of the heart. It is the means through which we understand what is broken, and violated, and injured, and lost, and what we're deprived of."
>
> —Deena Metzger

Even as change requires facing the unknown, change is accompanied by the loss of what I have known. Something comes, something goes. People I love move away or pass away. I get a wonderful new job but I have to leave my community of friends and the vegetable garden that's just starting to produce in my backyard. Or I'm happy for the wisdom of my years, but my face and body just don't look or act like when I was twenty. Some of these losses are insignificant to me; they go with the territory of change. Some, however, are deeply significant and impactful.

Personally, the loss of what is dear to me, the loss of what I have known and loved causes me deep sadness. Some days my heart is heavy for the loss of what I've known, and I grieve. I grieve the loss of my sister, my father, my grandparents. I grieve lost loves and good times gone by. On a different scale, I feel the loss of the disappearing forests to the paving of wilderness. I grieve for the elephants killed by poachers, and the mountain gorillas disappearing from their habitats. I grieve the poisoning of our food, our rivers, our air. My grief reminds me what is dear to my heart by what is no longer to be. Loss is a part of the movement of change, and the grief that accompanies loss is necessary in order to let the movement of change flow through. Tears are like a river releasing to open waters.

I know all too well, emotions have their own movement. They move like waves—huge tsunami waves, choppy rapids, or long slow tides. The best way I know to work with emotion, especially strong and difficult emotion, is to let it move like a wave, allow it to complete its movement and, eventually, to leave. If the movement gets held back, if it gets trapped and stagnates, or an inner turbulence stirs, the unexpressed emotion and grief can turn into physical illness, fatigue, depression, anxiety, or other displaced emotion.

It is vitally important to grieve for what we have lost, to feel the sorrow deeply as a way to honor the loss and to honor ourselves. There is no timetable for grief to visit or to leave. Yesterday was Father's Day, and I posted a photo of my father on Facebook like so many do. He was dancing with my mother. I burst out in tears. Though he's been gone now for nineteen years, I felt his loss. A wise friend of mine says, "Grief never goes away, it just visits less often and for a shorter duration, over time."

Sometimes, you just have to have a good cry, and let the waves of grief wash over you and return to the sea. Sometimes, it's good to dance and shake it up; bring in movement in some way. Or, speak with a therapist or a friend, or stare up at the night sky full of a million stars, or sit at the grave—or what feels like the grave—of a place you no longer can live.

It takes gentle time to heal from grief. And there is no timeline for the healing. All of the Seven Principles for Change play a role. There is comfort and safe ground to stand upon with each one. Have Hope, Spark Fire, Proceed Incrementally, and Find Community (including experts) are especially helpful principles in moving grief.

Amy McEachern, who is as much of a compassionate counselor as she is a mover-organizer, flew across the country to help pack up the country home of a dear friend of mine. My friend's life partner of twenty-two years died from a car accident. The house needed to be sold, and all the contents moved. My friend had heard Amy's podcast interview and was encouraged to reach out to Amy for help. Anyone who has lost a dear one knows how emotionally difficult it can be to deal with clearing closets and emptying rooms after they have passed. Selling that house was the acknowledgement that her partner would never again be there, they would never be sharing that house together, and so she had to move on. As Amy says, the reason for the move, the change, had already occurred. Her job is to help move the things that follow your change. We could look at the necessity of moving from the house as a context that had to change because of the drastic change to life. Together with Amy and a few good friends, they laughed and cried for several days until the last box was packed and what had been the cherished center of so many good times was now empty.

If we can't feel into the heart of grief, we can't truly move on to experience hope and joy. We can't be present to what is now, and what is next, because we are bound by the loss and sorrow that holds us to the past. Grief has to flow. It has to be carried, not just by you, but by the others with you, by your community, until it transforms to the next rightful calling of your heart to action.

Deena Metzger speaks about the necessity of grief.

Deena Metzger: At the last healing intensive, at the very center of it I asked people to identify themselves through the grief they carried, to go right into the heart of it, and don't step away from it. Particularly in these times. So for me, grief is the intelligence of the heart, it is the means through which we understand what is broken and violated and injured and lost and what we're deprived of. We hold that pain and it guides us. A particular grief tells us what we are called to do in the world. It is the compass, and if you step away from it then, very often, what you do in the world may satisfy other needs, but it probably won't get to that absolute work that you in particular are called to because you know it needs to be done through the grief you carry.

Grief is the intelligence of the heart, so when you're talking about change in that way, I think you're really talking about transformation; you're talking about what we're going to do. We're going to step out of allowing these conditions to exist, toward doing whatever we can so there can be a shift.

There is the grief from traumas and loss that seems impossible to move, like the personal losses of war, torture, or abuse, and yet the resiliency of our human spirit allows us that grace.

Amber Gray helps others to find that grace.

Amber Gray: Reconnecting to the things that created a daily rhythm and a routine in somebody's life, all of those rhythmic activities, if you will, the internal, the external connections, they're all rooted in the body. They're all rooted in how we feel in our body, how we breathe, how me move.

Restoration—it's a sense of restoring what we can. We can't put some things back, but we can acknowledge. Often there's a lot of grief and loss work involved in this work. I often talk about it in terms of increasing an awareness. When we live in fear we're not aware. Once we become aware of 'this is what I'm afraid of, this is what triggers me, this is what happened,' then there's a sense of shifting into ownership. That's my emotion, that's my sensation, that's related to that terrible thing that happened. Grieving it, acknowledging it, honoring it, divining it, praying to it, moving it, and then shifting into a deeper processing of that experience. Then, fitting it into the larger life.

Healing Communities

> "What should young people do with their lives today? Many things, obviously. But the most daring thing is to create stable communities in which the terrible disease of loneliness can be cured."
> —**Kurt Vonnegut**

Many of the guests speak about healing communities, or healing within a community, in order to bring about the most effective transformation. A group can hold the field for the one who is need of healing. The group shares the grief. The group helps carry the burden. The group can also be a field of health, coherency, and vitality that I can be sustained by. Often, it is my relationship to others that has been injured and needs to be restored with trust and sharing, and only a community of others can restore that. Isolation compounds or causes injury, contraction, and looping, creating a closed system where new information, new insight, and new support cannot enter.

The communities of Daré in Topanga Canyon, GRIP in San Quentin prison, Words and Waves, or the group work of Adam Wolpert in Northern

California, are all examples of how the strong context of community helps bring about and sustain health and healing.

Deena Metzger has run Daré for many years at her home in Topanga Canyon. Daré is council circle for healing that calls on circle members to listen from the heart and allow the sprits and the ancestors to speak through them on behalf of healing. From her website: "Wisdom comes from the combined voices and the presence of everyone who is participating. The purpose of council is to seek answers from the community that we can't find ourselves. Asking and addressing a single question coheres the community." And, "Daré is for the sake of healing, but we don't presume to say we know what healing is, how it occurs, or even how, always, to recognize it. We do know that healing calls us to wisdom and to living healing lives. We know that healing often requires another to assist in the process. Sometimes one is the healer and sometimes one is desperate for healing. Sometimes the two activities are one in the moment. Healing is, thus, an interchange, the dynamic of giving, and receiving."

> **Deena Metzger**: Daré, which is a gathering of the community on behalf of healing the individual, the community, the environment, the world, is a spontaneous community. Whoever comes through that gate on Daré day is a member of Daré. We support each person's vision and wisdom. We try to illicit from the pile of rubble that's on top of all of us what the intrinsic wisdom healing is, what spirit is calling them to, what it's like to live in a circle with people who may not have met before, and speak the most intimate stories and be heard. And to get support.
>
> So, what distinguishes Daré from many other ways that people meet is that we sit in council, but we don't give any opinions or ideas. We sit in council by telling stories, telling stories from around the experience. When you sit with people who tell stories that are deep and true, it changes everything. Their depth is revealed. I often say when we sit in council, that speaking in council is a commitment, and it's like when a native person offers tobacco. They're being true.

Rebecca Mark has a unique process of using the collective of community in the writing process itself. An award-winning writer, poet, and professor of English at Tulane University, she has published several books. For nearly thirty years, along with Emilie Conrad, she developed a unique creative process for discovering creative voice through movement, expressing what must be heard. Participants in the Words and Waves workshops write their own stories, which include marks, symbols, and drawings, as well as words, on enormous pads of paper. As the group shares their stories out loud, the characters and themes get picked up by the other group members and are intentionally woven into their own story work. So, in effect, while they are each writing their own story, they are carrying each other's stories, as well as carrying the emotional weight of those stories, which can be deeply personal, and at times traumatic. Rebecca describes the powerful effect of how the group holds the story for one another.

> **Rebecca Mark**: If I am given a very heavy rock to carry—let's make that the metaphor for my life—let's say I've been given a chronic disease, or I've experienced the death of somebody I love, or I had very abusive, traumatic experiences in my life. As we know, no one comes to any gathering of humans, whether we call them workshops or retreats or whatever, that does not encompass people bringing those very heavy rocks with them.
>
> If we're talking about healing as a narrative structure, therapy allows you to take your very heavy rock in your backpack to therapy, describe your rock from every angle, present your rock to the therapist. A good therapist is going to chip away at that, reduce the weight of it, not make it so overpowering in your life, and all of that; when we bring those rocks to Words and Waves, that rock is considered malleable.
>
> Language is a moving art. When you are dancing, you're moving that rock. When you are moving, you are moving that rock. When we have sound in everything, you're moving that rock. It's no longer actually a rock. It doesn't have the weight that it had. Particularly in community, everyone can pick that up. It doesn't weigh anything, because it starts to be just something that's handed around to everybody; everybody gets into it. "Oh my God, look at Sharon's rock. It has this cool thing on it," or, "I want to use that part," or, "I like that painting," or whatever, and it starts to literally dissolve and no longer have formal mass, so that what you are actually seeing is a dissolving of matter. After we begin to pick it up communally, then it dances, literally, on the cellular level. That's what's most exciting. That's the change. It's because it's been witnessed.

Community can be comprised of just two, and when **Harvey Ruderian** works with his clients, he steps into a healing bond where he matches his sense of healing presence with what he is receiving from his client, in order to invite and encourage their body, their essence, to restore itself to a more original state of health and homeostasis.

Harvey Ruderian: What's the difference between just holding a head and actually listening? When I listen, I hold your head, it starts to move, and I blend in, move with it, and all of a sudden I've got this thing as if I'm doing a little dance with my hands. It's microscopic but nevertheless that's what's going on. And so there's this dance that begins, and once it feels it gets a sense that I'm holding it, then it goes into a self-correction. It actually starts to renegotiate that which overwhelmed it because now it has my system there, too. We're all kind of like a fulcrum, you know. We're pendulums, we're fulcrums, and when we put our hands on, or even step in, somebody else's field— if a heart is open deeply, there's a place where you go into a harmonic where you unweight the interferences of our belief systems and our impressions that took us out of that place that's most connected to the earth and to our heart. And that's called healing.

So, in that sense, what you do with your hands when you've gone down and listened from that same place inside yourself to some place inside the person that is so deeply part of their actual embryogenic development, is that it actually holds the history of the person. It's got their history. It's actually constantly trying to self-correct but there are certain pieces that it can't do [on its own].

Some part of this thing called "being human" is communal. There's a magical piece that happens when two things come into communion and create what you might call change. I call it the evolution, or the heart of listening.

Amanda Foulger works with the largest sense of community, the community of belonging to the seen and unseen realms. She carries the restorative core of the natural world in her work as a shamanic healer. A form of spiritual practice, Shamanism connects us to the multidimensional network of spiritual support that comes from the natural world and the realms beyond, in order to assist with the many conditions, questions, and problems of human life. It draws from culturally specific indigenous systems as well as non-denominational core shamanic practice in contemporary life.

For over thirty years, Amanda has been a healer, practitioner, and teacher. She heads the faculty of the Foundation for Shamanic Studies. Whether working with individual clients or large groups, she works with the largest sense of healing in community. For Amanda, healing comes from drawing upon the sense of ultimate connection to all of nature and all of the worlds. We are individuals connected to a much larger source, and it's from that source we derive our sense of belonging and therefore restoration to wholeness, and healing. Like all indigenous cultures, her healing practices extend from restoring the individual in relation to the earth to restoring the earth, itself.

Amanda Foulger: In shamanic practice we talk about the middle world, the upper world, and the lower world. The upper world and the lower, cross-culturally, there's a pretty strong agreement about these other realities that are not physical realities, but they can impinge and relate to us in this reality. Then, we have what we call the middle world; Tolkien used the term Middle Earth, and it is this reality, it is this physical reality, which has a spiritual part, but it has a physical part, too. Everything about this reality is about change, and if we cannot learn to deal with change, and if we cannot learn to gracefully move with change, we are not going to evolve.

We get a little humble when we realize we didn't just create ourselves. The gift of life was given to us on some level. There is a kind of creative force at work in the universe, or at least as much as we can understand of it, within our particular solar system and galaxy.

There's a larger sense of being connected to something bigger, a creative life energy or a consciousness. People might call it "God," or people might call it the "creator energy" or something like that. In shamanic practice, we think that we all are connected to that source of power that has brought us into being. Therefore, we have power, and we can learn ways of cultivating power through our spiritual connections and through our spiritual practice—connecting with these forces that are beyond us that in a lot of traditional cultures they recognized as spirits or they recognized as ancestors, literally ancestors, or sometimes just the sense of beings that have existed before us, who have left, who may still have some interest in us here.

The Dalai Lama has spoken, as have other teachers spoken, that we all come from different parts of the universe as souls, but we come here to this planet because this is a place where we can have an embodied life and we get to learn things on a physical level, as well as in other ways.

In shamanic work, when we have a sense of connection to something bigger than us, then it's not so easy to be narcissistic. It's not an ego trip anymore. It's that we're in this together. We have a life experience that's a shared experience, not a solo act. Yes, there's a part of it that is a solo act, but on the more fundamental level, we are connected spiritually and from that great source. While some cultures may favor more being connected to, say, spirits of upper world, or spirits of lower world, or both, those are fine points. Those are culturally specific differences. What I think is not so culturally specific is that there is this deeper spirit, Great Mystery, that we are connected to that is beyond us, and that we get the opportunity to come here and do something with our lives as this evolutionary experiment here on the planet.

Healing the Earth

A large and necessary Restoration is the healing work of restoring the integrity of the Earth. Our environment is being assaulted on every front. Unchecked toxic air pollution in the new industrial China, the rampant spraying of pesticides and herbicides coupled with the rapid spread of untested GMO seeds for our most basic crops, the elimination of biodiversity, oil spills in the ocean, fracking practices polluting the water tables—it's a miracle there's still a bird singing in the sky or fish schooling in the sea. We are not separate from each other, from the land, the ocean, the animals, and all living creatures. The disregard for our surroundings is a disregard for all health and thriving. We are in desperate need to restore.

Penny Livingston-Stark is recognized internationally as a leader in permaculture design. For twenty-five years she has lectured, taught, and worked in land management, regenerative design, permaculture development, ecologically sound construction and design including natural and non-toxic building, rainwater collection, soil reclamation, edible and medicinal plants, and diverse field perennial farms. Penny cofounded, with her husband James Stark, Regenerative Design Institute and comanages Commonweal Garden, a seventeen-acre organic farm in Bolinas, California—a living classroom for learning from the wonders of the natural world, soil-based research, and transformational play. She articulates the interrelated nature of natural systems, social systems, and economic systems, and assures us that the ecological issues we face today are complex, and must be considered as whole and related systems in order to innovate new solutions to the rapid compromise of the Earth due to the effects of climate change, detrimental farming practices, fossil fuel extraction, and air and water pollution. We have to recognize the intricate complexity of ecosystems and learn from them, restoring the natural interdependence between air, soil, water, animals, insects, fungi, and microbes. Our failed approach to the problems of healing the Earth, she says, originates from the narrow way in which we are thinking.

Penny Livingston-Stark: We know how to grow food without chemicals. We know how to clean water biologically. We know how to build non-toxic buildings. We know how to design and build clean, renewable energy systems with what we have on this Earth without the need to continue mining more products. We know how to recycle the products that we have, and repurpose, and reuse. We know how to do everything. The technology is here. That is not our problem. The problem is, the question is, why aren't we doing it?

The answer is multifaceted and very complicated, but it has to do with the human worldview. The way I'm looking at it is that we need to change our worldview and our relationship to the Earth, herself, and I say "herself" on purpose. We need to recognize that we are related to this Earth, that she is our mother, whether you want to think about it the same as our biological mother or not, but we come from her and we return to her. She represents the feminine aspects of the archetype of the world; she's sick and she needs our help.

As long as we objectify nature, turn it into this object, this thing that isn't related to us, that isn't even really alive, it somehow allows us to justify doing her harm, extracting, taking advantage, exploiting, and ignoring the very clear signs of our impact through species extinction, ocean acidification, and all the things that are happening on the Earth right now.

It allows us to think like, "My car needs to go out and get fixed. Let's just go get some new parts and inject them or insert them here, and we'll fix everything." This mechanical worldview of separate parts that we can just kind of fit together isn't what's happening. It's much, much more complicated than that and it's much more interconnected and interrelated as a living system. Until we get this in our bones, and in ourselves, and in our spirit, it'll just keep justifying us to try to create these mechanical fixes that aren't really going to work.

As long as we objectify nature, turn it into this object, this thing that isn't related to us, that isn't even really alive, it somehow allows us to justify doing her harm.

Deena Metzger calls for a revisioning of medicine and healing, one that benefits the Earth and the individual at the same time. What is good for one must be good for the other. As is expressed through indigenous healing practices, they are the same. In our interview, I asked Deena if it was too late; can the Earth heal?

Deena Metzger: We can begin to learn, again, the ways of healing that are not only good for the person but also good for the Earth, and they're good for each other. I think you've heard me say many times that healing is contagious because if you find the life that's good for you to heal, that life, those principles, are going to be good for everyone around you.

You asked earlier can the Earth heal? I said I didn't know, but I also wanted to say that as long as it seems to me there are signs that gather us, or give us instruction, or show us how to walk that we never could have thought of ourselves, then it says to me the spirits are with us, and they're telling us if you shift, everything can heal.

Forgiveness

"I wondered if that was how forgiveness budded; not with the fanfare of epiphany, but with pain gathering its things, packing up, and slipping away unannounced in the middle of the night."

—**Khaled Hosseini**

To be able to open the heart again after betrayal, injury, or loss is a precious act. It requires both courage and compassion. It requires a new movement to emerge from the depths of grief. Forgiveness is one of the most certain paths to Restoration, and it is also one of the most difficult. However, it is an attempt to return to wholeness, once again, by letting go and freeing myself from the tight clutch and heavy burden of caution, anger, resentment, and the desire for revenge and punishment. In forgiving others, I free myself towards belonging and wholeness, be it with the person I am forgiving, or with myself. All the major religions and spiritual teachings speak to forgiveness: the Christian concepts of mercy, the Buddhist meditation practice of loving kindness, the Jewish holiday of Yom Kippur, the day of atonement—or as I like to say, at-one-ment, meaning a return to belonging to the self and the world through reflection and forgiveness. All these spiritual practices of forgiveness are pathways towards spiritual expansion with a sense of the divine, and expansion of the heart in human connection. Forgiveness does not have to mean reconciliation or condoning the offending act, but forgiveness can free up the constriction and allow us to move more freely with the movement of change.

In **Jacques Verduin**'s work with violent offenders in prison, forgiveness is an undercurrent of the experience, though Jacques will tell you, forgiveness is not always easy to come by. In his programs that create opportunities for dialogue between victims and offenders, forgiveness must come in its own timing. In the GRIP program with inmates, finding forgiveness with themselves for their crimes and actions is encouraged, as it opens the door for healing, but again, arrives when it is ready.

> **Jacques Verduin**: For some people in the [restorative justice] movement, forgiveness has moral value, is a goal, is something that is a desirable result. We don't have that because the way we look at it is you can't make that happen. You can't force that; you can't drive it. If it's to be there, it has to arrive by its own virtue. We do explorations on forgiveness meditations, but what distinguishes our meditations is that it really takes into account whether you're ready to engage in forgiveness or not. If you're not, there's a different exercise where you can say, "May I be willing to forgive you when I'm ready to do so." You can actively put that intention out so that you're in a different field where that can come to you. We've had victims come to us that want to meet with their offender. For example, "Because I want to ask him what are the last words of my beloved, my eleven-year-old boy. Not because I have some obscene fascination with that, but because it would set me free not to have to imagine what that was for the rest of my life." Who are we to say that you ought to forgive that person? That's entirely between the god of her understanding and her.
>
> We have a pretty pronounced clarity on how we work with forgiveness. It's not a desirable result on its own. You don't forgive the person; actually, you let go of the resentment and the energy of contraction. You don't have to excuse the act. You don't have to condone the act, but you just have the clarity that there's timing in this whole process. But when you get to that point, you have the clarity that says it no longer serves me in my power to hold this revenge or to hold this resentment inside of me. I wish to release that, which is, of course, very different than condoning what has happened.
>
> There are stages of this process. There's a stage where it's very important to be fully pissed off, and angry, and vengeful, and claim your statement that you don't agree with this, and to let somebody be in that for as long as they need to be. Like I said, it's like grace. It comes. You can't make it happen, so you create the circumstances for that, and then you respect the timing of everybody that wishes to explore that.

If my goal in ChangeAbility is to have more fluidity in meeting change, or more power in initiating change, then, as these guests have articulated, softening the effects of injury and trauma is necessary to allow for the movement of change. Injury and trauma create their own internal resistance to new change, even beneficial change, because of the compensatory holding patterns surrounding and protecting the site of past injury and trauma. Some of these resistances are known to us, while other remain hidden. But they are still impeding the flow of positive change.

In this chapter, my podcast guests and I have discussed that there are many ways to soften or dissolve trauma, and heal and restore a person, or an environment, to its sense of wholeness and balance. Context is very important in allowing change to occur; healing contexts are most beneficial. The context of healing in community, even a community of one other as described by Harvey Ruderian, supports the changes we cannot carry on our own.

As we seek Restoration for ourselves and our world, let us all join with others in softening and dissolving the obstacles to the free flow of change. Let us find lasting change though Restoration and healing, and a 360-degree stability in navigating the movement of change.

ChangeAbility = Change + Restoration

LISTEN
DEEPLY

BRING AWARENESS

FIND COMMUNITY

INCREMENTALLY

OCEED

WITH NATURE

HAVE HOPE

ALIG

MOVE WITH CHAN

PART TWO

INTRODUCTION TO PART TWO

OW THAT YOU HAVE BEGUN TO understand the Nature of Change, I want to invite you into a deeper and wider consideration of each of the Seven Principles of Change:

Bring Awareness
Listen Deeply
Find Community
Proceed Incrementally
Align with Nature
Have Hope
Spark Fire

In these next chapters I will discuss these seven principles and their application for the navigation of change in more depth, and you will read longer excerpts from each of the podcast guest interviews to illustrate these navigations. Each chapter can be seen as a mini-conversation between those particular guests and myself on the change principles they reflect upon most in their work and in their lives.

When it comes to ChangeAbility, there is much to consider. Change in the modern world is complex. Whether we experience the swift and sudden swirl of multiple events occurring interdependently, or we experience the stuck and stagnant resistance that prevents the rest of our lives from moving forward, we can become weighted by our emotional response to the complexity of change—and this can greatly cloud our perspective. Throughout this book, it continues to be important to carefully isolate and articulate each aspect of change for clarity and understanding—knowing full well that the navigation of change is not simple.

As you learn about each of the Seven Principles for Change, I hope you will continue to consider how each one interacts with all of the others. These principles for change are inseparable from one another, though at various times one may come to the front while others recede. Understanding how they interact as a whole will help remind you that they are all an essential part of the spiral of change that is moving all the time.

Again, it is my hope that you will take inspiration and instruction from these pages, and increase your ChangeAbility by the time you reach the last page of this book.

BRING AWARENESS underlies all the seven principles.

LISTEN DEEPLY informs all the seven principles.

FIND COMMUNITY supports all the seven principles.

PROCEED INCREMENTALLY builds all the seven principles towards realization.

ALIGN WITH NATURE creates proper relationship for all the seven principles.

HAVE HOPE lifts and inspires all the seven principles.

SPARK FIRE compels and animates all the seven principles.

FIND COMMUNITY

LISTEN DEEPLY

PROCEED INCREM

ALIGN WITH NA

BRING AWARENESS

HAVE HOPE

SPARK FIRE

1

BRING AWARENESS

Discovery, realization, notice, awakening, consciousness, knowledge, information

"Our lives end the day we become silent about things that matter."

—Martin Luther King Jr.

VERY JOURNEY TOWARD CHANGE BEGINS WITH awareness. *Where am I now? What are my circumstances? What do the sensations of my inner landscape tell me?*

If I'm seeking to bring about change, then the next questions come: *What are my needs? What are my desires? What is it about my current situation that is not working and needs to change—or what is changing in a way that needs my changed response?*

Awareness, like change, is all that we are. Awareness is what many spiritual traditions refer to as our consciousness, our essence of being. So, in effect, I cannot *create* awareness, because awareness simply *is* my state of being this being. I am awareness. I am consciousness. I am change, whether or not I experience myself that way. In fact, I may not even have an awareness of my awareness—which I think is called "clueless" in most circles. However, the word "awareness" can be used in other ways to describe knowledge, as that which we actually know with our minds or sense with all our sight, hearing, taste, smell, and especially for our discussion, our *felt sense* of internal and external sensation. When I'm lacking information, experience, or insight, it could be said that I'm lacking awareness. When I talk about expanding awareness I'm speaking about deepening my experience of consciousness—the experience of my essential nature or the nature of life. This is accompanied by insight and a deep sense of intimacy with myself in resonance with the natural world, the cosmos, other living beings, and other aspects of a shared consciousness. When I speak of the principle for change, Bring Awareness, I'm referring to the ways in which I bring a greater sense of knowing to myself or to others—in any number of ways.

Awareness can be cultivated internally or it can be directed outwardly to bring awareness to others. Externally, awareness can come to me in many forms of new information: from reading a book, a viral post on social media, a lecture, a film, to some gossip from a friend. My awareness can increase through my direct experience: I take a course in ceramics, I learn about my friend's religion by participating in her church events, I learn how to raise a garden by planting one, or how to care for my new baby, one diaper at a time. My awareness can come through observation: witnessing an increase in the homeless population on the streets of Santa Monica, seeing the beach littered with garbage from the storm drains after the rain, or sitting in on one of the GRIP classes inside San Quentin—an absolutely inspiring experience, by the way. Seeing is believing, they say. They also say that we don't know another's experience until we've walked inside their shoes.

The internal awareness of self-discovery can come with new insight, new ideas, new emotions—but, foremost, internal awareness comes through the awareness of my own internal sensation. How do I feel inside my body? What is my response? I'm aware of my sensation when I feel energized by a healthy green drink at Real Food Daily vegan restaurant, how my body feels awakened and alive in one of Fred Sugerman's movement classes, or how it feels to be sick or in pain. The sensation of strong emotion after I've broken up with my boyfriend—burning in my chest, tight breath, tight stomach, tears—gives me the awareness that I'm upset. The insight as to why we broke up brings another type of awareness.

Becoming quiet and still, learning how to heighten my sensations by using sensory awareness, meditation, listening to the wind blow through the trees, listening to an inner voice, or listening to the voice of my God or spirit guide: these are all ways that I can expand my inner awareness into a quality we call "presence." To have presence is to be fully aware of my surroundings and my inner landscape through the quality of my sensations. To be in presence is to fully inhabit my body and my being in this very moment. I'm not wandering off in thought to the past or the future. Presence is having all my attention in one place; that place is my sensation of being.

> "Meditation, mindfulness, yoga, performing arts, or athletics—all of these things require a presence or a state of mind that is directed into the present moment... If there's any secret, if there's any mystery school, they are all saying, 'be present.'"
>
> —Fred Sugerman

According to **Robert Litman**, all awareness begins with the breath. The awareness I place on the inhale, the exhale—and the empty place of suspension between the two—offers me the opportunity to know myself intimately at the most basic level. The quality of the movement of the breath—its depth, rhythm, and fullness—is my body's response to the ever-changing world within me and around me. Those same qualities of breath also shape my outward behavior and the capacity for interaction with my world.

> **Robert Litman**: I navigate change by merging, by bringing my awareness to the movement of breath as my primary resource for entering into my internal reality of existence. Not looking outside of myself for answers, but inside of myself for answers.
>
> Noticing as I watch the rhythm of my breath: what kind of response am I in? Am I anxious with it or am I comfortable with it? My breath will tell me. Learning how to create an internal environment that's receptive to the movement of breath means reducing my tension levels, and being more connected to ground. Whatever I do, I want to create a home for this force that wants to travel inside of me to be as welcomed as possible, no matter what. It's all in the breath.

Not only is noticing the quality of breath the primary awareness, it is also the basis of how I accept the movement of change outside myself. Again, I move in my life as I move in my body, and so it is also true for breath. I move in my life in the way that my breath moves. Therefore, how free or how constricted I am in my breathing both reflects and determines how I will move with external change, as well as how I will move with the awareness of that change.

Robert Litman: You can see that there's a change on the horizon, it's going to arrive and it's going to leave. Can I be receptive to how things arrive, to the movement of their arrival? If I go back in my breath, my breath arrives in me. How am I to welcome the arrival of my existence, right in this moment? How ready am I, when I breathe out, to say goodbye and wonder if I will have another moment or not? I'm willing to let go of this moment, although it is unknown whether I will get another. Things leave, things come back. I don't know how they do that. A mystery.

We're always connected to the processes of change. Changes in breath, changes in movement, changes in mood, changes in the way we hold our body, changes in our tiredness. Any place you look, everything is always changing. As the osteopath Bonnie Gintis said, "When we see ourselves in the solid form, we're just seeing a momentary aspect of spatially ordered metabolic activity." The metabolic activity of life is always moving, and change is constant. My awareness of that relaxes the anxiety I might have around change, for that moment anyway.

BASELINE

Awareness can begin simply by noticing—the feel of your breath, the thought that crosses your mind, the first signs of spring, the change of light from day to night. Often awareness comes by contrast. *Five years ago I used to be able to leap up these stairs without getting winded, and now I am out of breath.* Or, *I used to think he liked me, now I'm not so sure.* Or, *last week I walked by this tree and the branches were still bare, now I see tiny green leaves.* Or, *it's staying lighter later. It's not dark when I get off from work.* Contrast can also come with a more general sense of time comparison, *We never go out anymore. All we do is stay home and watch TV.*

Being able to find contrast requires first that I pay attention, *now.* If first I become aware of my current state of being and my current circumstances through my internal sensation and through whatever portals of information are available, then as things change, I know the way and the degree in which they are changing. The timeline of men's receding hairlines, from now to later, is a good, but perhaps rude example. The marker of the dropping water level on the summer lake is perhaps more kind: I understand the change through the contrast I had previously marked.

In Continuum we call it "taking a baseline," assessing where I am right now through feeling my internal sensations. When I sit quietly, what am I aware of inside my body? What sounds do I hear? Sights? Smells? A baseline could also be taken based on external circumstance and cues, often marked in time—*Today is my first day of school,* or, *This time is my personal best to beat in the swim race,* or, *I know where I was when JFK was shot.* People often use photographs to mark a baseline of how we are now. Today's family photos become precious, laughable keepsakes twenty years and a few fashion trends later.

Oftentimes I'm too busy, distracted, preoccupied, or insensitive to have awareness. I'm sorry, did I just describe my ex-husband? Just kidding. I have a friend who is forever searching for her keys. I tell her she can't remember where they are because she wasn't paying attention when she placed them down in the first place. It's true. I'm going to miss a lot if my attention is not with me in the moment. Can I sum it up in one word? Cell phones. All right, there are other distractions in life, too, but the habitual tick of checking my personal device constantly disrupts my attention and, therefore, fragments my awareness. Multitasking splits my attention and requires me to be fluid in my presence from one task to the next. It can certainly be done, but often in those situations where my attention is split, my awareness is of a sense of blur, confusion, anxiety, overwhelm, and of not being grounded in the presence of the moment. Those uncomfortable sensations will always speak more loudly to me than the task at hand.

Sometimes I want to have awareness but information or direct experience has no way of reaching me because where or how I live my life doesn't give me access. If I didn't walk by the beach that day after the rain I wouldn't have seen the debris. Or I can have a direct experience with the homeless people in Santa Monica as I pass by, but unless a news service is covering the problems for the homeless in New York City, or the displaced of people of Nepal after the earthquake, it won't come across my awareness. Maybe it's on the news, but I don't watch the news, or I don't see the news story that day, or I follow Fox News instead of CNN and the story is slanted in a particular direction, or the news item has already scrolled down on my Facebook feed—so I remain uninformed.

It's strange to think about: in 2013, a friend and I were about to walk into a restaurant in Ojai, California, when we heard the news over the car radio about the bomb explosions at the Boston Marathon. We were stunned and horrified, and our hearts were heavy as we went inside the restaurant in a state of disbelief. Looking around, it was apparent from the lively conversations and upbeat moods of other patrons that they'd not yet heard the news. This tragic event had already occurred; our awareness of the news had completely altered us. But, because these people were not yet aware, it was not yet part of their world. Not yet. Soon enough everyone would find out. As a public, we are always all in different states of awareness regarding information, all the time.

There are those people who find no value in learning about people, places, or events that don't have a real, direct connection to their own lives. I have easy access to information about the entire world at my fingertips, but that is an enormous amount of information. How can I be aware of everything, everywhere, all the time? At some point, the cacophony of messages causes me to want to shut out *extemporaneous* information, or soon, *all* information. I find that I create filters and categories of concern, consciously or unconsciously, as a strategy to contain the onslaught of information I receive. This may not necessarily the best strategy for social engagement, but it is a strategy for self-preservation.

When it comes to awareness, it could be that my attention is simply placed in another direction, not based on my distraction, but based on my interest. I have a necessary selection process based on my capacity, access interest, and the contexts of information I participate with—news sources, conversations, or even what I gather in observation walking in the woods. Providing new awareness requires "getting" my attention from all the ways it wanders, is distracted, or diverted. Advertisers have been challenged with this for years, and keep pushing the bar of what they will use to get my attention. Awareness needs to "hold" my attention based on interest, and that will have everything to do with my personal set of values.

INFORMATION

If only they knew! How often have I said this? Information is powerful. It can change the way I think, the way I feel, and the way I behave. All the ways in which information is shared—conversation, books, photographs, news, and media—are valuable tools for learning what I don't already know, and for sharing what I *already* do—but you don't. Sharing information, indeed, increases awareness. But, as I said, the Information Age in which we live has become the Information-Overload Age as I become assaulted and oversaturated by all the hundreds of messages that come my way from numerous sources and devices over the course of each day. As I prioritize what will filter through, I'll need to have direct experiences in order to have anything but a fleeting awareness. I'll need to have these messages be grounded in some sort of relevance to my life or my preferences.

The issues and information that directly impact my survival, my interests, or my concerns are the ones that will get my attention and have a chance to affect my awareness. Which is why information that is entertaining, provides pleasure, or refreshment is going to get more attention. That's why people are far more willing to watch funny commercials on television. I used humor and playful sex in my book *Donny and Ursula Save the World* for this very reason—to get readers' attention so I could increase their awareness of the much less humorous or sexy topic of an agribusiness takeover of agriculture through GMO technology. Some messages are far from funny or sexy, like police violence and racial hatred. Those messages must appeal to my heart and my sense of justice, to what I care about, what is right, and what needs to be corrected.

FROM INFORMATION TO ACTION

> "People don't want to know. They have to be made to know. Whether they act on what they know is up to them. But they have to know."
> —**Anthony Burgess**

When it comes to navigating change, the big question is: *do information and awareness necessarily lead to action?* No. Not necessarily. I could become informed and remain unmoved. So what could cause me to reconsider? If I became aware of something that ignited my sense of justice—*this is not right, something must be done about police violence toward African Americans*— or my sense of survival—*a hurricane is heading our way*—or just my good sense—*studies show that smoking causes cancer*—I might take action. Some would say we are compelled to action if the awareness engages our anxiety and sense of insecurity. That would be the advertising industry. *Are my teeth white enough? Do my carpets smell? Will I be loved if I don't have the latest version of the iPhone?*

My source of information or the source of my awareness also makes a huge difference as to whether or not I heed the message. I'm more likely to move toward change if I trust the source, if I care about the source, and if I have a direct experience with the source. I am more likely to protest a particular act of police violence if I am part of the community in which the violence took place. I am more likely to evacuate if I trust the weather service to be accurate. I am more likely to stop smoking if the request comes from my child.

For people interested in change, I would like to assume that simply giving information and raising awareness about an urgent and compelling issue would automatically spark an action to address it, but so often it's not the case. Surely, Americans finding out about the Ebola outbreak in Sierra Leone would have wanted to do something to help relieve the suffering patients and health workers. Certainly some did, while others simply took precautions to make certain they, themselves, didn't get sick, even though the outbreak was across the globe. Of course, if the public had no information or awareness at all about the dire situation there, they couldn't even begin to take action. They wouldn't even know to respond with money and assistance, or where to send help.

West Africa is very far away, and the story wouldn't hold attention for very long without a direct impact on American lives. If the danger from the outbreak is too removed, then it becomes just another piece of news. The closer the event or information affects me and my need for survival, the more my awareness increases. *Am I in danger? Do I need to fight? Do I need to run?* Will that awareness be enough to make me take action? It was not until the few cases of Ebola appeared in the United States that suddenly it was all over the news, and necessary precautions were taken at hospitals and health centers across our nation. The possibility of contracting the potentially deadly disease in our own cities got Americans' attention, and compelled us to action—in some cases, overreaction. The concerns over the deadly Ebola virus spilled over to the public panic over the forty cases of measles exchanged in Disneyland that had the public denouncing anti-vaxxers as bomb-strapped jihadist terrorists.

Claire Hope Cummings says that years ago, information used to motivate people to action. That is, she says, before we became so overwhelmed by the amount of information, and inured to horrible images that come at us through the media and social media to the point of making us numb. Now, startling information and images that used to compel us to action, in and of themselves, no longer do so.

Claire Hope Cummings: The Civil Rights Movement was brilliant at creating the pictures of the fire hoses on the protesters, and the bombings, and the horrors, and the church burnings. That's how we got that idea because the Civil Rights Movement, and the media at the time, told the story. The same was true for the Vietnam War. One of the reasons we ended that war was because information did work to alert people.

As a society, we also used to trust the news media as a reliable source, so that if we saw images of fire hoses on protestors or images from the Vietnam War, we believed what we saw was true. We believed the news media was unbiased and accurate. This is no longer the case. If I don't trust the source of my raised awareness, be it the news, my teacher, or even the signals I get from my own internal sensations about an illness or about my health, I will be far less likely to take action on my awareness. Bring Awareness requires trust.

Bringing awareness and building upon it is always the challenge in creating social change. Often, the information and awareness that activists and awakeners need to bring is about issues hidden from the public; often they are unpleasant. Two right-to-know labeling issues come to mind. The first issue involves the legal battles to label foods grown and processed from GMO seeds, and the second is in regards to government protection against labeling chickens raised in the USA that are then sent to China to be processed in unhealthful conditions and sold back on the US market. If I really follow my newly informed awareness, it's going to mean that I won't eat anything from a store or restaurant that's not organic, and I certainly won't be buying chicken. And even then, facts are hidden. Breakfast cereal labeled "organic" could still contain GMO ingredients since none of the ingredients are required to be labeled. For instance, I just found out that my favorite type of black tea that is sold in organic-type packaging is manufactured by a larger parent company that donated large sums of money to defeat GMO labeling efforts. So, now that I know, even though I love that tea, I can't buy it and still have integrity with my values. Bring Awareness is not always an easy choice.

Activists and awakeners also bring new perspectives to issues that are already known, and people may or may not be convinced, like correcting the public's misunderstanding about the relationship between federal funding for Planned Parenthood clinics, women's health care, and abortion. The majority of Planned Parenthood's services are for women's health care in general—only a very small portion goes to fund abortions. But spreading that information in order to change awareness requires money and resources to spread the word beyond the small circle of those with direct experience. This also requires receptive listeners who can appreciate, with open minds, the new information they are being told.

Michael Stocker has been advocating on behalf of marine life impacted by the detrimental effects of increasing noise pollution in the oceans. Military interests and business interests have not taken these animals and their natural habitat into account nearly enough.

> **Michael Stocker**: Cassandra was somebody who was a visionary. She had an ability to be able to see over the horizon, and nobody would believe her. That was her curse. I'm feeling like that a bit, because I have a systematic way of evaluating stuff, like these noise makers in the ocean…

Michael presents research papers and attends hearings to convince these industries to consider the habitats of these sea creatures that are being greatly impacted—in this case, by sonar.

> **Michael Stocker**: These people tend to think that when you put something in the water that's annoying, the animal will just leave the area. They will, but that's where they live. It's the same as…if you want to put a refinery somewhere, why don't you put it where the [poor] people are? Because they don't have a voice. That's the whole environmental justice thing we're not extending to animals. "Well, if they don't like it, they'll just leave." Okay, they'll just climb out and say, "I'll go to Central Park. This water thing is not working for me; it's too noisy in here." My empathic sense of these magnificent animals—they're innocent and we're subjecting them to all kinds of nasty, nasty stuff. These signals that they're putting out there, people can't hear them. What I have to do in order to get people to hear them is to take those signals and I lower them down in pitch and say, "This is what it sounds like to them."
>
> It's amazing how fast this stuff is being deployed and nobody is thinking about it. I've been saying this for years. One of the reasons I got on board is I saw in 1992, it was the beginning of the age of communication underwater using sound communication in water. Back then, it was acoustic thermography—there were low frequency signals they were using across the ocean base. It's not necessarily a bad idea, but if that were the only problem in the ocean right now, I wouldn't be doing what I'm doing. It's just they're using the ocean as a transmission medium

for all kinds of information, all kinds of data. It's not healthy for these animals. They're stressing out.

It just pisses me off when I hear people who are doing marine mammal studies saying, "Well, maybe they're just habituating to it and they're getting used to it; they're learning." That's what they said about the whales in whaling season when the whaling seasons were getting scarcer and scarcer with the start of mechanizing commercial whaling. For a number of years people said, "Wow, these whales are getting clever. They know what's going on. They hear it's coming now, and they can get out of the way." That's when I said, "No. They're just not there anymore. You killed them all." Then they started regulating, but it was that real naive argument. The Cassandra thing.

Awareness is necessary in order to begin to contemplate an action, but awareness, by itself, does not guarantee action. Whether it's because of apathy or overwhelm, unless I am so compelled by the intersection of my values with my new awareness, I may choose to *do nothing*. On the other hand, it may become essential to me that I *do take an action*. This was certainly my burning question when I wrote my novel: *When does our awareness become so full that we quake with its vibrancy and cannot sit still? When will we take action?* This was the question and its variations that I was asking my guests: *How have you raised awareness, and how have you been compelled to take action? How have your actions inspired others to take action?*

> "What makes you think human beings are sentient and aware? There's no evidence for it. Human beings never think for themselves, they find it too uncomfortable. For the most part, members of our species simply repeat what they are told—and become upset if they are exposed to any different view. The characteristic human trait is not awareness but conformity, and the characteristic result is religious warfare. Other animals fight for territory or food; but, uniquely in the animal kingdom, human beings fight for their 'beliefs.'"
>
> —**Michael Crichton**

Bring Awareness can be a challenge for creating social change; it can also be a challenge to personal change, because lack of self-awareness, or denial, can block even the perception of the need to change. Resistance to change often appears as the refusal to become aware, because once I know something to be true it becomes difficult to look away. And now, knowing what I know, there is more of an imperative to take an action. If I don't want to take the action, I will have to resist and deny the awareness of what is, else I'll feel too much tension, or even guilt.

Consider any number of patterns that I might need to change for greater health and well-being: a change of diet, more exercise, or to quit smoking. Or consider behavioral patterns that I might need to change: my need to listen to my partner more and not be so defensive, or the way I spend more money each month than I have, or how I don't take proper care of my car. If I am in denial, even when others have made these requests for me to change, I may not understand the consequences that come from these refusals, such as illness, my partner distancing himself from me, running high debt, or my car suddenly stopping on the freeway. These consequences may seem sudden. However, they are evolutions of conditions I was not willing to look at, embrace, or change. Ignorance is not bliss. Perhaps it can be—but just for a little while.

In the case of trauma, as I said earlier, patterns of behavior may be hidden from my awareness, and it will take healing at some level, often with professional, therapeutic assistance, in order to be able to move into greater awareness toward change.

RAISING AWARENESS

"Until you make the unconscious conscious, it will direct your life and you will call it fate."

—C. G. Jung

So, how do ChangeAbility artists, activists, and awakeners use novel ways to Bring Awareness and *keep* awareness on the areas they feel so passionately about? Awareness that they hope will spark action toward lasting change? I'll mention a few for whom artistic invention and clever creativity spark a certain fire of delight in attracting attention and holding it.

In 2008, the organization 350.org wanted to plant the number 350 firmly in the awareness of people around the world. The number 350, scientists tell us, is the allowable parts of CO_2 per million in the atmosphere to preserve a living planet. We are currently at 400 parts per million, which does not bode well for us. When the organization began, 350.org staged aerial photographs all over the world; people from diverse populations in a multitude of geographies held up signs, or formed mass human sculptures spelling out the number 350 in order to raise awareness. Now, the group is one of the leaders in creating a global climate movement to move us away from fossil fuels, in over 188 countries around the world.

Another surprising, creative action that gained world attention was the Ice Bucket Challenge to raise money and awareness for Amyotrophic Lateral Sclerosis (ALS). A simple challenge: make a video of yourself dumping a bucket of ice water on your head, post it on Facebook, Instagram, or other social media sites, then challenge friends to do the same within twenty-four hours—or donate one hundred dollars to ALS. Good fun! Celebrities, sports figures, even former presidents took on the challenge. They raised millions of dollars. So many charities were kicking themselves, wishing they had thought of that, but really, who knew the public would carry it so far?

And, as I mentioned, in my novel, *Donny and Ursula Save the World*, I used fiction, humor, and, quite honestly, sex, to Bring Awareness to the dangers of genetically modified seeds, and to the current threat of corporate ownership of the way our food is grown. In my view, while people are laughing, their mouths are open, their throats are open, and the important message slides right down. Understanding that I needed to get people's attention and keep it from the very start, there was lots of fun and playful sex involved. Sex sells; it gets our attention. Humor delights and disarms. That seems to be a universal.

The guests on the *Passing 4 Normal Podcast* all Bring Awareness through their intentions and their actions. They do it by being living examples of what can be accomplished by speaking up, speaking out, or creating new forms. For example, Claire Hope Cummings brings awareness by speaking up and out on the environment through her activism, writing, and radio broadcasts. Corinne Bourdeau cultivates awareness for important issues by promoting social change films. Ann Gentry creates daily awareness for healthy eating through her vegan restaurants. Jacques Verduin facilitates transformative self-awareness through group process. Deena Metzger brought compassion and courage to female breast cancer survivors through a single iconic image.

Corinne Bourdeau is a producer and marketing director for social change films about the environment, social justice and films that lift up the human spirit. The Passionate Filmmaker, she believes in the strong power of film to move the needle of change through information and inspiration.

Documentary films break open access, often shocking us with revelatory exposé about worlds we didn't know or couldn't imagine. Narrative films open our hearts to empathy for memorable characters and the crises they face. But without someone to cultivate a widespread audience and a plan for action steps through publicity, grassroots promotion and distribution, these films won't impact awareness at all because no one would see them. Corinne has brought her innovative expertise to impactful, award-winning films such as *The Cove*, *Fuel*, *Pump*, *Bottle Shock*, *Buck*, and *Boyhood*.

Coming from the film world myself, Corinne and I talked about the power of film not only to bring information and issue awareness to audiences, but to inspire and instruct people to take actions based upon their changed awareness. The story of each film she works with is a creative strategy in itself for enacting social change. I asked her, "How are filmmakers changing the world?"

Corinne Bourdeau: There are so many amazing filmmakers out there working on projects. Obvious ones are *The Cove*, which won the Academy Award and which got a lot of national attention, and also ended up helping to stop the dolphin slaughter in Japan.

There are also filmmakers that we work with on a smaller scale who are just as passionate, and affecting just as much change. For example, we worked on a film earlier this year, called *GMO OMG*, and it was a passionate band of filmmakers that really felt strongly about GMOs, and they did screenings across the country, and helped sign legislation into certain states that would cause GMOs to be labeled. While it's exciting to work on an Academy Award-winning film, it's also exciting to work with smaller, dedicated filmmakers that are making really worthwhile films also instrumental in social change.

Sharon Weil: Let's say, people see a film, and this really inspires them. Do you provide a way for people in the audience then to take a next step action?

Corinne Bourdeau: In a perfect world, that's what my company does. A lot of times, we're educating filmmakers. You have this great, amazing film, and people go to see it. Now what? I see this film about GMOs; what do I do? What are steps that I can take? We'll recommend that a filmmaker put on their website "Ten Steps You Can Take to Avoid GMOs" or "Five Ways You Can Help Fix the Health Care System" or "Three Ways You Can Stop the Dolphin Slaughter in Taiji."

Another thing we do is we encourage people to have dialogues after seeing the film. I just worked on a wonderful film… it's called *Ground Operations*, about vets who come back from the war, and a movement for them to start organic farms. I love this film for a number of reason: first of all, not a dry eye in the house when you see it, because it's just a well-made film, but also, because it's an example of a passionate filmmaker who didn't have a large budget, who wasn't nominated for an Academy Award, didn't have all those bells and whistles—but she has made great social change.

She has just gotten back from a tour of the Midwest, where she actually went to farms with vets, screened the film, and had the vets see how they could get involved with a farm, how organic foods could change their communities. She did this single-handedly, without a large budget, with just a lot of plumb and vigor and dedication. And, it just shows you how filmmakers can make great change, but they don't have to be a huge megaplex studio with millions of dollars.

Sharon Weil: Right, because there's the film itself, which is very moving, and very informative, but then there's this specific action that she is taking that is bringing people together and letting them use the film as a point of inspiration to actually take the action here and now.

Corinne Bourdeau: You can go on her website and you can say, "Oh, I could send a check and help a vet fund a farm," or "Perhaps I could go to my local VA and say, 'Hey a lot of these vets don't have jobs; how about if we hook them up with these organic farms?'" There are actual steps that people can take, and she has done a beautiful job of that. Like I said, I love these smaller films; they're where my heart's at, these smaller films that have great gusto and vision, and allow people to go, "Wow! That impacted me! I am going to go change something because of that!"

Sharon Weil: Absolutely. How do you determine the issues, the specific films, or filmmakers that you get involved with?

Corinne Bourdeau: The first thing is, we have to like the film. The second thing is, we have to know that it's going to be able to make some kind of change. We don't necessarily have to save dolphins…maybe the change is we just make the public aware of it. Change can be a lot of things, but we have to know that we can actually, what I call, move the needle, and make change.

Sharon Weil: I ask myself this all the time: how do you measure change? How do you measure that these films are actually having an impact?

Corinne Bourdeau: That's the sixty-four-million-dollar question, because I would not be exaggerating if I said we get this question asked every day—in some shape or form. The reason this question is so easy, and so hard to answer, is because change is such a broad thing.

When we worked on *Escape Fire: The Fight to Rescue American Health Care*, the Ford Foundation did a huge study of how much we impacted the health care system with all these graphs, and details, and statistics that showed that we did impact the conversation about health care. At the end of the day, I was more excited by the conversation I had with an acupuncturist who said he now includes his services as part of health care, after seeing the film. That did not show up on any study. The whole point of what I'm saying is, these small, little changes—the garden, the acupuncturist that decides to add health care, the example I used the other day where an artist saw *The Cove* and he quit his job and started doing dolphin murals around the world, to celebrate dolphins—none of that is covered, but to me, that's really change!

There's micro-change, which is these wonderful little day-to-day things, which I hear about every day, and that's my juice; and there are these macro-changes, where *Food, Inc.* caused five hundred gardens to be implemented at schools. It's impossible to measure the change; and yet there's so much change, it is beyond bountiful.

Corinne would not be bringing all these important, impactful films to audiences if she had not allowed herself to change. As the publisher of *Los Angeles* magazine, she was at the top of her field in a glamorous, well-paying job. The shock of 9/11 made her realize she wanted to be doing more about the things she truly cared about. Her passion for film led her to create her marketing company, 360 Degree Communications, whose role it is to Bring Awareness to audiences about issues that matter. Her own self-awareness about what mattered to her most compelled her to make her life's work about bringing awareness to others.

Deena Metzger has long been an advocate and activist for restoring the natural world, and restoring our connection to nature. She has spent her lifetime as a writer, teacher, storyteller, counselor, and medicine woman, using story as a portal to self-discovery and healing. Deena holds a vision and a value for a world that is returned to integrity and wholeness from the dangers of domination and fragmentation. At the forefront of many political and human rights movements, she has always been a bold and fearless voice for women, for freedom, for the animals, for indigenous peoples and their cultures, and for the healing of the earth.

I wanted to speak with Deena for the podcast because I *always* want to speak with Deena. After knowing her for over twenty-five years, she continues to be a model and a guide for the way to walk in the world. Her personal courage astounds me and inspires me. She has influenced the lives of multitudes of people both known and unknown to her.

In the 1970s, Deena was at center of feminist writing and culture in Los Angeles. During that time she had a mastectomy. In those years, the words "breast cancer" had to be whispered, and a woman whose body was disfigured from radical surgery kept herself hidden in shame. Not Deena. In her true style, she posed for photographer, Hella Hammid, her naked chest exposed, her arms spread out against a blue sky for all the world to see. The intricate tattoo of a vine covered the scar across her missing breast (tattoos were not commonplace then as they are today). This Tree Poster or Warrior Poster was also known as "I Am No Longer Afraid" and became the iconic image of claiming life after cancer, giving permission and courage to so many women to bring their cancer out into the open, then, and still. That image of her has been featured in articles, books, anthologies, and on book covers around the world. It was from her cancer that she discovered that disease and illness can be messengers to change our lives, and it was in that time that she began her healing practice of using story to reclaim health and healing on behalf of all.

Sharon Weil: How many women have taken inspiration and permission from that image of you putting yourself out there naked? Talk about being naked, you were naked out there. As a matter of fact, a couple months ago I was looking on Facebook and there was an image of a woman who had a similar thing. On her mastectomy scar she had a tattoo, and I thought, "If Deena hadn't done that, that women wouldn't be able to do this." We wouldn't have this permission in our vocabulary. I want to know: how is it that you are so brave?

Deena Metzger: Because I don't think of it as brave. I could say that "why not" is one of the wisdom statements that I carry. "Oh, here's a good idea. Should we do this? Why not?"

When I know that women's lives have been changed by that poster, how could I even hesitate for a moment? So many women's lives, in so many countries. It's on the cover of a book in Japan, across the world… Why not?

Sharon Weil: Yeah, why not? If someone is coming to you to find out, how do I step toward my healing? How do I step toward making change? How do I step toward working on behalf of the world? Would you just say, "Why not?"

Deena Metzger: No, I would say that everyone is given medicine or gifts—medicine in the way that native people talk about medicine. Medicine is your power, and your energy, and your gift, and your beauty, and your possibility. I would say, find out what that is and offer it. That will make the difference.

Truly, Deena's medicine is to speak so eloquently to the issues of our day, and to draw people near her, to teach about healing and to model living a life that is for healing. As a wise woman and medicine woman, she has counseled thousands to hear the calling of their hearts, and to live into the authentic life that fulfills that calling, on behalf of themselves, the spirits, and others. I am so proud to say that Deena Metzger has been my teacher and friend for all these years. In her presence, I have learned to craft my writing and use my voice in support of the life-values and earth-values we share. Her constant courage and "why not?" attitude has made her an inspiration to thousands of writers, students, feminists, seekers, and followers who have, in turn, cultivated their trembling courage to write, sing, pray, and speak out for a compassionate and integrated world.

For **Claire Hope Cummings**, her personal history of social activism is a history of the social activism movement in this country, starting in the 1960s. Claire's participation began at the University of California, Berkeley, and carries through to this day, though her efforts have evolved in form. Formerly an environmental attorney, she is now an author, a journalist, and a public speaker. Her strategies for how to Bring Awareness and change to the complex problems of environmental destruction and the detrimental effects of climate change are to uncover sound scientific research, and share human stories. She wrote one of the early, seminal books on GMOs, *Uncertain Peril: Genetic Engineering and the Future of Seeds*. Her persistence and continued flow of clear, scientific information has opened the way for the increasing awareness about the dangers of GMOs and the herbicides and pesticides that accompany their technology.

Claire's book not only created the fact base for my research for *Donny and Ursula Save the World*, but Claire, her book, her unwavering commitment, and all her activities on behalf of food, farming, and people have inspired me to be a stronger voice in these areas as well. She is creating awareness through the telling of research and stories. Her human stories, and stories of the land, create great affinity. Her factual research pierces the misinformation agribusiness corporations are trying to sell. Her voice is a call to relationship, and a warning of what can interfere.

Claire Hope Cummings: I was a young woman at Cal in the 1960s. I was raised very traditionally. I was supposed to be a white glove–wearing good girl, get married, and have a family. Being a 1950s-type housewife was sort of the expectation, and education was not considered crucial, but it was something that was, "Well done. Good for you." It's nice to have. If you really had to work, you could always be a teacher. In fact, that's exactly what my dad told me. If you look at the photographs of the Free Speech Movement that started at Cal in '64, it's amazing to look at the pictures…we do literally have gloves, and hats, and nylons, and high heels; and the guys are wearing ties.

I think a lot of people think of social change movements in the seventies, and anti-war in particular, as much scrappier, sort of hippie, but that's not how it started, and that's not who we were. Maybe it's that first point you're making about awareness. Here's this group of people who grew up in the forties and fifties seeing, in this case it was corporate control of knowledge. That's why it was called Free Speech. University of California, Berkeley was engaging with a lot of military research and things like that. Now, it's of course way over the top and sort of a lost cause, but back then in the sixties, we were going, "No, no. This is not okay."

It doesn't matter what brings you your awareness; if something's wrong, something needs to change.

It could be any kind of particular issue, but it calls to you, right? At that point, once I started engaging with social change at that level on the campus unrest, I never looked back.

I cut my teeth on the Civil Rights Movement because that was what was most apparent at the time and easy to understand. The African American experience in the United States very much influenced my thinking. I went on to work a lot with the Grape and Lettuce Strikes and farm workers…and then the Vietnam War started, so it was very much Mothers for Peace. The image of myself at the time was one kid in my right hand, one kid in a stroller, and one in the backpack. I had three kids under the age of five, and we'd go to the Mothers for Peace and we'd go to the marches. I didn't think anything of it. It's just what you did. Once you decide to participate in social change, it's not something you do because it's a fad, or "Oh, there's a rave going on." It's not like that at all, not for me. It's a commitment. It becomes a lifelong commitment.

This is the best way to put it: I decided my life was not going to just be about me, but it had to be about the world I lived in. Now, which cause I might be most engaged in at the time has been more of a choice, but I can no longer be uninvolved in the world.

I became a social activist and then, in the 1970s, I was in a lot of personal turmoil and engaged in a more spiritual approach to things. As part of that spiritual promise to myself and my life, I decided to engage in service.

I'd say in that first ten or twelve years, I was not consciously thinking of myself as a social change activist. I just did it; it was what we did. Eventually, though, I had to say this is who I am. This service is who I am. It's a lifelong, deep commitment.

Claire then became an environmental lawyer both to do good in the world and to make a living for her family. She specialized in representing native people in defense of their ancestral lands.

Claire Hope Cummings: The way the environmentalism was expressing itself back then was litigation, legislation, and public education, so I was not as involved in the public education part. Because I'm a lawyer, I'll take the case to the court. You, the environmental organization or Native American organization, you do the public education part. I'm just going to keep this issue, the development, whatever it was, I'm going to stop it for now, but you're going to have to go out and deal with educating the public about it. I might be at press conferences involved in articulating a lawsuit, but my job was not the public education part. Not at all.

Sharon Weil: So what brought you to public education?

Claire Hope Cummings: I burned out as a litigator. I mean, I was a sole practitioner. I was losing cases because that's what you do, and your clients hate it. There is nothing happy or good about this at all… I said, "Okay. I need a break." So, I shut down my law practice. I've always wanted to write, but at the time I did not know it would be a vehicle for social change. What eventually I was able to say was, I ended my litigation career and started as a journalist to continue my work on social change. Even then, we're not talking about trying to have influence. I want to make this really, really clear because I am not interested in engaging in persuasion. To me, one of the biggest faults in the environmental movement is all the finger wagging. I would say that the bigger fault, however, is that they over-rely on information as a way to try to say, "Oh, if people only knew how bad things were, they'd act." Well, that has not been true, has it? Well, no, and I knew that a long time ago. So my point was more to get down below a situation. I'm more interested in what's behind all that. What came up for me were the stories. It's not original to me, but basically putting the "culture" back into "agriculture."

And I love your navigation analogy. By showing how people navigate these different forces, it can inspire change. It can help support people in engaging in the hard work that change requires. That's more along the lines of what I was interested in rather than, "Here's all the information and let's persuade you to join." Wendell Berry told me one time, he said, "The problem is that we're acting by proxy."

When we talked about what was impeding change in the environmental movement. Claire surprised me with what she had to say.

Claire Hope Cummings: I think social media is probably the worst thing that ever happened to the environmental movement. A lot of people will completely disagree with that.

Sharon Weil: Why do you say that? Because it gives people a false sense that they're doing something?

Claire Hope Cummings: If you look at the well-reasoned critiques of social media, that's all that needs to be said. Then how it applies to this is what you said, partly, that we think we're doing something, but more importantly, this distractibility and overwhelm keeps us from being able to make a meaningful contribution. I mean, if you're running around in circles you're not going to be able to get anywhere… What were a billion people doing before YouTube? How are we using our time? How are we using our enormous resources?

I'm just saying that knowledge has not availed us, and the consumption of knowledge has not availed us of any improvement in the human condition.

And so now, with all her many years of experience in and around the environmental movement, having dedicated herself through litigation, legislation and public education, Claire sees her job as something else.

Claire Hope Cummings: Now, my job is to pay attention. It's like you see the hawk circling above. You have to know the right questions to ask to understand why that hawk is there and why you saw it like that. That's a very different form of navigation. Looking is a navigation of the nuclear submarine, maybe. I'm with the guys with the smells of the water and sea changing, the Polynesian star navigators, where there's a huge complex system that you learn through thirty years and then you know how to ride those currents.

Sharon Weil: It's like you're scanning the scene with all your responsiveness, right? And your responsiveness is very highly tuned.

Claire Hope Cummings: That's right. And that takes training and commitment, too. That's not something you can just say—that I'm going to do, mentally, and start. You have to train to be responsive in that way.

As you can see from our conversation, Claire has enormous clarity. She is an elegant translator of complex information for lay people to receive in-depth information that substantiates their concerns about food and land use. Her latest critiques center around our dangerous love and use of technology, and how it impacts our lives and the environment. Claire is, above all, a lover of the land and she is heartfully connected to the natural world. She sees hope in nature and the land and is compelled to share what she knows with others and she is committed to that service.

Ann Gentry's own personal quest for awareness prompted her to Bring Awareness to others in very tangible and successful ways through her well-known restaurant, Real Food Daily. I'd eaten at the well-known vegan gourmet restaurant before I ever knew her. Ann's delicious, sophisticated, healthy cuisine served me well when I was on a macrobiotic diet many years ago. The place is always packed, and diners leave with smiles on their faces and that glow to their skin that those vegans seem to have. Owner and creator of the Los Angeles plant-based restaurants, Ann shows you right there on your plate how pleasant it is to improve your health. All you have to do is put your fork to your mouth to begin to make the change. But her story has a larger implication. Ann began what is now a small food empire because of her own desire to make a personal change for her own health. Her change of diet as a young adult showed her such satisfying results that she made the preparation of this food her life.

Ann Gentry: I've been in this crazy restaurant business for twenty-one years. I started serving only food that comes from plants, which means I am a vegan restaurant. Exclusively a 100-percent plant-based menu that we're offering, which means no animal products or no animal byproducts: the cheese, the eggs, butter, et cetera. When I opened twenty-one years ago, I called it vegetarian: Real Food Daily organic vegetarian cooking. My first restaurant was in Santa Monica. Five years later, we opened in West Hollywood in the heart of LA where West Hollywood, Beverly Hills, and Los Angeles come together on a street called La Cienega. I jokingly said, "I came out of the closet. I'm really going to tell people who we are." I changed the byline from organic vegetarian cooking to organic vegan cuisine because I was part of a wave—a small wave of people, restaurateurs, and chefs that were really putting this vegan cuisine on the map.

But Ann wasn't always a vegan, or a chef.

Ann Gentry: I grew up on a standard American diet, Southern style. I was in a family of some amazing cooks, and I never took the bait to go into the kitchen and learn how to cook. I didn't really learn how to cook for myself until I was off in my young adult life and I stumbled upon vegetarianism. How about that?

I'm just a good cook. I'm not trained as a chef that had an incredible idea to open this type of restaurant in Los Angeles twenty-one years ago. I did it. I opened a restaurant. I learned how to cook through studying macrobiotics, which is an Asian philosophy about life. Macrobiotics means big, large life. Doesn't everybody want to have one of those? Hopefully, most people are creating that for themselves. I learned about food from a medicinal point of view, and everybody's different. We've all been born with our own constitution, the makeup of our heritage, our DNA, the nine months we spent inside our mother before birth. Then, we spend our life creating a condition. Everybody needs something different and at different times in your life…but we can change our condition by what we choose to eat. I've seen it work many times.

Ann is doing something I think is revolutionary. She's brought her plant-based cuisine to the Los Angeles International Airport food court.

Ann Gentry: What is happening to airports all over the world, and certainly all over our country, is that they're making a commitment to bring in the local brands that they have in the city. I was invited into LAX with a group of other restaurants. Each terminal at LAX is changing their food profile. Real Food Daily is in Terminal 4, American Airlines, in the food court with about five other LA concepts. Yes, we are the first of our kind in an airport across the planet serving a vegan cuisine—our strong commitment to organic produce and ingredients. This is a condensed menu. It is a quick service. It's for people on the go, and on the run, and ready to catch a plane, but you can eat there in the food court. You can take the food with you on the plane. Some people are getting off the plane and on their way home, stopping and grabbing food.

The most exciting moment I had was after we'd been open about two, three weeks. A woman walked up; she read our menu board. She had her bag on one arm. She dropped her other bag that was in her hand. She put her arms up in the air and just pulled them down in a big, *Yes!* Then, she said, "Wow, about time!" I ran up to her and I introduced myself. She just said, "Oh, I'm in heaven."

I have to admit, the airport is one of the last places I would expect to find healthy, vegetarian food. Any kind of healthy food! But there it is! And I am grateful. Each time someone from Kansas, or Iowa, or even Bakersfield walks by Ann Gentry's restaurant there in Terminal 4, they will notice a cuisine they might not be seeing at home. The awareness will be planted, and the opportunity will be right there to taste something new. If they are hungry enough, or curious enough, they might go stand in line.

In another example, somatic psychologist **Jacques Verduin** cultivates self-awareness through mindfulness meditation practice and through the Guiding Rage into Power (GRIP) program. The class helps bring the men to awareness of the sensations of their emotions, so they can slow their reactions down, observe, experience them and their causes, and make new choices. Many of these men are serving life sentences and will never see parole, but Jacques' perspective on being in prison is that the lock up is just as much of an internalized experience, and whereas they may not be able to change their incarceration, they can change their internal experience.

Jacques Verduin: I tell them, "Look, they have your body here, they have your movement, but they don't have your spirit. There's a lot of room below the gate and above that gate, but do you have it? Do you cultivate it?" Because having that kind of self-knowledge and having that way of connecting to yourself is probably the deepest experience that you will foster in terms of feeling free.

As an international speaker, Jacques also creates awareness with the public through public talks and presentations, and meetings with state prison officials. The GRIP program and these men serve as a model for curriculum to be implemented in other prisons throughout the state, and around the world.

Jacques Verduin: It's fair to say that we're in a trance as a nation about how we incarcerate—the levels and the ways we incarcerate people. Currently one in one-hundred-eight Americans is in prison. One in thirty-four is either in prison, on parole, or probation; that's over seven million people right there. One in twenty-eight school-aged children have a parent incarcerated.

Sharon Weil: This is unbelievable.

Jacques Verduin: I know, the numbers are incredible. In California it cost sixty thousand dollars a year to incarcerate someone, which of course is actually more than school tuition and housing for a year at Stanford. But 64 percent of the people released through this system are back within three years, and it's not just that they're back and they're going to cost more, it's also there are people that are victimized in the process. It cost $10 billion to incarcerate in California in the budget. Very little of that goes to rehabilitation, and none of what we do gets paid for by the government.

Thirty-four, a small but remarkable number of peacemaker graduates from the GRIP program have earned parole and release from prison. Some, upon leaving prison want to apply their hard-earned insight to give back and help prevent others from making the same grave mistakes they made in their young lives. In Northern California, Insight-Out takes the rage-into-power training developed in prison out to at-risk youth to give them awareness before they go down that road.

Jacques Verduin: We kept hearing from the guys, "Oh man, I wish I'd known this when I was fifteen years old, then maybe I wouldn't have gone this route." Because the men we're working with are violent offenders and they're life sentenced with paroles, they have a chance to get out if the parole board deems them fit. But, they're doing large chunks of time and many of them have taken a life. They've committed a murder, and so they said, "You know maybe we wouldn't have gone in there if we'd known." I finally I said, "I'm tired of hearing this, let's go tell them."
We had a few guys that had come out and made it past the parole board, and we went into Richmond, into a youth center there, and went into a high school

and pretty much end up with the youth that teachers don't know what to do with anymore, that are just sort of "hopeless cases" in their words. It is very hard work to work with these youths, but it's really neat to see that these men that have been there and done that recognize a lot of broken family situations, and neighborhood issues, and social justice issues. To see them work with these kids is such a beautiful thing, because they're trained. It's not just that they've been there and done that, but they're trained. We're training these men to become facilitators and they want to give back to the places they took from.

They have respect from these kids. They're called OGs. In the slang it's called Original Gangsters. "Hey, hey, OG, what do you think? What do you think about this?" We ride that pony of the fascination, but then turn a different direction; that's potent to see.

The type of awareness that these men are offering comes from such honest and painful self-reflection. Their life experiences and their transformation grants them their authority in being able to speak with young men who are at great risk of living a life of gang violence, crime, and incarceration. In the case of the GRIP graduates, awareness has led to changed action and changed lives, and the awareness they bring, combined with their training, will change the lives of countless others.

SUMMARY

So, how can Principle #1, Bring Awareness, increase ChangeAbility and begin the movement of change? Awareness, or a shift in awareness is the first step in recognizing that change has occurred. Awareness will also be the first step toward initiating change. The contrast between how things were and how they are now, or between how they are now and how I want them to be provides the awareness of the nature of the change, the degree of change, and the need for change:

◊   **Every journey toward change begins with awareness: where am I now? What is the nature of the change I am in?**

◊   **Awareness, like change, is all that we are.**

◊   **Direct, first-order experience is the most effective way to know what you know.**

◊   **Awareness can be cultivated internally or directed outwardly toward brining awareness to others.**

◊   **We often gain awareness through a baseline comparison between now and next.**

◊   **Information can compel us to want to take action, but information, by itself, is often not enough to motivate action or change.**

> "Some of the changes that are required have to do with extending our awareness of what is good or bad for us, to what is good or bad for everyone."
>
> —Deena Metzger

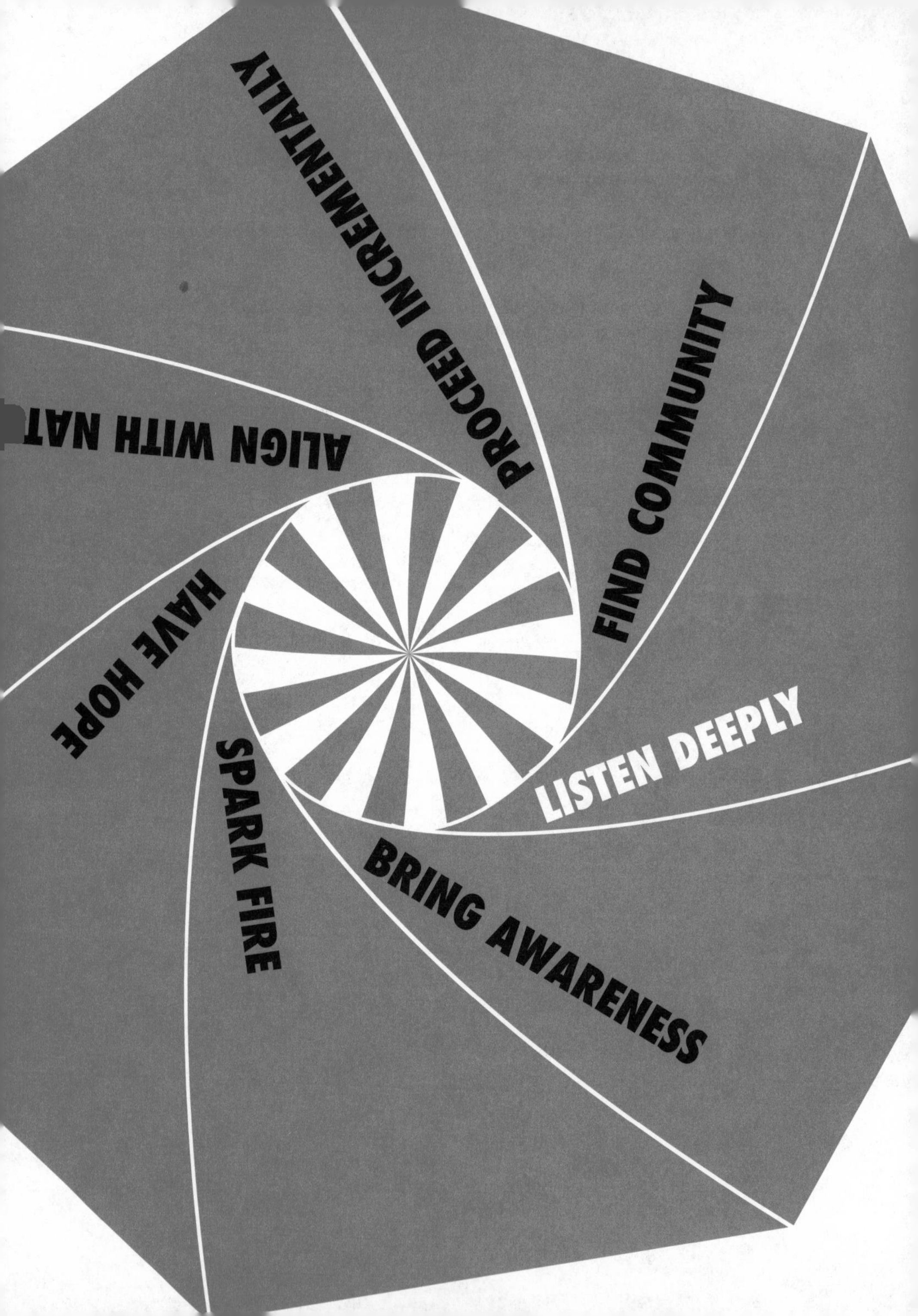
PROCEED INCREMENTALLY
FIND COMMUNITY
LISTEN DEEPLY
BRING AWARENESS
SPARK FIRE
HAVE HOPE
ALIGN WITH NAT

2 LISTEN DEEPLY

Hearing, receiving, perceiving, observing, understanding

"Listening is beyond hearing. It's listening deeply in deep respect. You hold the person in deep majesty, for who they are."

—Harvey Ruderian

PROGRESS DOES NOT MOVE IN A straight line. The same is true for change. As change evolves and unfolds, it meanders, it spirals, it reverses and goes back on itself. It moves—like all of nature moves—in undulations and waves: ocean waves, thermal waves, sound waves, electromagnetic waves. Even when change feels like it stops and starts, a slow, barely perceptible wave runs through it. Because, as my guests and I said before, change is constantly moving, no matter how slowly. But unless we are highly attuned, or highly optimistic, we may not feel the continuum of the wave of change, at all.

I set a course for change. I want to change where I'm living, or where I'm working. Sometimes change runs the course we choose, sometimes it runs off course in another direction. Let's say, I found the perfect apartment, but someone else got there first. Or I can't find another position in my field of work, but I'm offered a job in a completely different field and so then my work life, and consequently my social life, take a different turn. Change may seem to run off my intended course, but change is always right on its own course. The question is: *Am I able to recognize it?* Whether or not I *accept* it is a whole other thing. The paradox between feeling the free-flow movement of change, and wanting to direct the course of change toward a particular end requires that I be able to listen to the nature of change in a way that is beyond merely hearing, and that I respond accordingly.

How do I know what is taking place right now? How do I know what change is occurring or to what degree? How do I know what the nature of this change is: internal or external, fast or slow, of minor or major impact? And, how do I know what my response ought to be? Do I accept the change? Maybe not. But, at the very least, it is very helpful to *accept* that the change is indeed happening. I love my apartment and don't want to move, but I accept that my lease is up and the landlord is raising the rent. Do I adapt to it? I can try to negotiate a reduction in rent or get a roommate to share the increased rent. Or does the adaptation call for initiating new action? Perhaps I need to look for a new place to live. Each of these strategies requires a deep listening in order to receive the message of what is needed to respond to the situation. Whether that message comes from inside of me in the form of an idea or intuition, from the outside in the form of information coming from another person, or from events and results of the change—my awareness comes from Listen Deeply. What I mean by "listen" is also looking, sensing and asking.

Deep listening, or what might be called, active listening, often begins with a question. *What is happening right now?* Listen Deeply tells me what is. It can also tell me what isn't. I can know my heart's desire by knowing the difference between what is and what I would like it to be. I Bring Awareness when I Listen Deeply.

FEEDBACK

My environment is full of feedback. For every action there is a reaction. For every call there is a response. My environment is constantly sending me cues as to whether I am on course or off course based on either the ease, or the amount of resistance there is with the change. Everything, from the reactions and responses from the people in my life, to the effectiveness of my work efforts, to how my vegetable garden is growing in my backyard provides me with feedback. Whatever I put out into the world, I will get some sort of response, if I know how to listen for it. Let's say, I've been looking for a new apartment for several months and I can't find anything suitable. The feedback is: the rental market is very tight in my neighborhood in my price range. Based on the feedback, I may need to expand the geography of my search, increase the price I can pay, find a way to be the first in line to see any new rentals, or I may need to just keep on looking over time until something suitable shows up. I am constantly receiving feedback from my internal and external environment. How I receive that information, and how I let it shape my direction, determines my ability to navigate.

Listen Deeply (and then responding to what I "hear" back) is an interactive, creative play, one that is strengthened by curiosity, inquiry, flexibility, and attention to sensation. By "listening" I also mean observing, or sensing, through my eyes, through my hands, through my intuition, through hearing an intuitive inner voice, or feeling my way along the walls in the darkness. When things change, I have to change with them. How do I know when things have changed? By Listen Deeply.

HOW TO LISTEN

"There's a thought that the person who's sitting there observing is in a passive role. It's not at all a passive role, it's the deepest kind of participation."

—Adam Wolpert

The beginning impulse for writing this book arrived from the many conversations I had with the *Passing 4 Normal Podcast* guests, where many of them spoke directly about deep listening as the way in which they navigate their work and their lives. It was how Harvey Ruderian, Jackie Welch Schlicher, Jacques Verduin, Adam Wolpert, James Stark, Robert Litman, Deena Metzger, Rachel Lang, Amanda Foulger, Fred Sugerman, and Camille Maurine each talked about how they listen—whether with their ears, their hands, their hearts, or their intuitive knowing—that led me to begin to piece together the principles of change I am articulating in this book. So many people that I admire operate through deep listening, though they come to it in different ways. So many of those interviewed were saying a very similar thing about being guided by their listening; and so I started looking for what else they were saying in common.

Artist and group facilitator, **Adam Wolpert**, is a professional listener. He observes and listens deeply to the people in the groups he facilitates, to the nature that surrounds him, and to the creative impulses that arrive for his art. Adam then translates what he hears. All of his work is process oriented—which means that the way in which something arrives, moves, or gets resolved is as important as the results that come. It's a value of the process over the results, or certainly valuing it as much as the result. I find this to be true for all artists; their creative process is as compelling as what results from that process. Listen Deeply is at the beginning of any process, and is necessary for tracking how that process moves at any given moment.

In our conversation, Adam dispelled the idea that listening is a passive activity. He draws upon the work of the twentieth-century phenomenological philosopher Maurice Merleau-Ponty, about the foundational role perception plays in understanding and engaging in the world. Adam is an incredible listener. Over the years, I've had the opportunity to greatly benefit from Adam's leadership as a group facilitator, and I've marveled at how much he was able to glean from the text and the subtext of what people were saying when they spoke. I've also marveled at how effectively he synthesized what he'd heard. For him, the act of listening is the act of gathering—listening to the sounds of nature, to the intent beneath spoken words, or to the efficacy of structures is an engaged activity.

Adam Wolpert: I was very moved when I read Merleau-Ponty's ideas about phenomenology. He says, "Perception is participation." What he's saying that I've come to understand for group work is that the most profound kind of participation is perception—which is really listening, observing; really seeing what's going on. Often, there's a thought that that's passive, that the person who's sitting there observing is in a passive role. It's not at all a passive role; it's the deepest kind of participation. Then you move from that place of deep observation in a completely different way than you would move if you just came in with an idea, or you came in and said. "Here's the way I do things," and just proceeded. Deep listening—that seems to be the core of the practice.

Sharon Weil: Right. It's not passive at all; it's quite active. In the moment, it's responsive because it's from listening that you get your next impulse for what to do next, or what to suggest, or what color to use, or what to say to these two people to get them to come to agreement. It's all very responsive.

Adam Wolpert: I'm very privileged to spend a lot of my time alone, painting in nature. I'm always struck by how much time is spent listening; when I watch the animals around me. Even just watching the vegetation respond to microclimates or to other growing things nearby, you just have this sense that there's a lot of listening going on. That's so much the way things understand the right thing to do, the right next move.

INQUIRY

The practice of Listen Deeply is the practice of inquiry, without assumption or judgment. Purely asking the question: *What is happening now?*—then waiting for the reply, also without assumption or judgment. Not so easy to do. As a human, my life works efficiently because of all the assumptions I make. I wake up in the morning and I assume I'm in my house in Los Angeles, and that today is Tuesday because yesterday was Monday—and besides, that's what it says on my phone, and I assume that's right. I assume that the peaches I left in the refrigerator will still be there, that my car will start when I turn the key, that my daughter sitting next to me is indeed my daughter, and that I know the way to her school. I don't have to discover every moment or aspect of my life for the first time. However, making assumptions can limit my discovery and limit the possibilities of what else this could be. Assumption can limit my perception of what has changed. My daughter is a growing teen, and my assumptions about who she is are based on how she was last night or last week. If I am holding her to my previous assumptions, I may not notice that she's in a quiet and sullen mood, or that she changed her hair, or even that she grew an inch overnight.

Another example: so many arguments between friends, lovers, and foreign countries come from making assumptions that we don't even ask about. We use our assumptions as the basis for our behavior and response, and don't begin with an open question, or then listen openly for a fresh response. *What is going on here with you? What do you want, right now? What do you need?* The answer may be surprising, because things have changed; things are always changing. These are simple examples, perhaps. However, my point is that I need a certain amount of assumption and societal agreement in order to function with an efficient shorthand in my life so I am not reinventing the wheel every moment, but too much assumption will limit the discoveries

I can and need to make about changing circumstances—limiting new possibilities and limiting the movement of change.

When I begin the process of inquiry I have to begin with, "I don't know," because I don't—even if I think I do. Since everything is changing all the time, one of the questions in my inquiry is, "Have things changed or not?" This question is not coming out of fear, but out of curiosity. Curiosity is the lead word in inquiry. *What is new? What is different? What is the same? I want to know.*

One of James Stark's favorite expressions is, "Let's kick the tires on this," which, if any of you don't know, is a way you would test out an old used car, by kicking the tires to see if they were firm, if they had air, if they would take this car where it needed to go. "Kicking the tires" means let's test it out, let's try it out and see what it's made of. But please let's check it out by *trying it out*, and not by making assumptions.

SMALL COURSE CORRECTION

I use the principle of Listen Deeply to understand the "territory" I am in. By that I mean the literal territory or the metaphoric territory. Then, based on the territory—the climate, the mountains and valleys, the timing, and the destination—I map my course. I'm determined to follow the course, and stay the course, no matter what.

It's hard to believe that mapping a course and staying the course is actually comprised of a number of smaller course corrections based on feedback, and reading the signals along the way. So when I Proceed Incrementally, each new incremental step is based on feedback from the last, and thus I make adjustments for the next.

One thing I have in common with Adam is that we've both spent lots of time paddling on the river. Whether in canoes, kayaks, or rafts, there is nothing that has better equipped me for understanding this concept of staying the course through small course corrections. By reading the current in the water, I can watch how it moves over and around the rocks, how swiftly it churns and turns. I have to find the current, and try to keep my boat in the current, so its momentum moves me along. When the river takes a turn, the direction of the water takes a turn, so I'd better turn the boat too, or else I am setting up resistance that could flip the boat. When I come up upon rapids, I have to set my boat up so that the angle of my boat aligns with the direction of the current, just so, for a thrill ride and not a spill ride. That requires watching how the water moves, feeling my boat in the water, and making adjustments with my paddle to either hold the boat back, direct it right or left, or dig in and propel straight ahead. All of these are course corrections based on "listening" to the river, and then applying my navigational skill.

My doctor likes to say, "Keep doing what you're doing and you'll keep getting what you get."

He says this to patients who don't understand why their health is not improving while they are still doing the same old thing. Emilie Conrad often spoke about how doing things in the same habitual way creates a closed system that eventually loops the same information over and over, and causes the system to decline. Intentional change requires course correction, even for meeting strong and direct goals.

My father, when he was alive, was successful in the real estate business, and that was his goal. I believe one of his biggest talents for success was course correction—knowing when to get in, when to get out, and when to stay the course. He and his partner developed a new style of apartments in the late 1970s in the Westwood area, south of UCLA. Their concept of larger apartment buildings built around pleasantly landscaped, diverse courtyards with plenty of common room held great appeal. But the success was also in knowing the timing of when to sell the properties. When apartments were giving way to condo ownership—which was much less profitable—they went into commercial warehouses and light industrial centers. He listened to the movement of the market, and made adjustments.

My father would say to me, "If you shoot enough arrows at the target, eventually one will hit." But he didn't mean you just keep shooting the same arrows in the same way, time and time again. After you shoot each arrow, you study it, see where it went, figure out why, and adjust accordingly. Maybe you try a different kind of arrow. Maybe you try a different day when the wind is not blowing. Maybe you shoot them in really fast succession. Maybe you move the target. The point is that the answers to each of those inquiries produce new strategies for trying again. Each time a new strategy is offered, you look—you Listen Deeply—for what went right, what went wrong, and then you adjust.

In the days of the early railroad there was the expression, "Putting your ear to the ground," because you could put your ear to the ground next to the railroad tracks to hear the vibration if the train was coming. The expression means to listen for what is yet to come. The fashion industry is a great example of listening for what is to come. Designers may initiate styles based on creative whim, but successful styles are based on listening to what customers want, what they will wear, what they are tired of wearing, as well as updating what customers refuse to give up no matter how much things change. Fashion pushes change on purpose; that's how they make a profit, by changing up styles so I have to buy new things in order to be current and fashionable.

The ways that people get their entertainment is another example of an industry listening and making course correction according to the feedback of changing systems, driven by the competition for viewers' attention and their dollars. Historically, silent movies gave way to talkies in elaborate movie palaces; it was a special event to go out to the movies. Then television brought people home for their entertainment, gathering the family around the TV set to watch programs together. Then families began having more than one television set so they could watch different programs at the same time. Then cable television gave them more niche selection for the multiple viewers at home. Then came VHS tapes, video rental stores cropped up in every neighborhood. Then DVDs. Netflix started mailing them to you, or you could get pay-per-view on the TV. More recently, Netflix began streaming instantly, along with a number of other services online. Now, it's binge watching—on my TV, computer, iPad, phone. Pretty soon, I will receive it in a direct download to my brain! These are all course corrections based on listening and adapting. Where will it go next?

FAILURE IS FEEDBACK

I've been talking about the necessity for responsive course correction as part of successful ChangeAbility. If I am overly rigid and unchanging in my approach to change, I could go way off the course of my intention, or miss the cues entirely for adapting to change as it comes. When we see institutions that can't keep up with the times fall by the wayside, or people who are not constantly updating their thinking, their approach, or their "branding" become passé, it's because they were not listening and adjusting to change. So, I need to listen carefully, try things out, and make adjustments as I go. But what if I make a mistake?!?

Fear of failure, fear of making a mistake, can keep me from trying out something new. However, in the conversation about making responsive course corrections, mistakes are just another form of feedback.

Failure is a good indication of what did not work.

It's a good indication of what not to do again. If I bother to listen, I can navigate by failure just as much as I navigate by success. Shame often causes me to hide my mistakes from others. But really, when I make a mistake, I should make it loud and clear, so I can see that it didn't work as a strategy, and be able to make a course correction, either by myself or with the help of others.

CREATIVE RESPONSE

If I am listening carefully, and responding openly without assumption, then my response will be creative. The true nature of creativity is to respond with something fresh, and yet appropriate. So much of the artistic process is to allow impulse, information, or inspiration to emerge into form. An artist courts the "muse" and listens for the discovery of how the collaboration of the materials, craft, imagination, and the magic of the moment cocreate what comes forward to be shaped and reshaped. Whether I am writing a book or a movie, creating a dance or a painting, creativity is the uninhibited response to Listen Deeply. It's not surprising, then, that the podcast guests who spoke to Listen Deeply were either artists working with the creative-artistic process, or somatic practitioners working with the ongoing creative process of the human body.

Jackie Welch Schlicher is the ultimate artist. She has been working with the call and response of creative play, on stage and off. One of her primary areas of talent is as an improvisational performer—and she is one of the best!

She is a master of the art of being fresh, authentic, and funny in the moment. In recent years, she has turned her creative interests to clay. As a ceramicist, she is able to "listen" to how the clay is taking shape on her potter's wheel, encouraged through her hands. It's a magical, creative, and surprising process to be guided in this way. Her creative experience is totally translatable from form to form. I asked her what was common to all the art forms she's worked in. It all has to do with how she faces the unknown.

Jackie Welch Schlicher: I would say the thing that is common in it all is the creative aspect. There's a listening involved. There is a communication involved, and there's a sharing. Whether it's singing or directing or writing, there's dialogue going on. Even with pottery, there's dialogue going on. You're connecting with your inner world, you're connecting with the outer world. There's a lot going on when you're in any kind of creative expression.

Sharon Weil: Let's take that into clay. You said to me that clay is your current teacher right now, and that this is where you meet yourself. How is that happening?

Jackie Welch Schlicher: Earlier, my play was with my emotion, and feelings, and thoughts, and body when I was acting, when I was doing improv. Clay is a different scene partner, if you will. It's got its own language. When I'm improvising with my clay, when I'm sitting at my potter's wheel, I'm in a question of not just what will this be, but how will this become what it wants to be with my assistance? Or, how can I shape this piece of clay into something that I see? Can we collaborate on this? Can we agree that this is going to be a bowl—and what kind of bowl will it be?

It's teaching me from a different perspective—drawing on my past experience and using that as the foundation like what I'd be putting together for an improv performance. It's giving me something fresh, and new, and different that sits outside of me, and yet is very much connected to me through my hands—through my desire to create a new shape, to explore what happens when there's a "mistake." Can I build on that? Can I find the end of what's just happened and accept that into what's to become? Yeah, it's teaching me in a way that's literally hands-on. I can't sit at the wheel and not have that experience.

Adam Wolpert knows, firsthand, the path of the creative artist.

Adam Wolpert: "We're supposed to be lost." In the creative process; it's absolutely critical. Many people have discussed this, and books have been written about how our most creative state is the state of muddle: the state of confusion. The giant place between waking and sleeping, that place where we really don't know what we're doing. Out of the muck comes the lotus. Out of that confused place, emerges something which never could have been imagined without going into that confusion or that muddle.

People can do this without having any idea that what they're doing has been done before. They're part of the human pilgrimage toward change. It's much easier when you understand the system in some larger sense. That's something that facilitators can do for groups, and it's something that artists can do for themselves. I've been mapping paintings for almost thirty years now. When I get into that difficult muddle, I can recognize and appreciate it for what it is, rather than panicking and thinking, "Maybe I got lost on the way."

Both Adam and Jackie speak from years of experience of going down into the process of meeting themselves in the creative unknown and being able to bring forward what wants to emerge through their craft. So, when they are "listening," what are they listening for? Writer, poet, and English professor **Rebecca Mark** says that we are listening for what is new.

Rebecca Mark: We have to listen deeply, and we also have to really train ourselves to listen to what is new. We have to train ourselves to see that spark, or that light, or that thing that we didn't know before. So when I'm listening in that [writers'] circle, I'm listening for the moment when there's a crack, or a little something that's just so exciting and different.

Rebecca describes the process of how participants work in the Words and Waves workshops, where sound and movement inspire deep discoveries of words, marks, symbols, and drawings on paper, evoking stories of an entirely different order. The participants in the group share their work with each other, reading aloud in a "chorus" of shared story.

Rebecca Mark: If the piece is brand new, I just want to listen to it. Listening without judgment—and that's perhaps the training that I have to constantly practice. When you're brought up in a Jewish-Irish family, you learn judgment, like, day one. Shame, judgment, criticism—it's all part of the mother's milk. I had to really get away from the notion, "Is this good literature or not?" I don't even care anymore. But, I can tell when something is dancing, or sparking, or bursting into flames, and so my listening is for the intelligence of life making itself known.

I'm literally listening for excitement. I'm listening for the stutter of, "Oh my God, I'm hanging over a cliff and I want to let go, but I'm terrified to let go." I'm listening for that. I'm listening much more for these "states of emergence."

I would call it where you are like a little chick cracking out of that shell, and you're emerging, and you're letting us see your wet feathers, and your webbed toes, and the wing that hasn't come out yet. Change requires a field of emergent expectation, and a whole lot of "listeners" who are there just waiting to see what the little chick's going to look like, because we've just been so excited by it.

It does really midwife our listening, and attentiveness, and cherishing, and empathetic midwife-sparks are essential to this work. You have to have that. Gertrude Stein said that without Alice B. Toklas, forget it. She worked all night. Every morning she handed her writing over to Alice B. Toklas, and Alice B. Toklas read it, typed it up, and by lunch they went over the writing.

That is essential. The artist as despairing, cutting off the ears—all of that stuff—it is because they do not have a listening community. They cannot make that next leap, that transformative leap, because they don't have a listening community. I think you're right on about that. The deep listening, and I would say deep parenting, and caring, and all those words where you're just allowing the thing to flourish—then somebody can hear, "This image really works, and this one needs work," and then she'll go home and do it, because she has the support. Then it doesn't become criticism, it just becomes, "I love what you're doing, and I want to see it blossom even more."

TRACKING SENSATION

How do we Listen Deeply? Just as in how we Bring Awareness, it comes down to engaging the felt sense of internal sensations—my emotions, responses, and the nuances of my physical body—as the primary source of knowing. If I have a direct experience in sensation, then I can know it to be true. And if I can understand that experience in a larger matrix of meaning, then I can appreciate the message and the significance of what is being offered.

For over twenty-five years I have studied and taught the art of tracking sensation. Through the movement practice of Continuum, I've learned to attend the movement of the breath, the ripples and tingles of the nervous system, and the quality of tension or release in muscle and connective tissue. I've learned to be able to identify within my own body the physical sensations that accompany my emotions. For example, when I am angry I feel heat rise in my chest, my breath quickens, my muscles tense, the muscles of my face begin to form a snarl, my eyes narrow, my upper lip curls. Or, when I am nervous, my breath quickens and also wants to stop, as in "my breath catches." My stomach tightens or churns. If I'm really nervous, I can feel my bowels loosen. I might break out into a sweat, or feel perspiration push through my pores. I want to move about quickly, or I might want to freeze and not move at all, holding all that impulse toward movement, inside.

Jacques Verduin uses sensory awareness as the primary tool for self-understanding in his GRIP program in San Quentin prison. Triggered unconscious, unchecked, or undesirable impulses can lead to lashing out and violence, in a moment. Jacques' training asks the men to first become intimately aware of their own sensations—learning their own sensation vocabulary, if you will—so they can begin to slow down the moments when anger or rage is triggered, and understand the mechanics of their response. Once they have that understanding, they have the ability to make new choices of response and behavior. They can disrupt the automatic patterns, and make new choices. Practicing with understanding, in a controlled and slowed down context, can prepare them for situations when they might be truly triggered outside the controlled context. They are listening deeply to both their impulses and to their responses.

Sharon Weil: I'm so interested that you talked about identifying the sensations that lead to emotions. We're not really talking about emotions, but the sensations that lead to them. I know that your background is in somatics, and also in meditation and mindfulness practice. Because of your body orientation, the idea of sensation being different than emotion is not something that people necessarily know how to separate or identify.

Jacques Verduin: It became really important. If you're trying to work with impulse control then it implies you have to also understand how to track what's happening. After some careful observation through the years we found that there's a certain order in how what happens, happens. Everything starts with what the body registers through its portals—these openings in our body: eyes, ears, nose, taste buds, pores in the skin. Information comes in, and then depending on whether we like it or not, we have an emotion about it. Then, when that emotion becomes clear, there's a thought. It filters through the memory banks, based on what you've experienced already, and then that's followed by an action.

What we learned...okay, prison speak. We go like, "Okay, you're in your cell. Your neighbor is playing the radio too loud." They all nod their heads. They've all been through that. The first thing that happens is you cringe, there's a contraction, you maybe frown your forehead or your eyebrows and there's a feeling in the body of violation, perhaps. Then, there's an emotion. In this case, "I don't like it. I don't feel good." Then, very quickly there's a thought, "I feel disrespected. This guy is not with it, maybe I should teach him a lesson." Then the action, "I'm going to go over. I'm either going to jump on the radio or on the guy; it depends on whether he turns it down or not."

All that can happen, and it does happen, very quickly, right? To learn how to break that down and stay with the sensation as the main skill-building piece in that exercise proved really important because the very person that then is disrespected begins to be validated, right there, by being heard—in this case by himself—about what's going on. These feelings can start knocking the door down because somebody's home to receive them and validate them, and then they change. Sensations change constantly. Life is movement, so if you're registering something that's changing, you're at least not as stuck with something, or not as set in your ways as to how to deal with it.

PATTERN RECOGNITION

In identifying the impulses and the sensations that lead to emotion, we can see underlying patterns that emerge based on strategy, repetition, adaptation, and response. Recognizing patterns is a good way to assess the terrain of any given situation or problem, and an effective way to navigate change. However, being locked into patterns will limit the movement of change, and keep change traveling in the same configuration, repeatedly. **Adam Wolpert** says that patterns reveal relationship: between objects, people, and responses that lead to behavior. As an artist, Adam reflects the patterns he observes in nature. As a group facilitator, he observes the patterns that have formed in organizations and in human dynamics. Rafting on rivers, he navigates by recognizing the patterns in the water, which tell the story of how to make a safe journey over rocks and ledges.

> **Adam Wolpert**: Pattern is the language of change. If you can see the pattern and the structures that underlie that pattern, then you can engage something that's more stable and static—even as the surface keeps reinventing itself, and keeps moving and changing.

> **Sharon Weil**: As an artist, what patterns are you observing? What patterns are you working with?

> **Adam Wolpert**: You can see that relationship is being expressed all throughout nature. When you're looking at something, you're usually looking at the expression of a relationship. For example, if you look at fish—try to depict them or understand them visually—you see them swimming around in the water. You see that the form of the fish is the expression of its relationship with the water.

The form only makes sense in relationship with what it does and how it is, in its place. All of these relationships are expressed over and over again, around that form. That's a fascinating thing to also look for, in groups. When I'm doing group work and I have a group that's changing, there's an underlying pattern in how that change will be expressed. When you find the pattern, then you can engage in a more meaningful way.

Sharon Weil: Are you finding the pattern because you're so experienced with working with groups, and so you see, "Oh, this is this pattern; I've seen this before," or are you actually observing, "This is the shape of the wake of their coming up against each other in certain ways?"

Adam Wolpert: I think both are true. There's a lot of ground that's already been walked in this field; it's a really rich field. There's been so much study of group dynamics that goes all the way back to the early twentieth century. Kurt Lewin brought up this whole idea of group dynamics. One of his core ideas is to change something in a group, there are these three steps: "unfreeze, change, and refreeze," or sometimes it's said "freeze, change, freeze" or "freeze, melt, freeze." It's this idea that if you've got a big circle of ice and you want a square of ice, you don't try to carve the circle into a square. You melt it, and then freeze it into a square.

Change is usually a journey. There are these stages from one frozen state, or stable state, to another. Moving from one state to another usually involves a process which engages discomfort and misunderstanding, or difficulty, or chaos, or things falling apart.

If you can locate a group in those stages, you can work with them much more effectively. There are some moments when groups need to fall apart in order to come back together. There are other moments when groups are just about to crystallize the new thing, and there might be a rush of anxiety or a panic about the discomfort. When groups change, they often move out of their comfort zone, and people become uncomfortable. Then, the facilitator's job is not to let it fall apart, but to let that process end and let the new crystallization form fully and take on its own new stability.

One of the things I've learned over the years of facilitating is to, as much as possible, give the group a framework wherein they can locate themselves. If you have some way to locate yourself within a process, within a broader framework, you have a better chance of surviving, not getting too caught up in the trees, seeing the forest.

In looking for patterns, I can also locate the patterns of the obstacles that divert the flow of the movement of change, much like the rocks beneath the river current, that Adam mentioned earlier.

In an earlier chapter, **Harvey Ruderian** discussed holding patterns in the body to be still or stuck places where movement has compensated, *going around* the places that are not moving. Harvey is able to make these discoveries in clients with his highly trained eye, easily identifying structural compensations in how a person stands or walks. He also Listens Deeply with his own hands and his full presence to the movement, or lack of movement, in the cerebral spinal fluid, and the tissues of the body. In that way, he uncovers and unwinds deep-set holding patterns caused by injury, trauma, stress, and even ancestry. He shared with me an expanded vision of how he perceives the body when he listens.

Harvey Ruderian: There's a wonderful word that we've incorporated in the work called "listening." Listening is an interesting word in itself because when we talk about listening, we oftentimes think of that which we're engaging when we're hearing. For me, the word listening is something deeper.

Being present as a practitioner is not to diagnose too deeply what you're feeling, but just to simply feel.

The more you've learned how to feel—it's like listening to an orchestra and you've learned to be able to hear like the conductor, right? That's an incredible ear that conductor has. [As a practitioner] over the years, your hands get more and more sensitive. So, what you're doing is not manipulating, you're simply able to listen. And it's able to listen to you because there's an intelligence there.

It's an extraordinary gift to be here in our bodies on the planet. When you start to really inquire as I have over many years of being with people in fifty or sixty or seventy thousand sessions, people just start to share with me about how their lives are stuck.

They may be the only person, or maybe all the people in their lives see them as being in pain, and being fixated, and being stuck. Perhaps their whole world is what we call "repetitive strain injury." In many ways, people live whole lives in a state of repetitive strain because their deep divine self—the part that I see walking in the door—is stuck.

Somebody walks into my room and they want to tell me the story of their holding pattern—their fixation, their illness, their calamity, their pain—because that's what brings people in. I used to be a Rolfer and give people ten sessions. I've done lots of fix-it work. I grew and grew over the last forty-plus years. In the more biodynamic way that I work, I move more and more into listening, a partnering, you might say, which is part of the evolutionary wave that is flowering in this person. This wave is coming out of evolution itself. It's evolution manifesting itself.

Harvey places his hands on his clients and feels the subtle, long and short, slow and fast waves moving through the person's tissues and fluids. In joining with those waves, he can help resolve holding patterns in the deepest places that lie beneath the daily tensions, and beneath the central nervous system. The holding patterns then open up into a field that is much more spacious and expansive, where the true nature of the person's divine self—as he calls it—can be met and encouraged to come forward. He describes the feeling as "…a different language. It's a bit more shamanic, you might say. It's listening to, and feeling, the spell of the sensuous."

CONNECTING

Shamanic healer **Amanda Foulger** teaches others to be able to "listen" to helpful and healing spirits from the upper and lower worlds—as she refers to them. Amanda also acts as a translator for these voices to come through. In shamanic practice, she recognizes that listening doesn't just take place through sound, or through our ears. There are many ways that we can make contact and receive helpful messages, depending upon our own strengths of orientation.

Amanda Foulger: Some people are very visual. Some people are very auditory. Some people are very kinesthetic and feel in their body, or some people have a very clear message of some kind that comes as a thought or a feeling. The idea, over time, is that you need to learn your own language of spirit. What is the way you connect? Ideally, we want to have all of the senses involved, and we want to have a very complete experience—but it doesn't always happen that way.

You have to learn through a lot of practice and experience. Sometimes, people have experiences in dreams that are very compelling. This world of myths and dreams, it's very much the kind of world we get in touch with consciously in shamanic work, and it usually has very specific reasons. We want to be in touch with sources of power. We want to get help or healing. We want to get some kind of guidance in our life, or for somebody else. Those are the things that we're after in classic shamanic practice.

TRUST

When I Listen Deeply to myself, or others, can I trust what I hear? Especially when the messages I receive come from places or realms I can't really see or locate—can I trust that? I believe that the lack of trust, and self-doubt, are two of the greatest forms of resistance I can encounter, and therefore two of the biggest obstacles to change and ChangeAbility. It's one thing to be able to hear the voice, whether it an internal voice speaking to the artist, a voice of the spirits speaking from other dimensions, the voice of people giving us counsel and advice, or the voice of consumer surveys and focus groups. But once I am listening, can I trust what I hear? Can I trust what I have come to know? As a writer it's taken me a very long time to be able to trust the creative voice that comes from within, or to be able to distinguish between the many. It takes practice to overcome the doubt and to trust the free-fall of change.

Jackie Welch Schlicher talks about how important it is for an artist to follow the impulses that guide her and to trust where they might lead. This is the artist's way. This is what others admire when they see an artist trusting their creative impulses enough to follow through and let the work come forward in form.

Jackie Welch Schlicher: I'm going to start first with improv and big-theater improv. Often, you come on to the stage with your brilliant idea. Before you have a chance to get it out, someone else is sharing their brilliant idea. I have to listen, and be attuned to that, and respond. Now, my idea may assist that one, but I may also have to let it go. That's what I think of when I'm at the potter's wheel, being aware that I have ears in my ears and I'm listening to the clay. The question I'm asking is, "Are you too wet; are you too dry? Do I need to speed up the wheel here? What's going to happen?" Because the clay has been sent to go where it wants to go, or where the scientific forces are sending it by virtue of it being on a spinning wheel. I'm listening and learning how to communicate so that it understands, and so that I understand. It gets that I want to make a belly here; that I want it to bow out this way. It's telling me "I can't do it that fast. Go slower.

Take your time. Not that much pressure. Oh, a little more pressure here." There's a listening that's going on in everything. Of course as a singer you're listening. You're tuning into the music, and the rhythm, and energy of what's going on around you. And the writer—there's all kinds of conversation going on with the characters, and stepping into imaginary worlds, and tuning in, being aware of what's coming forth.

Sharon Weil: When I am writing, a character talks to me. Can I trust them? Are these really the characters' voices? Is this just me making it up? For so many years you've been in this listening-trusting response cycle. So many people struggle with this, and want to know, "Now I've learned how to listen, how do I trust what I hear?"

Jackie Welch Schlicher: That's a great question. In my experience, the act of trusting connects you to that guiding principle, to the spirit behind whatever it is you are doing. I mean, it's not just an empty action. If I say to you "I really trust you," there's something that happens just in that communication. There's a reciprocation of trust in that.

There's room for the learning, and the teacher shows up. There's room for the learning and having that trust to say, "I have come far enough to be ready to take this step," because we're all learning how to trust ourselves, number one, but also to trust that we've got all the support we need. If you are in doubt, that drains a little bit of that trust, doesn't it? It pulls the plug on it a little bit, but you want the full feature. You plug up that hole and let go of the doubt. It's better to jump off the cliff—as they say—sprout your wings, and the floor arrives to meet you.

Sharon Weil: Sometimes that leak that you're talking about is just the unwillingness to trust, especially as we're learning a new thing. It's like when I was writing a script, and this character started talking to me and telling me what to do, I'm like, "Okay, I'll listen." When you listen, it happens. When you listen to what the clay is saying to you, flow and creativity open.

Jackie Welch Schlicher: I like to think of it as hacking away the sticker bushes. It's like clearing the path to connect.

Sharon Weil: Clearing a path to connect. I really like that.

Jackie Welch Schlicher: Clearing away the fog, the sticker bushes, or whatever you want to call it. The stuff that's in between you and where you're headed takes time. It takes patience. It takes love. It takes listening to yourself and being kind in those moments, being gentle with yourself in those moments of doubt and giving yourself the patience to go again, and to go again—and every time you probably get a little further. At least that's worked for me.

I like how she says that clearing the path from self-doubt takes patience and practice, just like any art takes patience and practice, and the willingness to throw the clay over and over again onto the wheel.

As an intuitive healer, **Rachel Lang** hears a voice that few others can. Since she was young child, she has had the gift of being able to "see" and to "hear" from spirits and ancestors from other dimensions of reality, including those who are no longer alive. Rachel reads for clients, translating from other realms, so to speak, the answers to their questions. Also a gifted spiritual healer and astrologer, her many years of practice have given her an authority all her own, as well as a validation from the voices that she brings through. So many clients rely on her to advise them from information they don't feel they have access to, but that she does. So I asked her, "Since trust is crucial to making choices for change, how do you trust the information that comes to you? How do you trust yourself?"

Rachel Lang: That's a great question. Sometimes I don't trust myself. You can't rely on external validation. That has nothing to do with how much you trust yourself. The only way to trust the information that's coming in is to continue dialoguing with everything in my environment, to continue a spiritual practice where I'm constantly tuning in and I'm listening to myself.

I can hear my voice. I can hear the voice of my ancestors. Sometimes I hear myself and it sounds like my mother. Sometimes I hear myself and I sound like Eleanor Roosevelt. That process of hearing, of being in constant communication with spirit guides, with people guides—people who come into our lives who we trust—it's really important to cultivate trust.

I think we're always in this process of returning back to our two-year-old selves—the time when we had our Mars return, and we knew what we wanted.

We were developing our egos, and we said "no," and we said "yes," and we meant it. And we didn't want to share, or we did; or we didn't want to eat that, or we wanted to eat this. I think we're always in this process of going back and finding that inner voice that gets repressed, and shaped, and formed by our culture. Having a spiritual practice where I'm listening to that voice, having people in my life who can reflect back for me certain things about myself that help shape my own relationship with myself is very important.

Sharon Weil: What happens when I don't trust and don't heed that voice?

Rachel Lang: When you don't trust, or when you don't heed that voice, then it puts you back in that place of separateness. When you're in a place of separateness, yes, you can function, you can still move through change, you can still make decisions in your life, but everything just feels so dense. There's a certain absence of joy, or not an absence of joy, but you're not fully living into your joy. I think ultimately our souls want to be joyful. Trusting, even when you have no proof that there's any reason to trust, returns you back into a state of bliss.

Sharon Weil: Returns you to a state of bliss and therefore…

Rachel Lang: You might trust yourself implicitly and still get into a relationship where someone's cheating on you, or still get into a bad financial decision. We think that if things aren't good, if we have losses, or if we have deception or betrayal, that somehow that's not part of the divine plan, or we view it as negative, or we want to assign a judgment to it rather than seeing it as magic, or seeing it as something that we cocreated.

When we can start to see that even the challenges in our lives are magic, even the losses—loss of a loved one or the loss of a job—are a cocreative process. There's magic, there's a miracle in there; it's opening up something else. And when we can see that, and we can live into that, then we can trust anything, because trust ultimately allows us to live a full, rich, complete life experience and sometimes life experiences have things that the external world would judge as bad. They just are. They're truth, that's what they are. They're truth and they're cocreation.

Writer **Rebecca Mark** speaks not only of the trust the writer must have for bringing forward the internal voices she hears, but Rebecca also talks about the need to be able to bring your work forward to be met by trustworthy listeners. Every artist needs at least a small circle of trusted listeners, as she referred to earlier, in order to let the new emergent work flourish.

Rebecca Mark: Part of it is the communal, because you will get a sense of the shared resonance. When that voice comes forward it's almost like a bell goes off in the room, or there's a tension released, or there's a sense of reverberation that occurs. That's what an important communal setting allows… "I know I hit a chord here."

I was doing a piece a while ago, and I just was missing it, and missing it, and missing it. I could tell, when I read it to the group, I was missing it. Then I just went into the movement again, and when I came out I was right where I needed to be. You have to have enough of a dramatic awareness to feel the cellular transformation, because in my understanding, it is occurring within the neurological pathways of the brain and the body, so that you are actually sensing newness. You are experiencing the thrill of that newness.

You are hitting on what's the most exciting thing about innovators, and transformers, and change-makers, that they keep hearing that bell, and they keep being willing to go into that cave. Everybody else might say, "It looks like it's just stuff here," but they're going to be like, "No, no, no, no. This is very important."

This profound and unique way of using words and drawings in an interdependent, interchangeable way of storytelling can be very unformed and tender when it first emerges. I asked Rebecca whether or not she involves a large number of people in her own creative projects.

Rebecca Mark: When I'm working on a project, I don't bring in a lot of voices [from other people]. I bring in only those voices that I can trust, and that is something you're saying here with trust. I know I can trust this person, and this person, and I will show them the work, but I'm not going to show it too prematurely to people who just don't have any idea what's going on.

We are pretty lonely, those people who are doing something new, and we have to surround ourselves with really trustworthy people.

Sharon Weil: It can't be done in isolation.

Rebecca Mark: No. No true change will take place. Some people become famous very, very early, and they get a lot of either very positive or very negative feedback, that kind of works their own self-trust. Those of us who aren't famous get to do a lot more self-trust. How did you know if this was the book you needed to work on? You *knew* this was the book you needed to work on. That's really important. When I'm following a line on a paper I trust that my body, my hand, my gesture, my everything is in line with each other, and that's the line that wants to come forward, and when I'm in that sweet spot, then I can.

I'm in the gush of that particular cellular move. Often, all I'm doing is trusting the cellular movement, and just recording it on the paper. Which is really fun. That's one thing for trust, is that it's fun. What is debilitating is then you come home and you discount that, and you give it no value.

Trust gives me the confidence and the willingness to dissolve my resistance to change. Even if I don't trust the change I am about to enter, or trust the unknown outcome of that change, when I find the touchstones of stable ground I can rely upon, I can allow the movement of change to flow, and I can find courage, willingness, and as Rachel put it, joy.

BUILDING FROM THE INSIDE OUT

Jacques Verduin first developed his programs through the organization he helped to found and then directed, Insight Prison Project. He told me that his current organization is called Insight-Out because the programs were developed from the inside need to the outside form. The development of these programs is a wonderful example of how Listen Deeply and making small course corrections as you go creates results that truly serve the need, and therefore can be most effective.

Jacques Verduin: We went into a major prison, San Quentin State Prison, a little naive, thinking, "This is great. They have time, we teach meditation, we'll make a monastery." Well, that was not what happened. First of all, that was more about us than them. It became more important to ask, "What's needed here?" and serve that. Some of [the prisons] had over five thousand people in prison, and there was no violence prevention program. Rather than ideology, our perspective was informed by what was needed on the ground. We started getting informed by relationships.

Rather than providing a service, as it's called in business, we engaged a relationship and said, "Who are you? Ask us who we are, and what can we do together." That was different, and it was very important for us not to fall into the polarity of us and them, which is probably nowhere bigger than in this field. You have the "good people" and "bad people." The bad people have nothing to say because they're bad, and the good people organize very well so that they have fully say, politically.

From the get-go, on the team we had victims, we had correctional officers, law enforcement—so we couldn't be packed down as a bunch of crazy liberal volunteers that don't have a life that need to find some meaning somewhere or something. That was done purposefully. As an innovator I understood that if you want to build a movement you can't just have something that people can be against. It's got to be something that they can be for. It's very important.

We thought, "If we work from the inside out, we're informed through relationship. We serve the *needs* rather than come with our own shtick." Something could develop from the most unusual angle inside the belly of the beast that would, on every stage, involve and amplify the voices that are of the population inside. In the program, that means, for example, that they make their own learning agreements. We divide them up in four groups. This group has confidentiality, this group has participation and attendance, this group has communication, and this group has respect. They make up the rules for the learning community.

It's a really beautiful thing to see, actually. It's like democracy in action, because these are people that are institutionalized. All of them have served over twenty years. They don't get asked, "What do you think?" Or, "How should we do things?" They're rusty, and you get to see which ones of them have internalized their keeper's MO. Like, for example, on confidentiality, some people will say, "If somebody doesn't keep confidentiality, you've got to throw them out." Then somebody else said, "Wouldn't we all like a little forgiveness?" It's just fascinating. Then, at the end of the group, the solution is for us, by us, about us. That's a salutation. The other way that works out is we have inmates teaching inmates more and more, because we're training them, and they need places to exercise their training. That brings in a different dignity, when people say, "Well, I could be like that." And, "Wait a minute. Some of these guys are getting hired? I could get hired for dedicating myself to my own transformation so that I can offer it to others?" It does bring hope and it does bring dignity.

SUMMARY

How can principle #2 Listen Deeply increase the ease and responsiveness of ChangeAbility?

For every action there is a reaction; for every call there is a response. The world is full of feedback in many forms. I can best utilize that feedback by learning to be attuned and by listening into the particulars of my circumstances. By "listening," I don't just mean hearing with my ears, but I also mean sensing with the felt sense of my hands, my intuition, my empathy, and the sensations of my inner landscape. Listen Deeply originates with inquiry; led by curiosity. The genuine inquiry of *what is going on here or what do I need to know* comes best without judgment or assumption so that I might make new and fresh discoveries which can then lead to new and creative responses. Listen Deeply is the art of recognizing feedback and having the ability and flexibility to respond most appropriately through course corrections in order to maximize ChangeAbility.

◊ I Listen Deeply by tracking my sensations: sight, sound, taste, smell, touch— as well as an internal felt sense, my intuition, and my artistic impulse and guides.

◊ The practice of deep listening is the practice of open inquiry, without assumption or judgment. What am I perceiving about this situation? What do I need to know?

◊ Everything in my environment is offering me feedback, if I will only listen.

◊ Even mistakes and failure are forms of feedback about what is not working and needs to change.

◊ An important aspect of ChangeAbility is the recognition of the need for small course corrections on the path of change. I determine the need and the strategy for these corrections through listening to the feedback I hear, and then adjusting my course.

◊ Recognizing patterns is a good way to assess the terrain of any given situation or challenge. Patterns reveal the underlying structure beneath what is changing or what is not. Recognizing patterns is an efficient guide for navigating change.

◊ Establishing self-trust and trust of others allows me to take action, without resistance, on the feedback I receive, or the impulses I feel.

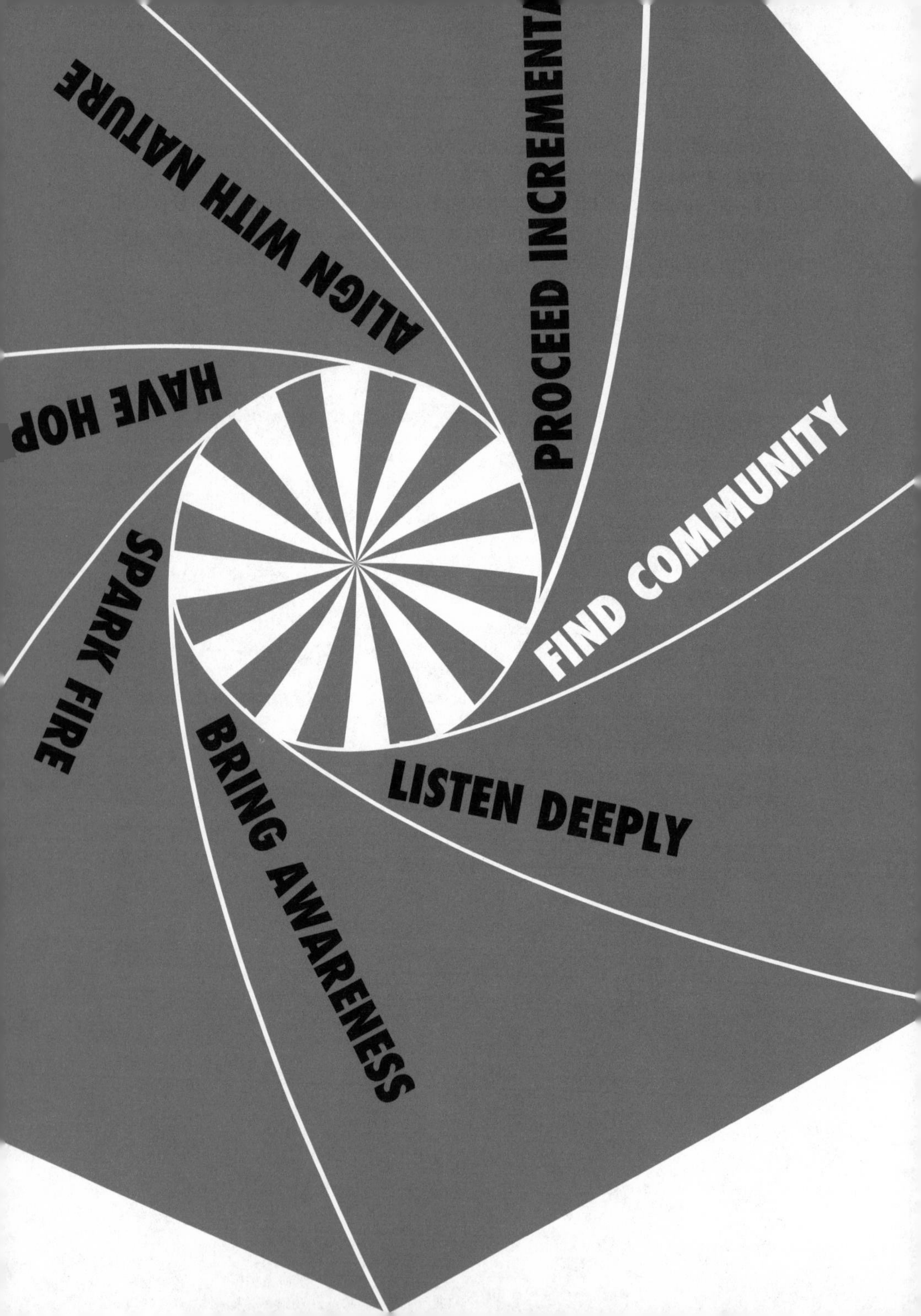
ALIGN WITH NATURE
PROCEED INCREMENTA
HAVE HOP
FIND COMMUNITY
SPARK FIRE
BRING AWARENESS
LISTEN DEEPLY

3 FIND COMMUNITY

Tribe, family, neighborhood, village, society, relation, relationship, support, connection, cooperation, alliance, partnership, organization, affinity, affiliation

"I alone cannot change the world, but I can cast a stone across the waters to create many ripples."

—Mother Teresa

THIS CHAPTER ON PRINCIPLE #3 FIND Community can be short and simple: get help for everything you do!

It's a radical thought, because though we know this to be true, it seems to come hard for so many people. *I'm shy, I'm embarrassed, I'm fiercely independent, I've been let down by others and disappointed, I don't know who to ask, I can do it better myself, I think I have to do it myself, I can't afford it, I don't deserve it, or I don't need help*—these are the excuses I tell myself.

None of us ask for help nearly enough, and we need to! If you were to look at any change in your life right now that is not moving well I would ask you, do you have enough assistance? Is there room for more?

"Human beings, for the most part, are herd animals and pack animals. We don't end here. We exist in relationship and the give and take on every single level from energy, to touch, to community."

—Deena Metzger

It is our nature to belong to one another. In order to navigate change or even tolerate change, I need to Find Community. By Find Community, I mean find support. Find whatever ground, strength, expertise, or companionship that joins me with others to lighten my load and ease my way. Find the thoughts, feelings, and feedback from my environment to allow me to remain whole within myself. Find like-minded compadres, dedicated coworkers, numbers of supporters, playful cocreators, and sympathetic hearts. There are so many ways that I can find and offer support. The movement of change has less resistance and more joy when I share with others. We are social creatures; the unknown, as well as the known, is best not faced alone.

BELONGING

"Harmony and unity are deep principles of shamanic practice. It's not just about being nice, it actually is about what can you contribute in a situation with others that creates harmony and unity? Can you operate from that place? We understand now that the heart, in its resonant field, is most expanded when people are happy and appreciative. That's when people are harmonizing and making that kind of an effort to harmonize."

—Amanda Foulger

Our greatest joy comes from communion, be it with another, with the energies of nature, with a universal spirit, or with a sense of self. Though **Deena Metzger** often works alone in her writing, all her activities involve creating community, nurturing community, holding community, and using community as the most nourishing way for creativity and healing to emerge. Deena's sense of community not only includes individuals, but extends to all creatures of the earth, the earth itself, the ancestors, and the helpful spirits that guide us.

Deena Metzger: There's no separation. The native people of this country, the first people—in this instance the Lakota Sioux people—have a phrase which they say after anything that's sacred or important, in the way we say blessings. They say, "Mitakuye Oyasin, *all my relations.*" When we develop the ability to think "all my relations" before we act at any time, everything will be changed, extending concern and compassion to everything and everyone.

Socially, the herd or pack nature of humans, that innate need for belonging, was addressed by forming the tribe. Historically, the tribe was defined by genetics and geography, and was not only a means for belonging, but was a necessity for survival. However, as peoples dispersed over continents, over time, we have come to define our sense of tribal belonging differently. We now organize ourselves in tribes we call communities, based on locale, interest, or affiliation. We have belonging to partners, families, neighborhoods, coworkers, causes, and religions. Because we are tribal beings, for whatever activities there are in my life, there is some group I belong to as a result, and I derive my identity, to a greater or lesser degree, from the groups I belong to.

I find that the word "community" is used broadly. Any time a group forms for any purpose it seems to be called a community. There are so many types of communities and so many levels and purposes. Some are meant to be temporary, existing for a period of time: the community of parents at my daughter's school during the time she is attending, or the very temporary community that gathers once a year with Heal the Bay to clean up trash and debris from the Santa Monica beaches. While some communities are meant to be short-lived, others are longer lasting and a have more essential commitment: the community of family, marriage, and relationship.

Sometimes, people are considered a community merely because of their proximity of geography, like my neighborhood, even if I have nothing to do with my neighbors except to wave when we are walking our dogs, or gather in town for the Fourth of July parade. That geographical community can have a more specific purpose, like a community watch for suspicious activity in the neighborhood, or say, if I lived in a co-op apartment building where we all own apartments in the same building and need to make some common decisions together about the garbage cans or maintenance fees. We are a community strictly because we happen to be near each other, and, therefore, need to make some decisions together; but we didn't form into that community necessarily to become one.

There are those who do choose to live near each other or live together as an intentional community, like Adam Wolpert at Occidental Arts and Ecology Center. There, a group of families, the Sowing Circle, are choosing to live together in a community with common goals, common rules, and common ownership that comes from an ideal of how best to live in relation to others. And in their case, also to live in relationship to the natural world. Families can also be intentional communities, until they're not.

Then there are communities that form because of shared backgrounds or cultures, like the Jewish community in West Los Angeles, the Filipino community in the Bay Area that Beth Rosales works very hard to support, the American ex-patriot community living in Bali who watch the results of the US elections together, or the American-Armenian community that marched in protest in cities all over the country this year when President Obama would not recognize the mass killings of Armenians under Ottoman rule (1915–1918) as genocide.

I could have the same common background with the cultural community and still not identify because of personal differences. This can often be seen in people who "move away" from their countries, cities, or families of origin. Melting-pot cities like Los Angeles or New York City are gathering places for people seeking to make a different way of life from the communities in which they were raised.

However, we have seen how when a community comes together, they can increase their power and increase their voice. Only in recent years has the gay and lesbian community called themselves the LGBT community, coming together as one to include bisexual and transgender people. That community has grown in its own inclusivity, and has become a more powerful, unified voice that was strong enough to bring marriage equality laws to the Supreme Court and finally win. Truly, the support for same-sex marriage is shared by a much larger group of Americans beyond the LGBT community, for the marriage equality decision granted equal rights for all of us.

Social media is an incredible tool in building community for the purpose of support for my ideas and activities. It's a great tool to Bring Awareness and to Proceed Incrementally through vehicles like crowdsourcing or signing online petitions. These allow us to become part of a community, or a community action, by way of a click. Social media played a large part in the call to action for the Occupy Movement and Arab Spring. In those cases, virtual communities' calls for support became real communities of activists standing together in protest. Social media is now an essential part of communicating and community building. However, as Claire Hope Cummings warned, the sheer load of information coming from social media is overwhelming how we spend our time, and is distracting us from real issues that need our attention. She also warned that participating online can give us a false sense of action on issues. "Liking" an action page on Facebook is not the same as taking an action, although it can increase awareness and contribute support.

It's obviously important to know the difference between real communities and virtual ones; they should not be mistaken for one another. Twitter, Facebook, Instagram, or LinkedIn may help me find a community of agreement and assistance, but true support involves real contact. My Twitter followers may help me spread the word about my latest book event, or about the latest action request on behalf of the fight against GMOs. My Facebook friends might even create a groundswell of "happy birthday" wishes that make my day, or I might find out of someone's recent success. Many of my Facebook friends are my *actual* friends. Social media is just one of the meta-levels of communication that we share. Others are acquaintances, or people who I am happy to stay in contact with in Nashville, or New York, or around the world—in places I no longer live. But when I am sick I want real friends to show up with real soup. Though these days, social media may be the way they find out that I need it.

ISOLATION AND SEPARATION FROM COMMUNITY

"Everything in our culture is designed to isolate and fragment, so when we come back again into community, and then we come back into a community of human beings that's true on land, that is a community in the presence of the spirits and the elementals. When we reconstruct the entire world that is necessary for anything to thrive, and the ecosystem is back—complex, diverse, intact—then healing is possible…and sanity. And without it, it doesn't exist."

—Deena Metzger

Separation is the underlying cause of all suffering. If we are change, if we are one, then our being cannot be separated from all existence. And yet, each one of us has felt a sense of separation, loneliness, rejection, or feeling "other." It's a profound sense of disconnection. I can feel disconnected from my own felt sense of feelings and emotions, from my sense of purpose and value, or from the structures of my family, my partnerships, my school community, my work community, or my religious community. *Do I belong?* If I am a pack animal and a tribal dweller, then a sense of separation from the group will be at the root of all of my discomfort, regardless of the shape or purpose of the group—even if the group is just myself and one other. Feeling separated from the group, I become fragmented within myself, and do not have the sense of wholeness that is crucial to my well-being; that sense that Amanda Fougler calls "unity and harmony."

Separation can lead to isolation, and because we need social contact, physical contact, and emotional contact in order to thrive, isolation cuts me off from the very nutrients of contact that I need. I am robbed of the bio-signals from other beings and from nature itself that provide me my most needed contact for belonging. **Robert Litman** speaks of how separation leads to isolation.

> **Robert Litman**: Circumstances outside of ourselves can make us feel unsafe. We don't feel like we belong. We separate from the belongingness of it all. When we get separate, we feel even less safe, because we are not taking in information from the environment. We feel isolated. In defense, in our isolation, since we're no longer in communication with the whole, or being part of the whole, we become less permeable. We pull in.

There are so many ways I might separate myself from my sense of belonging, mostly through my thoughts and reactions, and a lack of trust in the ever-changing scene of life. I can be shy at a party or in a group of strangers. Walking into the group, I am aware that the way in which I enter is the way in which I will be responded to. If I tell myself no one here cares about me or wants me here, then I will be guarded, hang in the corner and isolate myself. If I tell myself I have affinity with these people, even if we haven't met, then I enter more open, curious and friendly. I may still not receive a warm welcome, but I might still remain open if I believe there is a possibility.

My sense of separation comes from my thoughts, but there are times when the community can actually turn against me if I am not aligned with its purpose, or follow the rules. If I stand on my desk at work and shout at the boss, I may be asked to leave. Or if I turn against the town where I live and I rob the bank, I will be arrested. The classic nightmare that is repeated over and over again in kids movies is of being ostracized in school by the cheerleader in-crowd. Or where your friends suddenly turn on you and close rank against your without you knowing why. Sometimes the rules for belonging are clearly stated; sometimes they are not.

Feeling alone, or the *fear* that I'll be alone is often what stops me from taking a risk and making change. It drives so much behavior. The illusion of separation can be acted out in so many ways. I might convince myself that I'm the only person in the world who cares about, say, the dangers of genetically modified food. Or worse, my fear of being criticized or ostracized for proposing to you that you change the way you eat, the way you buy, keeps me silent. My friends might not invite me to dinner anymore. They might think I'm an alarmist health-nut crackpot for alerting them to something they consider a non-issue. It would require that they change out of their comfortable eating and buying pattern and they don't want to be reminded by me, so they might exclude me. So I won't share my ideas, or my book about GMOs—I might not even write it. Or I might feel alone and in real danger, as I did when writing *Donny and Ursula Save the World*. I had a large underlying fear that I would be "messed with" by Monsanto by alluding to them in such satirical protest, that at times it did stop me in my writing tracks. It wasn't until I found allies who were also working in the anti-GMO issue that I felt more safe.

Our basic human need is for belonging, and to find safety in belonging, whether it's belonging to another, to a tribe, or to a biomorphic field. When the message is *be like us or be banished*, it can be very threatening to make a change. Whether the fear is banishment, or simply embarrassment…

WE HAVE TO ASK FOR HELP!

We need to join with others, and have them join with us.

Sometimes the support that's needed is from an expert. **Amy McEarchern** heeds the call. As a moving and organizing professional, her job is to do what most people think they ought to be able to do themselves, but can't or don't; organize their own stuff and move it. Before calling Amy, her clients suffer, feeling overwhelmed by the accumulation of their possessions. They're often embarrassed at the state of their mess and their inability to manage it. I know—I'm one of them!

Sharon Weil: So many people feel like they have to move on their own. They think, "Why should I hire somebody?" Unless you need a mover to take your things to a location far away, most people think, "Oh, no, no. I have to do this myself or I should do it myself," right?

Amy McEachern: I get that one a lot. People are like, "Well, I don't know…" Then they start self-flagellating over the fact that they really should be able to do this, and I have said to them, "Here's the thing. During the day you go away and do what you do, and I go away and do what I do. Whether it's being a mother, whether it's being a producer, whether it's being a plumber, whatever. That's what you do. This is what I do. I've got all the equipment, I've got the know-how, I've got the knowledge, I've got the repetitive training from doing so many houses over and over. So there's a pattern to it that happens." Maybe I could fix my own toilet if I got a book and tried to figure it out, but I can go to work and make a better income to pay somebody to do it rather than the aggravation of trying to do somebody else's job. That's just what I have to tell people. "You do things better than I do in many, many areas. But this…I got. I love it. I love doing it, and you don't have to do it alone. It can be scary. But that's why I'm here."

Deena Metzger works with many manifestations of disease that come from isolation and fragmentation. The healing communities she gathers help hold the individual so they do not feel so alone or ashamed of their pain, illness or the ways they cannot fit in with the larger world. She describes a healing workshop gathering that included physicians and patients, where participants volunteered to receive healing from the group.

Sharon Weil: I think one of the main signs of disease is isolation, whether it's isolation of a person or it's the fragmentation of the Earth. Community is the antidote to isolation and that is what allows an environment for healing to take place, for it to spread, and be shared, and carried. I know you're doing this with the Daré circles, and pretty much with everything you do. You're always gathering people together, right?

Deena Metzger: Obsessively. Yes. We were twenty-two people over this President's Day weekend and we only thought one person was going to be sort of the volunteer patient but it turned out we had at least three official people and then more people coming at the end. If you can imagine you have an illness. You haven't been able to find the way to heal it. You're afraid and suddenly instead of being locked up in a small office, often without a window, with a physician you don't know, if instead of that you're in a circle of people and you're telling your story, and it's not shameful to be ill. It's nothing you did wrong. It's what happens to all of us, and speaking about your condition with these people who care, it's an entirely different world. Time after time, whether it was a physician or a patient, they said, "Oh my God, what it is to be in community."

Regardless of the task at hand, it's important to reach out for support, and it's an illusion to think that we do *anything* by ourselves—or should. We are influenced by those around us, whether known to us or not, and we influence those around us, whether we know it not. I often say we have no idea, really, what effect we have on others. Something I said might have stayed with a person for years, and I won't even know it. Or a kindness someone did for me, that they brushed off and forgot about, changed my life. We are not in this life alone, not any part of it. So, offering tangible support where I can is very important to me.

It's how I am with my friends—many of whom are writers, artists, and performers. We make a point of showing up to each other's shows, fundraising events, and workshops, bringing other people with us to create a warm audience. Or, how a friend needs the support of a listening ear about a troubled relationship; or I need a family member to sit with me during a hospital stay; or a buddy to help me stay committed to my health regime, or my spiritual practice, or to get me to the gym. Find Community and offer community, especially on the sharp turns of change.

COMMUNITY IS CONTEXT

I spoke earlier about the context for change having a direct impact on the change itself. And I spoke about how groups can be a context for healing. We can look at *all* community as a context, whether it is an accidental or intentional community, a traditional gathering or a temporary one. The social agreement creates the context for how individuals behave in groups, and within a particular group. The agreement of the group, as well as its makeup and purpose, determines how well the group functions and supports its members. The type of change that can take place for an individual will be determined by the context of that community. On the other hand, a community can and does advocate for an individual, and protect them from certain types of adverse change, such as attacks from the outside, or other harmful outcomes. This is some of the protection that union, guild, or gang membership provides—we take care of our own.

Jacques Verduin is well aware of the importance of community as context in the GRIP program in San Quentin. Forming a trustworthy community of support in which the learning work could take place was key in order that the real work of transformation could take place. Jacques reports that what they needed to do first was to create a genuine place of belonging.

> **Jacques Verduin:** What we found is the context is actually more important than the content. Meaning that, for this learning community to come alive in its full potential, we had to provide, and discover, and explore a way of being together that would provide the right context for the learning process. This learning community became the tribe, and the tribe was inspired by this Navajo saying. The Navajo describe a criminal as a person who acted as if they have no relatives. That makes sense. Where's the accountability if you're not bonded in a communal structure?
>
> My God, is that ever the malady, the disease of this nation, at this time, where so many of our young people don't experience the meaning of interacting with something that gives them a place? It's not just young people, it's all of us. It's me. It's you. If we're honest enough, there's a difficulty to feeling where you do belong. We radically addressed that by creating this tribe.
>
> Every bit of it has to do with preparing ourselves, creating this context so we can do the work. The learning agreements, the pledge, there's a tribal membership form where they write the names of all the people that do time with them: their victims, their families, their communities, their kids. They're not just numbers and a last name. Because that's how you're identified in the prison, with a record that you're forever guilty for. The men stand up in these circles and learn to discover their pride. "I am so-and-so. Ethnically, here's where I come from. Geographically, here's where I come from. These are my spiritual beliefs. These are the names of my victims. These are the names of my children." That testimony, as it goes around, is so powerful. They're just stating the facts, but these facts for decades have been ignored as a part of their identity, and the tribe says, "Come in."
>
> I think it was Fritz Perls that said, "Contact is the appreciation of differences." Real contact is the appreciation of differences. We get to discover our wealth as a tribe. We've had Samoan-Irish people, we've had Belizian Rastas, you name it, and it's in that room. For once, it gets to pronounce itself to the world with some new pride. All of that goes in the tribal book, and the tribal book has its own chair. All those people are evoked to sit around us every time we meet, to encourage us, or to be a witness, or to take account of what we're doing. There's cultural

expression. We ask people to write songs, or to sing songs, or do raps, or spoken word pieces, because you can't say you're a tribe if you don't have some artistic expression of that tribe.

All of that's built under the understanding that the art of working with people is to get them ready to do the work. When they're ready, then you can actually do the work. It's very simple, but it's very potent, too.

As with all contexts, it has to be the right fit to benefit its members. It can't be too constricted or limited as to block off the possibility of emergent change. If the context of community is too tight, the movement is restricted. Like a boarding school with strict rules of admission and regulations, or an ethnic group that doesn't allow mingling with anyone outside of the group, there's no room for innovation or change. If the context of community is too loose, then the movement is dissipated, diffused and does not hold together—like a preschool with no teachers and no fences, or a town hall meeting with multiple agendas and no real leader. We need structure to hold community together, but too much impedes new possibility.

However the context of community is held, that context has to make way for the certainty of constant change. Healthy communities, whether it's a marriage, a nonprofit organization, a religious institution, a school, a club, or a committee, need to allow for the movement of change and be responsive to the change that is best for the group. Not always an easy thing to determine or to implement.

James Stark embodies the principle of Find Community as he connects individuals and groups to the community of the natural world though the Regenerative Design Institute at Commonweal in Bolinas, California, and through the education he codirects in the Ecology of Leadership program. As a visionary community organizer based in the principles of permaculture, James understands that communities are as dynamic as ecosystems, and that healthy communities need to accommodate constant change, whether they are a community of one hundred or a community of two. He speaks to the complexities of group dynamics because, as in nature, all the dynamics within the community are "dancing with change."

James Stark: A community is changing every moment. If you walk down the street this morning it's different than it was when you left it last night. Things are moving. Things are always changing. People are coming. People are leaving. People are dying. People are being born. It's an organism that's on the move.

As we begin to explore how to develop community, it's developing the capacity to be able to dance with change. The inherent part of change is there's an unknown, and that really scares us. I want my strawberry to look exactly like it did last time I ate it, right?

Sharon Weil: Right.

James Stark: I don't want it to be different. I want to lock in on this; but we can't lock in on anything, because it's impossible to lock things in. They just move. The preparation for our inner garden that we talked about before… Can we unfold each moment and each day rather than sourcing from fear that the unknown, or the mountain lion's going to eat us? Or all this stuff that fear has generated, can we move into the possibility of embracing that maybe nothing bad can happen to us? Stuff just happens, and then we deal with it. That opens up our capacity to stand in our community and realize, I may have a vision of what this could look like, but it's probably not going to end up looking like that because I take that desire, or that vision, and then another person comes into it. Already, that ecology has grown into a level of complexity, and from the perfectness of two things uniting, a third thing emerges, but it may be a surprise. It's how we dance with the change of the change.

Sharon Weil: When we're talking about communities, we're talking about anything that's more than one, so we're talking about couples as a community of two, we're talking about groups, larger groups, neighborhoods, cities… You're saying that when I have this idea, my idea is going to change as soon as I interact with someone else. I also hear you say we can replace fear with curiosity, as our base.

James Stark: Exactly. And with the complexity that a community is, it really isn't something we can figure out. There's just way too many moving parts, so it really encourages and calls us forward. We need to be operating from a different center rather than from upstairs in the attic in our head, trying to think out things. That's part of shifting from fear to shifting to loving, and gratitude, and curiosity, and building the intuition. The quiet mind and spending time with nature are essential to being a community vision holder.

I spent five years working in Asia, and one of my mentors there, in his mind, the community unfoldment looks like this: if you had an initial idea come through you, it's not your idea, but an idea that came through you. When the champagne comes and the celebration of it manifests in the community, if no one knows that idea had anything to do with you—then that is the cleanest form of doing service.

Then, the community feels that the community did it, which they did do it, but that goes counter to our culture of the lone wolf, and planting the flag, and getting benefit. A community visionary who has an idea, or is committing to community service, when they come from a place where they're not needing anything out of that, they're full and complete themselves and all they're doing is serving in a clean way, then it's irresistible and you can't become a target. As soon as the ego gets involved, then all the friction starts to happen.

Sharon Weil: There's the rub. I've spent many years in the film and television business, in many different capacities, and certainly as a writer you cannot go into a film or television production expecting that the script you wrote is what's going to end up on the screen. There are many people, in their capacities, who contribute to that vision, and if it's working well, it is a collective vision, like you said, and it's something that no one of you would have come up with on their own. In an ideal world, it ends up being better. Now, of course, you bring up the idea of ego, and if people are very invested, not just in what their vision is, but that it's their vision, it doesn't even matter what the vision is, if they're invested in *this is my opinion and the emphasis is on me*, that's when you run into trouble, right?

James Stark: From the wisdom cultures, especially Buddhism—Buddhism non-attachment—that's a big gift. That just increases your capacity a million times by not being attached and holding onto what you're feeling. The possibility that you can feel inside and hold it like a feather, rather than a clenched fist around it, opens you to go, as you said, way beyond what you could even imagine could happen. If the ecology of visionaries who come together to move something forward in their communities come from that place, it becomes unstoppable, and goes like wildfire. If six egos get in a room, you might as well go and have a coffee break!

The way in which James approaches the ecology of community has within its philosophy and practice a way to accommodate the movement of change within a group, while at the same time bringing the group together around a common mission, vision, and agreement. This accommodation of the movement of change within a group allows for the context of change to be strong, but flexible, so that individuals can remain in the evolving community, rather than have to leave in order to have their needs met.

GRASSROOTS COMMUNITIES

"Never believe that a few caring people can't change the world. For, indeed, that's all who ever have."

—Margaret Mead

For Find Community, sometimes, people gather themselves into a community or an action, sometimes the need for action gathers them. Both philanthropic advisor **Beth Rosales** and author-activist **Paul Rogat Loeb** work with gathering grassroots activism within communities, and with growing the communities themselves. Beth guides foundations and individual donors to primarily support the work within the communities impacted by social justice issues of inequality. In many cases, she also works directly with the communities themselves, helping them to raise funds and awareness for needed services and resources. Paul currently works with engaging students in the election process through the Campus Election Engagement Project, a non-partisan effort to help colleges and universities enroll millions of students to participate in elections. He has written and speaks extensively about social engagement, and tells the stories of many inspirational leaders who gathered grassroots social action on behalf of freedom, equality, environment, and the social good.

Beth Rosales defines what is meant by a grassroots community, and a grassroots community action. She describes a grassroots action in Richmond, California, that took place in response to toxic fires at the Chevron refinery in the neighborhood.

Beth Rosales: The definition of grassroots has always been that it's a group of people that are impacted by a problem or by an issue who become aware of how that issue or problem impacts their lives—how it affects their families, their children, etcetera—and then they become part of finding the solutions and implementing the strategies to fight for those solutions. So, I can give you a little example, the Chevron fire in Richmond.

Actually, there's been now three fires that have happened at the Chevron refinery. The first fire, there was not a system of phones by which people could be notified to close their doors, to not go outside. There's a fire at the refinery and those with asthma, or with babies, old people... I can't remember how many people died, but old people and young babies. So then by the second fire, you then have an organization that was organizing in Richmond so they were able to organize their people to go out, physically, because they knew where the families were living. These are primarily Black families, Cambodian, and Laotian families. The organizers knew where the families were, so they were able to send out the kids and the people and the churches. And by the third fire, there was a little system—a warning signal, a sound signal, and there was a phone system, and what they called a trusted advocates system. All of these solutions were coming from the community, and the fire department, and the city. And, so I think that when the problems are embedded in those communities that then figure out the solutions, then it works better. You have culture and language.

The first point of contact for the community is the churches, because they are such a strong influence in the Black, or Latino, or the new immigrant communities. It was the combination of the Rainbow Coalition, the churches, and a bunch of young kids that were just tempestuous organizers…and Chevron had to pay for all of that—as they should.

What I mean by "grassroots" is involving the communities that are impacted by the problems. Otherwise it doesn't work.

There is safety in numbers; there is power in numbers. We can be braver when we feel the support of others. We can be more effective when we share our vision, hopes, and the task of the work, itself. Most of the time we don't know where our actions will lead, or how we can gather others to join us in our cause.

Paul Rogat Loeb talks about the importance of taking action, not knowing where it will lead. He speaks about a piece in his anthology, *The Impossible Will Take A Little While*, that was written by psychologist and author Mary Pipher. She is the author of many books including the bestsellers, *Reviving Ophelia* and *Another Country*, but she was never an activist. Her story in the anthology was called "Reluctant Activists," and it tells about how she was compelled to action when the TransCanada Corporation came into Nebraska to buy up the land to build the Keystone XL Pipeline, proposed to run from Alberta, Canada, to the Gulf of Mexico. Mary Pipher's action gathered others in ways she never could have anticipated.

Paul Loeb: It's interesting because she's not, by nature, a political activist. She's somebody of strong ethical values, but she's not an organizer by temperament. The Keystone Pipeline—they came to Nebraska and everyone thought it was a done deal. They just lined up all the money to every single elected official in the route to potentially rent their sled porch or backyard or whatever. Not quite bribery, but basically it is. They bought up all the airtime. Everybody knows it's going to happen.

She didn't know what to do, so she does this very radical action of holding a potluck and gets three or four friends, and they have some good food and they talk. It's not like they have a magic solution, but they think maybe they can make something happen; and then they do another one. They bring in some more folks. They started reaching out in these towns and communities, and they found this guy named Randy Thompson who's just a rock-red Republican rancher, who I'm sure, looks like John Wayne. His response to TransCanada, the company pushing the Pipeline, is "I will not be bullied. This land has been in my family, and I'm not going to sell it to you folks." They make life-size cutouts of him they make him the symbol and the face of the movement, "I Will Not Be Bullied" and "I Stand with Randy."

It just starts growing and then there's a certain point… It was a Cornhusker's football game. I think it's eighty thousand people in the stadium. Of course, the TransCanada ad flashes on the jumbotron and the stadium erupts into boos. Suddenly this is not going according to plan. Because of that, our national groups get inspired; they feel like maybe they actually can stop it, and so the national environmental groups are organizing, and I think there's eleven or thirteen hundred people that are arrested at the White House, pressuring Obama. You look at all of it, and you end up with this very significant movement. We don't know the ultimate story, but so far it's delayed, I think it's four years now. That's very significant. To me, it's an example of how when you act you just don't really know where it's going to lead. [Note: President Obama rejected the permit for the Keystone XL Pipeline in November 2015.]

We align with people and form community through shared values. One important way we support individuals, organizations, and causes is through the money we give. Individual donations to nonprofit organizations are by far the larger contribution over foundation grants. Religious institutions receive a large portion of all individual charitable donations in this country. Crowdsourcing sites like Kickstarter and Indiegogo form a group of support from individuals unknown to each other, and oftentimes unknown to the person raising money for the project. The individuals become a community. Each contributes their small part, and together can raise significant amounts of money for startup companies, activist initiatives, and art projects. A friend of mine just raised close to two hundred thousand dollars for a historical documentary project about artifacts uncovered in the Warsaw Ghetto. Another friend raised money for her theatrical show about lesbian herstory.

When I interviewed **Beth Rosales**, I had wanted to speak with her because of her commitment to social change and her absolute expertise when it comes to understanding trends in progressive charitable giving. For over thirty-five years she has been helping to strengthen social justice movements through strategic funding. I was surprised when Beth told me just how much Americans donate per year, and why.

> **Beth Rosales**: Generally, people give because they've had a personal experience. For example, having a close relative or friend as a cancer survivor. They also want to make a difference, they want to do something about a problem or take a stance. People say that people are motivated by personal recognition or benefits, but that really has not been the case.
>
> Also in many cultures, there's been a tradition, as you know, of *tzedakah* for example, in the Jewish community. There have been traditions that are actually not even rated as contributions. Contributions are generally acknowledge and measured through IRS filing, and so many people do not itemize these gifts. Even those gifts, which are considered informal gifts, are not counted—but they're billions. In 2013, contributions in the US totaled $335 billion.
>
> **Sharon Weil**: $335 billion?
>
> **Beth Rosales**: Yes. And 95 percent of households give on an average of about twenty-nine hundred dollars a year, so that's very impressive. People who make less than fifty thousand dollars, generally have given up to 15 percent, but historically records show that people who make all the way up to about two hundred fifty thousand dollars stay at about 2 percent of their annual gross income. And then actually the higher the income then it starts pulling up. Records show that people who make five hundred thousand dollars a year and up, give about 4 percent of their adjusted gross income.
>
> **Sharon Weil**: Which is a large amount.
>
> **Beth Rosales**: Very, very generous Americans—average household, about twenty-nine hundred a year.

As generous as individual Americans are, it is the *totality* of their giving that makes such a large impact, reinforcing the idea that the strength is in the community and in the numbers. **Paul Rogat Loeb** speaks about how it's never just a lone individual doing the work, even when it appears to be that way. There is always a community of support in any social action, and needs to be. Paul tells the story of Rosa Parks, the brave civil rights activist who in 1955 defied the Jim Crow laws of Alabama and refused to give up her seat on the bus to a white women—which was required of her as a woman of color. Her action set off the year-long bus boycott by African Americans in Montgomery, Alabama, the first large-scale demonstration against segregation in the United States.

Paul Loeb: In both "Impossible Will Take A Little While" and "Soul Of A Citizen," I used the Rosa Parks story and the example of the myths of the lone superhero, because the image is that she comes out of nowhere. But in fact, she's part of this community with the NAACP. She's been at it for a dozen years. She's taken training sessions at this Highlander Center in Tennessee to meet with other civil rights activists. Instead of the image of the lone hero, what you see is somebody who jumps in and a very, very radical triggering action is *going to a meeting*, which any one of us could do. Or *calling people* to a meeting, or *taking notes* at a meeting…because she was the secretary at the NAACP chapter. Anybody could do it. What we have to do is to be able to jump in to those more accessible places; and we don't really know where our involvement's going to grow.

Sharon Weil: That's right. We don't know what's going to come, or who's going to join with us, or where we're going to find support.

Paul Loeb: The *who's going to join with us* is really important because if I trace Rosa Parks back, we know that her husband Raymond Parks founded the NAACP chapter in Montgomery, so he was obviously an influence on her. But what we don't know is who influenced him because people write about her and they don't write about *him*, keeping him in the shadows. *We* could be a person bringing in the next Rosa Parks.

Tracing back the history of social movements—even before the Civil Rights Movement, and in social movements since—**Beth Rosales'** view is that social change requires more than just funding; it requires bodies on the line, and coming together to sound a large and collective voice that speaks out for change in order to create movement in social structures and social values.

Beth Rosales: If you look at all of the large social movements, such as labor in the early twenties, or the suffrage movement, or the Civil Rights movement in the fifties, and the student movement, the anti-war movement against Vietnam in the sixties and seventies, and now, most recently, the whole issue of lesbians and gays being able to marry… However contemporary the social change movement is, or going back to the early nineteen hundreds, all movements required some kind of very organized community voices being heard, either by politicians or the public. As they say, social change is really a large transformation of a culture's values, and social structures, and social institutions.

I'll give you an example: the environmental movement, for the last ten years has received, I call, a whooping $50 billion worth of contributions around climate change. But, those funders and grantees were saying they were not winning. They're not winning in terms of the policy and structural changes in the country. Now, there's a recognition that a mass movement of environmental activism is important. I think you've noticed that in that last march, last September, four hundred thousand people showed up in New York.

Again that was a very concerted effort to include those communities that have been most effected by climate change. There's was a real effort to bring people from New Orleans, people from New Jersey, people from the Midwest that have been taking the brunt of floods and national disasters.

All these movements have required some kind of mass organizing and grassroots groups. Really, if you look at the history in the country, it required that level of bodies It's not enough to just fund organizations that do policy work or that do advocacy work. It's really becoming important to work with just regular ordinary people. I guess for me, that really is what social change is about. If people can be awakened, they will rise up and do something about their conditions. So, that's what I look for when I work for foundations. I've always encouraged, "let's fund the small grassroots organization, that have a base in community." As progressives, you don't always want to be speaking to the choir, and I think that's our biggest challenge is to organize our next door neighbor.

The younger donors—I call them next-gen donors—are unlike the older donors, in that they're much more vibrant, they're more engaged; they want to volunteer, they want to sit on the board, they want to share their skills, they want to share their contacts. Now, I think as grant-makers, it's not enough just to give money, but rather a social justice funder really has to be a reliable and a consistent supporter. I also want to add, actually more than just giving, and also more than the social action, is the importance of listening. If more funders listened to the nonprofits, "Why do you do what you do?" or "How do you do what you do?" I think that would be such a joy.

I formed a different type of grassroots community around the promotion of my novel *Donny and Ursula Save the World* by "seeding out the book."

Utlizing the principle for change #5 Align with Nature, we used the seeds and mushrooms element of the book to inform how we did the marketing. Inspired by the mycelium—the tiny root-like network that connects all fungi to all other plant roots beneath the ground in a system of shared bio-intelligence—I wanted to hook up my own kind of mycellial web, connecting like minds and hearts in support of the book, and its anti-GMO message.

We identified twenty-five "seeders"—influential people who had their own lists of like-minded followers. I asked them to promote the book to their list for action on the launch date of the book. In marketing terminology, I believe they call it "connecting the connectors." We called it our seeders, because they were seeding the book out into the community.

We also had another clever way of seeding out the book. Because the main character Ursula was a travel agent, and because the plot involves much global travel (no spoiler alerts here) we wanted to get the book going around the world and be able to see where it traveled. We created copies of the book to be seeder copies, meant to be passed hand-to-hand. The idea was that you read the book, put your name and location at the back, notified us through a square code at the back of the book, and passed it on to a friend, to a stranger, left it on a park bench or in one of those lovely little library kiosks that stand in public places. We then would track the book and post it on a giant map of the world on our website. It was fun. It had a purpose. It created reader involvement. It got the book into many hands, in the most unexpected locations. It created the D+U community: a grassroots effort for a grassroots type of book.

COLLABORATION

Collaboration—working together with others for mutual benefit and for the strength of numbers—is an important strategy for Find Community and is a mainstay of **John Weeks**' approach to effecting change in the health care industry. He is the former executive director of the Academic Consortium for Complementary and Alternative Health Care. ACCAHC envisions a healthcare system that is multidisciplinary and enhances competence, mutual respect, and collaboration across *all* healthcare disciplines. These include integrative disciplines of acupuncture and oriental medicine, chiropractic, naturopathic medicine, and massage. ACCAHC has made great strides through the strategic alliance of educators, policy makers, and practitioners for the "little guy" to have a larger voice and penetrate the enormous industry of mainstream public health. John speaks about making alliances and building a collaborative infrastructure as a way to increase ACCAHC's effectiveness and reach with policy makers.

John Weeks: We say that we practice collaboration *internally* in order to foster it *externally*. Instead of working from a single guild's perspective—whether that be chiropractic or acupuncture—we realized early on that there would be force in numbers. Senator Tom Harkin, who has been the strongest elected official supporting this movement, suggested twenty years ago to a group of us that if you really want to be effective in Congress, why don't you figure out what your shared issues are and come together with them? That is a principle that we followed.

So, by aggregating a set of now seventeen national organizations representing all of the councils of colleges, accrediting agencies, and certifying agencies for these organizations, we can knock on any door and not say, "Hey, we're acupuncturists, let us in." I'll introduce myself as John Weeks. "I'm an executive director of the Academic Consortium for Complementary and Alternative Health Care and we are from five Department of Education–recognized disciplines, and together we are connected to three hundred seventy-five thousand licensed practitioners in the country, and we know that you're thinking about setting up a committee to basically set the direction for pain care research and education in the US and we think we should be at that table." An honest broker will listen to that and say, "You're right." At the Institute of Medicine of the National Academies, we have found truly honest brokers, really fine public servants who will listen openly and honestly, and invite us in. That's been a key way we've been able to impact, by first building our own house internally. We kind of surprise them with who we are when we knock on the door.

I've always realized that in writing about a subject where people are trying to create change, they're working hard at it. So I would interview somebody, but if I knew somebody else was working on the same problem, I'd finish the interview or interrupt the interview and say, "Hey, you really ought to be in touch with so-and-so," and help connect them.

Artists form interesting collaborations amongst themselves. Music, dance, film, television, and theatrical productions are collaborative mediums; more than one creative spirit is needed in order to fulfill the artist expression. Even solo artists—painters, sculptors, writers, standup comedians—create collaborations with their readers, viewers, and audience when their visions and communications impact those on the receiving end. Sports teams are dependent upon their fans for their rankings, ratings, and their big salaries, and fans form impassioned community in stadiums and sports bars.

Deena Metzger speaks to the collaboration between the writer and the reader.

Sharon Weil: I think we forget, especially when we're nervous, to put something forward, that there's always community around us, whatever our ideas.

Deena Metzger: A writer is in conversation with a reader, always. If I'm reading a book that really deeply moves me, that means the writer has spoken words right into my heart and I'm being changed, and fulfilled, and enlightened through those words—so that's a very profound, intimate relationship.

This, then, extends into the spoken or unspoken ways in which a group of writers can support and affect each other in community, even when they are not directly collaborating on a common work. By listening, giving feedback, and responding to shared written work, and by remembering and referring back to each others stories, holding them tenderly until they fully emerge as formed, a community of writers provides a context of support. Deena talks about the writing circles she has been leading for over thirty years.

Deena Metzger: That's what always mattered to me teaching these classes where we'd come together as a real community and after a while—and sometimes not such a long while—we really love each other, and we care about each other, and we're thrilled by each other's gifts and beauty.

In the Words and Waves workshops, **Rebecca Mark** encourages each of the writer's work to be influenced by one another's themes and images, as a way for the shared experience to make way for even more unexpected material to reveal itself.

Rebecca Mark: That, I think, is what you're documenting in your book. You're documenting what happens when the neural transmitters actually allow for a multiplicity of imaginative connections, and that's where the communal is so powerful—because I don't have to think up everything. Erla brought up something, Emma's brought up something, Sharon, Linda…and I've got twenty-five things to work with.

It's potentially very subversive, and very radical, because it takes away the notion of the individual artist working alone in their turret and producing something.

Somebody's aunt who died, I remember once, oh my God. That aunt had a very interesting name. The name of that aunt became part of everyone's writing. Well, that does something that we don't even know yet what it does. It takes the charge off of individual trauma, for one. If you've gone through a terrible thing, but everyone in the room is holding it, and writing it, and weaving it into drawings and creative expression and imagination… Here's another fire, and here's another wave. Here's another excitement around that. You are not carrying that story in a way that is either painful or somehow paralyzing your tissue, or doing something to your psyche that's not allowing you to speak. You are suddenly being held, and you're free to speak. You can speak as a poet. You can speak in one hundred different ways—even silent people. I've seen one person who all they did was draw grass for a day. Grass. Just grass. Just drawing this grass. Underneath the grass heap, these words started to emerge. I mean, it was just phenomenal. She was silent. She barely spoke, but the words would emerge with a full story of a sexual abuse incident that she had had as a child, which she had no idea about. She never knew it had happened. The story was told just like you were reading it on the newspaper. It was so clear.

CONFLICT

Ah yes, conflict. As soon as we separate and split away from wholeness, we have duality and the opportunity for conflict: differing opinions, differing needs, differing experiences, differing sense of timing. Difference does not necessarily put us into conflict, but if differing parties feel they must occupy the same time and space—and one must win out over the other—then conflict will arise. The potential for conflict, or the surety of it, can steer people away from choosing to seek community, or from working within a context of community in order to bring about change. "I'll just do it myself" seems to be the exasperated response that comes from the discomfort of engaging with conflict. The inability to adequately address conflict within personal relationships is at the heart of the high divorce rate, and makes people gun-shy to enter into new relationships. Very few people like conflict and even fewer are skilled in navigating through conflict to come to mutually satisfying resolution.

Adam Wolpert is incredibly skilled at navigating conflict and bringing groups of people to new understandings and new structures of operating and cooperating with each other. As a group facilitator, Adam brilliantly uses a consensus style decision-making process where groups seek full agreement by cycling through the articulation of the needs of the entire group on behalf of their agreed upon vision, rather than majority vote where surely some will win and some will lose. In our interview, he spoke about the work of Sam Kaner and his book, *Facilitator's Guide to Participatory Decision-Making*. According to Adam, divergent thinking, or conflict, is a natural part of group decision-making.

Adam Wolpert: Sam Kaner has a wonderful book about participatory decision-making. He has this diagram that he drew, which on the left side has something called a Point of Initiation. Then on the right side is a Point of Closure. When a group sets out on a journey to change something, it might be in the form of a proposal. The group first goes into this realm of divergent thinking, which is at first very exciting, but then quickly becomes very unnerving and anxiety producing. Everybody's moving away from each other in their thinking.

Then at a certain point, the anxiety that's produced by all this divergent thinking begins a dynamic of convergence. Then, people start thinking convergently and build on each other's ideas. It's almost like if you imagine on a molecular level, a bunch of big molecules getting pulled apart, and all these little particles are floating around, and then start to come together and form new molecules.

When you move into this convergent zone, you move toward resolving your situation in a positive way. In between divergent and convergent thinking, is this thing that he calls the Groan Zone—which is very much like the storming period in group evolution. A bunch of people together suddenly have this panic, this sense of "Oh no, it's all wrong. We're doing the wrong thing, we're with the wrong people, this is taking too long."

If you can, at that moment of panic, show everyone from a higher altitude, where they are in a bigger process, there can be this extraordinary, not only relief, but refreshment and empowerment that comes into the group. People say, "Oh okay, there is a light at the end of the tunnel and there is something right about this very difficult part of the journey."

Conflict, when escalated and unresolved can become violent, whether that's between individuals, communities, or nations. **Amanda Foulger** has great concern for the levels of violence we express in our world. In our conversation, Amanda refers to Council process based on *The Way of Council* written by Jack Zimmerman and Virginia Coyle. Council process is a communication practice of open, heartfelt expression and attentive, empathic listening for conflict resolution and visioning. It moves participants away from a hierarchical structure of decision making to a partnership model, through deep trust and community building.

Amanda Foulger: What I think is very disturbing in our world is the resort to violence on a human level to solve these issues of differences and different views, different ideas, all these different kinds of things. This is the part where human beings are destroying themselves. It's an illness, this lack of respect for and consideration that each life is precious, that each life is important. How can you live a life that is in unity and harmony, and how do you deal with conflict?

Think about the Palestinian-Israeli conflict, which has been going on for God knows how long. There are these outbursts of terrible violence, and then times when things kind of go along peaceably for a while. Now, the kind of terrorist action that's going on in our world, it's very challenging to us. I don't know that I have big answers at all but this principle of unity and harmony in our shamanic work, that's one of the most important keys. Every day you have a choice about being in unity and harmony or not. Yup, we have disagreements. Yup, we have problems and we have issues that arise for us, but how can we deal with them?

Sharon Weil: You were saying that change is our nature, and that change is the nature of the middle world; it's the nature of our reality. Yet, why do so many people have such difficulty with change, and why does it lead to conflict?

Amanda Foulger: It is in thinking about one's life as *separate*. We are individuals, of course, but again, we have these principles of unity and harmony. Now you think about the people who are involved in Council process, for example, which was certainly derived from indigenous practices. There's now a whole modern iteration of Council process. It is about getting a group of people together and speaking and listening to one another, so that you don't just yell at each other.

You talk through the issues. You talk through the problems. You talk through whatever it is, so that each person has their own way of arriving at a solution.

The Council process recognizes that everybody needs to be heard and that there is a point where you have to give it up. You might come to where, "Yup, this is what I always wanted and I always thought it was right, but you know what, not everybody else is on that page, so I can offer my thoughts and maybe we can find some way to arrive at a solution that is more inclusive." That's the challenge of everyday life.

In February of this year, **Jacques Verduin** was invited to a conference in Jordan. Two hours after the conference ended, images appeared on television of a captured Jordanian pilot burning in a cage, set on fire by ISIS. As Jacques describes, "People literally were running out of their houses screaming for revenge. In no time, there were 40,000 people out. The embassy called, 'Out of here, out of here.' There were jets flying over and bombing sections; prisoners were being executed. It was like, 'Holy shit.' I'm looking upwards and going, 'Why am I here?'"

Jacques Verduin: Every conflict has a history. That's a characteristic of conflict. It's not always respected for the power that it has. It fuels the conflict, if you don't address it and heal it. There's so much history on the conflict in that region. It's a steep task, because there's so much identity, and it begins to form around being victimized by the conflict. Jordan is interesting. Jordan has taken in millions of refugees, from Iraq, from Syria, from all these places where the Arab Spring exploded.

On another trip last year, Jacques traveled to Bosnia to train professionals about his transformational GRIP program.

Jacques Verduin: There was a flood when I went to Bosnia in May last year, and as it goes with disasters, people were helping each other out, people that were really at odds with each other. I was very hopeful.

Once, the flood was so bad that it wasn't clear that the training was going to happen, but since it was in Sarajevo, which is a little higher, they decided it should happen, so I went over there. A couple of days in, the water unearthed one of these mass graves, and all of these bodies started floating on up, so boom, that whole thing's back again, right?

The longer you stayed, the more everybody had a war story, and everybody on the team were all professionals: sociologists, psychologists, criminologists. The woman organizing it actually had a father tortured in one of the prisons we visited that became sort of a camp during the war. Badly tortured. The Muslims and the Christians for centuries lived next to each other. You had churches and temples right there, right? Until that whole Serbian fascism came in.

I saw a lot of mass graves and a lot of memorials, and I had the same thing, like, "Why is this happening?" I don't think I'm a fiend for this. I hope not. But there's something about encountering people's despair when the light is right next to it. Just that ability to show up when there's intense suffering and bear witness to it, just that. No qualifications, no taking positions, just bearing witness to it and letting it work you, and meeting incredible people that somehow, for some reason, are called to show up. To be part of that is pretty humbling.

It's like this, too: Desmond Tutu, who was part of the truth and reconciliation process, talks about an old Swahili word called Ubuntu. Ubuntu, he says, is how we're inextricably connected: our mutuality. A person with Ubuntu knows that, and carries the joy and the wisdom of that.

Something bigger happens than the crime or the mass slaughter of people itself; you lose something as a society. Not just as an ethnicity or a group or an individual, but as a society. Like all this stuff with ISIS. Now, there's possibility you've sort of given up on humans, right? This process of bearing witness to it, and going in to hear people speak their bitterness and their suffering heals that greater piece, where there's a way back to being human again.

I think, in the absence of that, a lot of us just turn it off. It's like, "I don't want to hear about this shit. Put these prisoners behind walls. Flip the channel." Or just denounce people and be done with it that way, right? To witness it without judgment is powerful. And for someone to actually be heard, to feel that their story is heard, is also very powerful.

All three of these guests who speak about conflict, Adam, Amanda, and Jacques, talk of the need to Listen Deeply, and bear witness to one another in order to resolve any sort of conflict. The history of any conflict needs to be recognized and helped to heal before new visions can come forward and be implemented. This type of healing must be done in community, and *within* the community where the conflict has occurred.

SUMMARY

To summarize the principle for change #3 Find Community, this simple motto suffices: get help for everything you do! Find support and companionship in all areas of your life. If you are struggling with change, chances are you are not finding enough community. Or if the struggle is within the community, find additional supports to resolve conflict so that every member of the community can benefit from the support from others. ChangeAbility increases when the work of change, or the response to change can be carried by more than one person.

◊ **Find support and companionship.**

◊ **In ChangeAbility, all our navigations move with greater ease when we have support. They are also more pleasant, and more fun.**

◊ **Socially, we are pack or herd animals with an innate need for belonging.**

◊ **Community is a context, and can either facilitate or inhibit the movement of change for the individual.**

◊ **Separation from the community creates isolation. Isolation is the source of most physical, emotional, and spiritual disease.**

◊ **There are many ways to gather and form community.**

◊ **Grassroots change, change that comes from within a particular community to serve its own needs, is a most effective strategy for change.**

◊ **Collaboration—working together for mutual benefit—is a helpful use of community.**

◊ **Celebrate differences. Look for creative ways to resolve conflict. The best methods involve inquiry and listening, rather than operating from assumptions.**

ALIGN WITH NATURE

HAVE HOPE

SPARK FIRE

PROCEED INCREMENTALLY

BRING

LISTEN DEEPLY

FIND COMMUNITY

PROCEED INCREMENTALLY

Incremental: gradual, step-by-step, a minute increase in quantity, regular consecutive additions, phased

"Give me a couple of years, and I'll make that actress an overnight sensation."

—Samuel Goldwyn

HOW DOES THE SAYING GO? "AN overnight success is fifteen years in the making"? What appears to be an instant flash of success usually isn't. We simply see the end result without the backstory to explain how that all happened. Results are what happen in the wake of a process, and that process always takes its own time. The results come from incremental step-by-step progress or principle for change #4 Proceed Incrementally.

Most Hollywood stars' careers have begun with obscure B movies and TV bit parts. They can go through long periods of unemployment, or be continually employed but basically unrecognized, until one day it seems like they are in every film you see (they've had a lot of #3 Find Community helping them get there, by the way). Or like at my bank, employees enter as a teller, then become a supervisor, then a bank officer, then the branch manager, then on to regional manager, then out of my sight; but I imagine they could become the president of the bank! That's more or less a straight line, though each position would be considered an incremental step and its own result. They are smaller steps on the longer ladder of life.

Most of the time the process of change is not direct. If I look back on my own life, it's only in hindsight that I can see the story of where I've come from to arrive at where I am now. I can't see the whole story when I am standing in the middle of Act Two. And, of course, as my story moves forward, I have more that I can see behind me. My current story is the culmination of all the jobs, experiences, activities, and people's influence that have built upon one another to bring me to what I am doing today—writing this book. All my film jobs, writing jobs, work with nonprofit organizations, study of movement, good work habits, bad work habits, friendships, marriages, and my endless curiosity have incrementally brought me to share these pages with you. I feel that the way each of the podcast guests have lived their lives to create the successful bodies of work that they have are fascinating roads of process, and they recognize them as such. Each twist and turn brought unexpected, sometimes undesirable results, but they learned to make course corrections, through #2 Listen Deeply, and to keep moving on—not always forward, sometimes to the side, or even a few steps back.

Perhaps it's because I was born under the astrological sign of Taurus that I know how to put one foot in front of the other and value that kind of steady progress. I understand how valuable it is that a process not only be incremental, but be consistent and committed, for the best lasting results. The word incremental implies units or segments, breaking up the larger whole into smaller pieces. My life is not only measured incrementally, I experience it that way. I go from breath to breath and from moment to moment. The yardstick is marked in inches, the long road trip is marked city by city, the year until Christmas is counted down in days. Given that anything can happen at any time, and that change can happen quickly as well as it can take forever, an incremental approach is the most comfortable and accessible way to view the larger movement of change. It's also the most manageable way to employ ChangeAbility, finding ways to refresh Have Hope and Spark Fire along the way.

On a personal level, whether I am trying to lose weight, run a marathon, or save up for a new car, change is achievable in small steps toward larger outcomes. The same is true for social change. For so long it seemed that the equal right to marriage would never come. The state-by-state battles for same-sex marriage rocked back and forth between passed legislation and court appeals. And then one day, the Supreme Court decided in favor of Marriage Equality for the entire nation. But it did not happen overnight; there have been years of incremental steps, setbacks and course corrections. There are still county clerks who are defying the law by refusing to issue marriage licenses, signifying that there are more incremental steps to come before the ruling has full acceptance.

> "Sometimes there are days like this, when that slow, steady effort is rewarded with justice that arrives like a thunderbolt."
> —**President Obama**, in regards to the Supreme Court ruling on the Marriage Equality act

The final decision to end Apartheid in South Africa was preceded by decades of struggle and failed attempts to abolish the heinous laws. Today, the discrimination against African American citizens in our country is still being played out in police violence and shootings of young men and women, and in the killing of nine people in the historic Emanuel African Methodist Episcopal Church in South Carolina by a declared white supremacist. The incremental victories leading up to the Civil Rights Act in the 1960s have necessitated continual incremental actions for civil rights, still. The American folk song popular during the Civil Rights Movement tells us to "keep your eyes on the prize." Little by little and step by step, the goal is set in front of me, but the path is made of many incremental steps, circuitous as they may be.

If I am moving from moment to moment and breath to breath, then the spaces *in between* the moments and the breaths are the intervals in the movement of change, just like the intervals between musical notes in the movement of music. (Sometimes it feels not so much like I am moving from moment to moment, but that I'm moving from resistance to resistance, and the intervals are just the rests in between.) It is in the intervals, or the quiet space between actions, that I can receive feedback through listening deeply, making small course corrections, or huge course corrections, and proceeding.

In addition to being a breath and movement educator, **Robert Litman**, is a master-level swimmer. He explores change principles within his own movement as he attentively glides through the water. Robert explains how he experiences this process of Proceed Incrementally: gathering feedback from his sensations and from the water itself, making adjustments, and continuing on as he tries to improve his swimming performance.

Robert Litman: The definition of the word incremental: it's an adjective. It means adding on, especially in a regular series. If you went to system theory, the organism is learning incrementally. It tries something, it learns and feels into it. It uses it. Everything gets in relationship to it. It adds on and moves into the next stage. It's a cocreation with whatever intelligences are working to create movement.

Sharon Weil: We talk about in movement if you're moving too quickly, or you're moving too suddenly, then the system goes, "Ah, too much!"

Robert Litman: I do this in the pool sometimes. I can feel the detail here. I'm going to see how fast I can go with this kind of gross knowledge of where I'm headed. I increase the speed, and I get to a point and think, "Okay I can't go any further. This is my edge now. I see where my edge is." I go back into my perception and I start working the details. Let's connect this to this. Let's feel this whole thing incrementally building into some form of grace and movement in the water.

I get to a point where I'm feeling like I'm really connected. Moving through the water, I feel graceful. Less effort. Breathing is easy. "Let's go up to that edge and see where it is now." I push out into the speeding. Okay, I'm beyond that edge now. I'm out here much further, and my ability to get out further faster, more graceful, more coordinated is much larger.

We play back and forth between our edges and the detail in between, so we can gather incremental strength to move beyond our edges.

I like what Robert says about a play back and forth between our edges and the detail in between. The detail is where I receive the feedback and make the adjustments; the edge is what I come up against when I try it out. *Has it moved? Has it changed? Can I swim faster now having adjusted my stroke and my breath? Has the edge of the law in our country moved enough to allow marriage equality?* That edge has moved, yes. Do all people in this country embrace this decision? That edge has not completely moved, so more adjustment in the detail, and incremental movement will be needed.

In fitness, the way to build reliable strength and stamina is through gradual increase in weight, repetition, and effort. When you exceed your own strength, go too quickly, or push too hard, this is when you get injured or your muscles literally recoil from being overstretched, and then you not only end up with a torn hamstring muscle, you also become disappointed and discouraged. In approaching any task where you are building something new, it helps to find the rhythm of change.

RHYTHM AND PACE

> "It doesn't matter how slowly you go, as long as you don't stop."
> —**Confucius**

I have come to understand that the movement of change has many rhythms, and those rhythms drive how we receive and work with change. When Proceeding Incrementally, the pace of those incremental steps could be rapid and syncopated, as well as slow and predictable; whatever its speed and duration, it's by utilizing and adjusting to the rhythm of change that we can manage best. When I can find the beat, or get in the *groove* of the movement of change, the rhythm itself can carry me through the navigations. Once I find the rhythm of this change I can keep it going if it's facilitating ChangeAbility; if it's not, then I can slow the rhythm down, or speed it up, depending upon what is needed.

As always, I begin with #1 *Bring Awareness.* I ask, *What is the rhythm of the change I am in? Is this like a Viennese waltz or a free-form jazz improvisation? Can I identify not just the speed and pace of the change, but is the change smooth and regular or syncopated and erratic? Does it form a pattern like the daily change from day to night, or is it completely unpredictable, like a sudden earthquake or an accidental death? Is there anything about understanding its rhythm that can help me anticipate the pattern and plan my next moves?* Adam Wolpert spoke about looking for patterns in change in the chapter on Listen Deeply, and I will be discussing more about nature's patterns and rhythms in the following chapter on Align with Nature.

Either as a strategy for initiating new change or for adapting to existing change, finding the rhythm of change and staying on the rhythm carries me through the times when I am not "feeling the love" quite so strong. Like with exercise: if my rhythm is to go to the gym at 7:00 p.m. Monday, Wednesday, and Friday, then that rhythm and regularity can get me there and keep me there even when I don't feel like going. This is certainly true for writing and is why most professional writers have a writing rhythm that includes writing every day. I like to call it a "rhythm" rather than a "schedule" because it implies I *want to* rather than *have to*, and it turns my regularity into music and dance, rather than a clock.

A rhythm becomes a habit when we can no longer hear the music.

At times, I can choose the rhythm I want. Musically the rhythm can be 3/4 time, 4/4 time, or something syncopated. It is harder to keep momentum going with stop-start, stop-start. I know this for a fact, because when I was younger, I used to dig my heels in when change started moving too quickly. I couldn't tolerate the speed. Then, once I had time to adjust and calm my reaction to too much movement, I'd have to restart the momentum all over again from the stopped position—and that required a lot of effort. It's the difference between pedaling a bicycle uphill from a full stop, versus coming up to the hill with speed and momentum.

At times I can choose the rhythm of change, but more often, the rhythm of change chooses me. It is dictated by something or someone outside myself, like when the harvest comes early, when my infant needs to sleep, or when my boss announces I've been promoted, transferred, and have to show up for work in a new city next week. The fast pace of rapid change can create a momentum that carries me, and I'll have to make quick decisions. Chances are, if I Listen Deeply and trust, those decisions will be clear and sure. A slower, more gradual pace of change can give me more time to weigh my choices, or simply more time to wallow in indecision.

Amber Gray said earlier that events that happen "too much, too fast" can cause trauma, or certainly overwhelm. Overwhelm also applies to tasks or events that appear too large. Emilie Conrad often spoke about the need to slow down in order to feel the nuanced details of our experiences so to not have them whizz by our awareness. Our awareness needs time to reorient and readjust after any change. Our system has to settle and find safety and balance once again. The way in which we integrate change is essential to our ability to cope with more. When we have high hopes, huge ambition, or necessarily large goals, how can we really manage and integrate the change?

BREAKING IT DOWN

It is very helpful to break larger tasks into smaller, incremental parts. These parts can have an order to them, step by step, but you cannot skip steps—no matter how much you think you can. It never works; you'll have to make up for it in the end.

As a screenwriter I have learned that a script gets written draft by draft. Even if I can feel how the entire story is supposed to go—even if I can visualize the whole thing, and know how it ends—I still have to get there draft by draft. Each draft serves a different purpose. The first one is for simply generating all I know about the story, just getting the first draft out of me. Then there's another draft to perfect the plot, another to deepen the characters, and then one to polish, tighten, and do the final edit. Eventually, it all comes together with the intricate weave that is necessary for integrating all the elements of story and the layering of thought and action. Many young writers try to rush to a finished product—perfecting scenes and dialogue before the entire story has even had a chance to appear. Writing is rewriting. And though rewriting can be a pain in the butt, the script becomes polished through incremental steps. If I know this and plan for this, my navigation can be more pleasant, with less resistance.

As for the story itself, it is most compelling when it is filled with incremental and unexpected twists and turns—just like life. The great screenwriting teacher, Robert McKee, who has schooled practically every working screenwriter in America at one time or another, has a very insightful thing to say about storytelling that I will attempt to paraphrase. He said that we are told that each scene *progresses* the story: I go outside, I get in my car, I drive to my job. But he says that what makes for compelling drama is that every scene *turns* the story: I go outside, I get in my car, my car won't start, I take the bus to my job, I get fired, not for being late but for something that happened three months ago. Every turn is a change: I am thwarted but I triumph, or I fail and don't know what to do next. How the character navigates these incremental changes is what draws us in to his or her story. Just like what keeps me interested in the incremental movement of my life. I don't expect it to be easy, but do expect it to be full of change.

Keep it simple. One day at a time. You can't skip steps.

"Keep it simple" is not a motto that I personally know how to live by, but I do have great respect for its value. Simplifying, downsizing, purging, and spring cleaning are incremental ways of reducing to a more fundamental state. The change is going from more to less, and from excess to essence. The process of simplifying cannot be complicated (as it would be in my hands) or it misses the point entirely. Breaking a large overwhelming task into smaller ones seems the best approach to arrive at simplicity.

When it comes to the daunting activity of moving the contents of an entire house, **Amy McEachern** gets clients sorting, clearing, cleaning, and moving—one box at a time. Her system of sorting makes the decisions easier because there's already a place for each item in question to go.

> **Amy McEachern**: When I help people organize, I set up a bunch of boxes and I call them "Dump," "Donate," "Send to Aunt Margaret in New York," "Move to the New House," "Trash." When people touch things it becomes a multiple choice question. Which box does this go to? *Boom, boom, boom, boom, boom.* It's easy; it's less thinking. I try to do the same with my own moving forward. How do I make this less scary? I can say, "I'm going to do A, B, C, D, or E."

YOU DON'T HAVE TO START BIG

I don't have to start big when making a change. And I don't have to know what I'm doing in order to get started. Phew. That's a relief, right? If I wait to initiate an action until I know exactly how things were going to turn out, I might never get started at all. So, start anywhere, start small. We don't know where our actions will lead, so just begin—and begin with something that is doable and manageable. This applies to personal moves for change, as well as the ones that take me into public spheres of participation. **Paul Rogat Loeb** names the rationale we tell ourselves for not getting involved in political action until we are sure that we have it all together, are an expert, or at least will not embarrass ourselves. Paul's remedy is to start small. Even some of our greatest heroes had small beginnings.

Paul Loeb: In "Soul Of A Citizen," I talk about taking things step by step—that suddenly you don't jump in and have to become a super activist all at once. One of the notions that challenges us is this notion called "the perfect standard," which is the idea that you have to be this absolutely impossibly eloquent, confident, knowledgeable person—who nobody ever could be. I used the story of Gandhi. Gandhi's family basically mortgaged everything they had to send him to law school to land the jury, whole hopes riding on him. He graduates. When he gets up in the court, he was so intimidated, he's literally tongue-tied, can't get a sentence out. Loses his case. This happens again, and again, and again and they don't know what to do. Finally, there's somebody that had always got a case in South Africa and they sent him off there, and hopefully that will change things. He literally and metaphorically regained his voice in the struggle against what became called Apartheid. It's not to say that he had permanent laryngitis or something like that. He could talk, but suddenly in that public moment, he froze.

I love that story because it says that even Gandhi, when he started, was completely intimidated, and shy, and tongue-tied. He changes, and this is where he ends up. You've got to be able to jump in and not feel like you need to know everything, and you need to be perfect, and all the rest of that because this is just never going to happen.

Everybody, all the giants of history, they also started in a relatively modest steps and then something leaps.

I like the term "bite-size action." Like bite-size candy bars, and the new trend in bite-size appetizers, a bite-size action is just enough. One full bite, and that's all. Bite-size actions are simple one-offs, like the annual beach cleanup with Heal the Bay in Santa Monica, or taking part in a political rally that wants to demonstrate numbers for the cause, taking just one step toward your personal health—like not eating the bite-size candy bar!

Main Street Moms Organize or Bust developed bite-size actions to increase voter turnout, starting in 2004. Women gathered in one and others' homes and wrote over 500,000 peer-to-peer letters to unregistered women voters in key states across the nation. In Northern California, MMOB holds Soups and Solutions to engage local community in civic action. Bring a bowl, share some soup, and become informed about climate issues such as fracking and the Keystone XL Pipeline—and then take one action.

Amanda Foulger works with the largest sense of connection and belonging to the natural and spiritual world, yet she encourages us toward bite-size action on personal commitment. She asks us to find what it is we can each do on behalf of our values and on behalf of the changes in the world we want to see. When Amanda and I spoke, she talked about the inspiration she has found in the twentieth-century futurist inventor and designer, Buckminster Fuller. A true visionary, Fuller was an expansive "comprehensive anticipatory design scientist" working to solve global problems surrounding housing, shelter, transportation, education, energy, ecological destruction, and poverty. Fuller held twenty-eight patents, authored twenty-eight books, and received forty-seven honorary degrees.

> **Amanda Foulger**: He was amazing. He put his mind to it and figured out all these different ways—like solar energy, building the geodesic domes, building cars and houses that were energy efficient, and the World Game—which were a way for people to recognize all the resources that we have on the planet and that if we work together, we can make them all work. He was a great teacher because he really saw it so clearly at a very critical time. I know he tried to reach as many people as he could possibly in his lifetime.

> **Sharon Weil**: He was an incredible visionary. He began a certain level of thinking that carried on through many others after him.

> **Amanda Foulger**: Exactly. I think all the stuff about climate change…he was a real early player in recognizing what the issues were. He knew he couldn't do everything, but he knew that it came down to each individual person being in integrity with themselves. If I'm going to use a car, if I'm going to buy these products, if I'm going to use water this way—I have to have integrity with it.
> The problem is, of course, you can feel totally overwhelmed by the immensity of what it is, so you have to figure out something that you can do on a personal level that is meaningful. What is that going to be and how are you going to do that? The guy who did the work with zero trash and wrote his book about it, he just said, "Okay, if I'm going to have integrity, this is what I have to do, I have to be responsible for every piece of trash that I collect at my house and I have to put it some place where it's not going to be harmful." That's where he took it. I think each of us has to find what is that arena where you really feel you can be effective and do something meaningful for yourself and hopefully for the generations to come.

Sharon Weil: And it doesn't have to be an enormous act either. This is one of the points that I'm trying to make in the book. It can be small and simple. It can be bite-size.

Amanda Foulger: I quite agree. I think if it can come down to something pretty simple that you can agree to do, rather than feeling like you have to be another Buckminster Fuller—because we're never going to be another Buckminster Fuller. But at least take inspiration and say, "There is something that I can commit to in my life that I'm willing and able to do," and do it so that there's some sense of connection from a very personal level to what's going on the planet.

Amanda suggests that we find one personal thing we can commit to in order to improve the state of the world. Social change film producer and marketing director, **Corinne Bourdeau** has a simple approach for that. She talks about working on what you are passionate about for a short time every day. Just start with a small amount of time each day and let it grow from there. Gradually increase the time you devote to your passion, and you will find that more of your day is filled with what you want to be doing.

Corinne Bourdeau: One of the trite phrases we always hear is "Follow your bliss, and the money will follow"—well, yes and no. I have a little bit of a twist on that: spend part of every day, no matter what, doing something that you're really, really passionate about.

I left a high-paying, comfortable job and jumped in…but maybe another way to go about it is if you have a job, or you're doing something that you're not crazy about, find out what it is that you do love. Anything—whether it's food, or saving the environment, or painting, whatever it is…making quilts, it doesn't matter. Start spending a small time of every day doing it. Then, increase that every day.

When I started doing things that I really loved, just a little bit each day, at some point enough gates opened that I could switch over to doing it all the time. It might not happen overnight.

Sharon Weil: It's fabulous! Because we always have ten minutes somewhere, right? That's a start…ten minutes.

Corinne Bourdeau: I'll give a great example: I have a friend who loves the food industry. Her whole life is food, good food, planting gardens. I finally said, "Susan, just every day, start doing something in the food industry. Go to a conference, plant a garden, visit the farmers' market, do some volunteer work." Well, she now runs a PR firm, and her clients are all foodies. It happened over three years, but eventually she went from, "Oh, I took on a volunteer project at the Farmers' Market" to "Great! Now let's have somebody turn into a client!" It doesn't always have to be this leaving day jobs wondering if you're going to pay the mortgage. I think it can be a softer change, and eventually you'll get to the point where you are following your bliss and the money did follow.

HOW SMALL GROWS TO LARGE

> "If every American adult who drinks coffee gave up a morning coffee, we'd have two hundred twenty million dollars we could give to charity. Amazing, from giving up a five dollar Starbucks."
>
> —Beth Rosales

Starting small or simple doesn't mean staying small and simple. That's just the place to begin. So in Proceed Incrementally, what are some of the strategies for growing change, growing support, and growing funds? Find Community is an important strategy for incrementally growing change, person by person, as I have mentioned with the example of Main Street Moms Organize or Bust. Another strategy within community is the raising of money in small increments that add up. I mentioned crowdsourcing in the previous chapter as a great way to be a small donor and have your dollar pooled with others to make a much larger impact than you could on your own. Just so you understand, individual, small donations are the majority of charitable giving in this country. Surprisingly, it's not large foundation grants that provide the main support for nonprofit organizations, it's small, individual donors. In fact, according to philanthropic advisor **Beth Rosales**, many donors giving small amounts together can be more effective and more helpful than single large donors. Just as each vote matters, each dollar matters.

Beth Rosales: A small donation of fifty dollars is just as great as a $20,000 gift. If you're in a nonprofit for example, you want to bundle smaller gifts in; you actually want to have a larger base of support, rather than one person who stays with you for a year or two and then walks away—and there goes your $20,000 gift. If you had fifty or one hundred people giving a hundred dollars each, not all of them are going to go away at a certain time. There is strength, actually, in small gifts. I think generally if one is giving what is meaningful for them, that really conveys that level of support.

For example during the Civil Rights Movement—you remember the freedom summer—probably, those were supported by individual gifts between fifty dollars or a hundred dollars. The buses, housing the young students who went down South to help register people… Small gifts do make a difference. Obviously foundations that give twenty thousand dollars and up are very, very helpful, especially to grassroots organizations, but still…

Beth tells us how we can make incremental progress for the issues we value through the nonprofit organizations we support. She gives us strategies for charitable giving that help sustain the organizations over a longer period of time—which is essential for their planning and sustained efforts on behalf of their causes.

Beth Rosales: There's 1.5 million nonprofits in the United States. In California alone we have about 127,000 groups that are registered with the IRS and with the Secretary of State. I think in terms of being strategic, it really depends on the individual, though I think there are some similar practices that we can all employ. One, is to give general support: meaning as a donor, you don't dictate what the amount should be spent toward. And as an individual, I would say, it really helps strategically when you stay with that organization over time. You don't just throw fifty dollars here, fifty dollars there. Let's say, especially during the holiday giving, you have a list, and hopefully one would stay a good ten years in supporting whatever cause, especially your scrappy grassroots organizations that really struggle because they don't have the budget to have a development person, to have those fancy brochures that reach us by mail or online. Strategically, I say, work into your values and what causes you to really want to support them. In many ways your giving really promotes the position that you hold about a cause.

Let me just give you an example: Planned Parenthood. As you know Planned Parenthood has been around for quite some time now but they're up and down, up and down, depending on the political environment. Planned Parenthood has been able to keep their funding even though federal grants have been removed from them by the current Congress—and it's been through individuals. I don't want to run all kinds of statistics for you but within that $335 billion that's given every year in the country, 70 percent is given by individuals.

I know that there are foundations, and that's the field that I'm in, and we get a lot of credit for charitable giving, but only 15 percent of money given is given by foundations.

Sharon Weil: Wow. So, really individuals do make a difference.

Beth Rosales: A big difference. So I think whether you give $50 or $50,000 it really, really does make a difference.

RIPPLE OUT

Start with the circle of who you know, then ripple out.

Another highly effective strategy for growing from small and simple to something larger and more complex is the idea of rippling out. Just as a pebble thrown in a lake will cause ripples in the water—pushing out circles of current that reach father and farther out from where the pebble landed—a single well-placed action can have the same effect. It's a very efficient, exponential strategy for growth. Depending upon the rhythm and pace of the change, it can also be a very rapid strategy for growth. Teachers are a beautiful example of ripple out, because the messages they teach are carried out through all their students. When you teach the teachers, then you are multiplying the reach. Pyramid marketing strategies are based on this idea of expanding territory and reach through selling franchises to others. And the type of social action described in the story about Mary Pipher's reluctant activism, utilized ripple out as her strategy for bringing out the message to stop the Keystone XL Pipeline in Nebraska.

Michael Lerner, the president and cofounder of Commonweal, first introduced me to this idea as a way to effectively grow an organization and let it thrive, a model which I now thoroughly embrace. He has grown many organizations this way. Commonweal incubates and supports a number of highly effective programs in the areas of health and healing, arts and education, and environment and justice. Their programs include the pioneering Cancer Help Program, Regenerative Design Institute at Commonweal Garden, Collaborative on Health and the Environment, and the New School series of conversations with the thought and action leaders of our time. His model is, you begin with the circle of those you know. Gather people that are invested in their relationships with you, and with whom you already have trust. It doesn't have to be a large group, but it is group that is well-connected, or deeply involved in the field you are trying to affect. Then those people reach out to who they know, with the same degree of personal or professional relationship or respect. Then those people reach out—and out and out it goes. Slowly. There is no rush. Ripple out doesn't just go out in one direction. There will be feedback, course correction, and other ways of inclusion and expansion along the way.

When a social media post goes viral it's traveling on extreme ripple out—very short and rapid increments, click by click. For that matter, a *real* virus, like a highly contagious flu, also has ripple out, working very much along the same lines of infecting those with closest relationships first, then to their relationships—and out and out.

> "It is from numberless diverse acts of courage and belief that human history is shaped. Each time a man stands up for an ideal, or acts to improve the lot of others, or strikes out against injustice, he sends forth a tiny ripple of hope, and crossing each other from a million different centers of energy and daring those ripples build a current which can sweep down the mightiest walls of oppression and resistance."
> —**Robert F. Kennedy**, address on Day of Affirmation, University of Cape Town, June 6, 1966

PATIENCE

> "Rivers know this: there is no hurry. We shall get there some day."
> —**A. A. Milne**, *Winnie the Pooh*

Maybe patience should have been at the top of this chapter, because it is the most necessary and the most difficult aspect of Proceed Incrementally. I don't do simple; nor do I do patience very well. Patience may be a virtue, but it sure isn't easy! Don't we all want to just get there already?

Patience is not the absence of action. When I Align with Nature and I Listen Deeply, patience allows for the rightness of proper timing. In patience, I will find the most expedient and fortuitous opening for action or reception. Patience is not waiting. Patience is the quality of waiting; it's the way in which I wait.

"I want it later...now!"

My favorite expression about patience is from of my goddaughter, who at three years old wanted an ice cream. Her mother patiently told her, as all us patient mothers do, "You can have it later." To which she cleverly replied, "I want it later...now!" I repeat that often, both as a joke, and as serious reflection of how difficult patience can be. Patience requires hope, fire, and discipline to sustain it. Having patience requires a steady perseverance and the ability to somehow suppress or dissolve anxiety, restlessness, and the annoyance that comes with delay. Things happen in their own timing whether I wait patiently or not. I will get through this traffic when the accident blocking the road clears. My time spent waiting will either be pleasant or unpleasant depending on my level of patience and the resources I have to keep renewing my patience when anxiety arises. Every time I think about how late I am for work I need to renew my sense of patience, or I will, as my grandmother would say, "burn my kishkes out"—which translates to "get very upset." I could say that patience is a necessary constant across the incremental steps of change, but it also needs to be renewed in increments. If patience doesn't come naturally, patience can be learned. And sustained patience must be renewed at every turn. It only appears sustained because I keep renewing it.

Proceed Incrementally doesn't mean that change can't happen swiftly. It can and does. But that's not where patience is called for. It's in the interminable waiting, and the enduring of disappointments, setbacks, and seemingly lost causes that requires the steady holding of the goal and the dream, and the renewal of patience.

John Weeks and his associates at ACCAHC are a great example of how sustained patience and incremental effort can bring good results, even in an enormously frustrating uphill battle. As I said earlier, the movement of external change is complicated by the number of people, the number of agendas and the amount of resistance involved. Starting small and building as they could, ACCAHC has influenced significant movement, and continues to do so, for the inclusion of alternative and complementary disciplines into the health care industry. By addressing common values, slow, incremental movement is taking place in the system overall.

John Weeks: The secret weapon in so much of this is that a growing percentage of all of us are using some form of health care that is not typically provided in a hospital, or in a regular doctor visit, or in the health system, so we encounter people right and left who actually may not be representing the ideas that we have, but they are actually agents for the change themselves. So, we'll knock at the door and we'll find somebody who is saying, "Finally, at last. Welcome! Let's see if we can manifest this."

The big turning point in this whole dialogue was in 1993; before that, it was ugly. When I started the first decade, if you mention naturopathic in the media, you had to quote somebody saying they're quacks and frauds—and that was what was routine.

But when the report came out of David Eisenberg who happened to be at Harvard—which put the right brand on this survey—they found out that a third of adult Americans were using some form of unconventional medicine, as it was called then, and there were nearly $14 billion being spent out of pocket. At that point, not only did all of these major stakeholder groups say, "Huh, maybe there are customers there; maybe they're potential insured employees who would like these benefits." The media began to think, "a bunch of our readers actually like this stuff, maybe we should treat it differently." Politicians started to think, "Oh, there are voters who like this stuff." In fact, a lot of single-issue voters think that this is about the most important thing in their life.

But the other thing that it did, which will speak to the grassroots nature of this movement and this secret weapon in all of our organizing work, is that people throughout all these stakeholder organizations felt empowered. They could sit in their office and look around the room and go, "Well, if a third are using these things, then my quiet use of acupuncture that I never mentioned to anybody is probably reflected in the practices of other people in the room here."

Sharon Weil: That's right.

John Weeks: So, people began to step forward empowered by that data. Then as the numbers grew… Today I saw in a report that a full 80 percent of women with breast cancer will use some form of alternatives. With right conditions, the numbers that you see from studies, it's between 45 and 90 percent of people are exploring non-conventional things.

Sharon Weil: It's certainly about time that policies and insurance companies; that these practices and disciplines be accepted as what people are already doing. This is what people are already doing.

John Weeks: The other major help for us right now, and I would say since the Affordable Care Act was passed, I tell people who are interested in these fields and disciplines that whatever else you think about that plan, it actually empowered integrative thinking, integrative practice, and the complementary and alternative medicine fields in ways they never have been before in federal policy—which is itself valuable to have for the first time.

So, knocking on the door, and walking through the door, we not only are finding people who are more likely to have grown up with using non-conventional care, people who are using it now, but they're also living in cultures that are beginning to say out loud what we need to be doing is creating health. That's where we need to be.

In John's case, patience has paid off. Having the quality of patience has allowed him to stay the course through all its twists and turns.

SETTING GOALS

I am told that it's best to set reasonable goals. Sometimes I hear that and it feels like a put down. Like I am being told *don't be too uppity*, or *don't reach too high—be reasonable*. Why would I want to be reasonable when most of the success stories I hear are when people reached beyond reason? Like space exploration, or the eradication of polio. So, I'm not saying here to set reasonable goals. The podcast guests don't set reasonable goals, in fact most of their goals hold an incredibly high vision for how humans and for how our world can be restored. But they set the *right* goals. And the strategies for their dreams and visions are made up of smaller reachable goals, and are recognized as such.

There is great satisfaction in reaching a goal. It gives me confidence to try for the next one. But the higher my goals, the more patience I will need, as well as a large amount of compassion for myself for inevitably missing the mark a time or two.

One area of change that can be very challenging when it comes to setting goals has to do with our diet—what I eat, and how much. Setting goals about my own health and how I achieve it is an area where I can easily become overly ambitious and miss my mark as each New Year's resolution dissolves by the first week in February. **Ann Gentry** and I discussed the many different approaches to diet and changing health through healthy eating. Our conversation was meant to cut through some of the clutter of all the different healthy diets that are out there. Ultimately, Ann's approach is to simplify and choose a diet that works for you—one you can maintain, incrementally, as a lifestyle.

Ann Gentry: Twenty-one years later, and I've seen a lot of trends come and go. A lot of diet modalities peak with interest and then lose interest. Really, when you look at them, they're all the same. We're all trying to get to the same place… balance. What works for you?

Sharon Weil: A sense of well-being.

Ann Gentry: Well-being, good focus, an ideal weight. Food is fuel. It's not just celebratory; it's the fuel we're using to get through our days. You want to choose wisely when you think about it that way. Everybody's going to tell you something differently out there. Everybody's got their take on it. Now, the paleo diet is very intriguing, and interesting, and popular—with hundreds of cookbooks. I've watched it leave the Zone and be the Atkins diet. Everything rehashes through with a different cover, so to speak, a different title. The whole juicing, and cleansing, and raw food…when I got into this movement back in the late seventies, early eighties, that was around then, low-key. Now, it's really reaching a larger mass of people. It's got a different flare to it and a different look, but it goes back way past the seventies—out of this hygiene movement that started in the thirties and forties in this country.

I think, at the end of the day, you've really got to find what works for you. Stay committed to it. You don't have to get on your holier-than-thou preaching pulpit to think that everybody around you has to do that exact same thing because again, it's back to your condition, your constitution, and what really works for you.

Sharon Weil: You and I were talking that sometimes the best thing to do to change your diet is to get certain things out of what you're eating. Other times the good thing to do is to add them in to what you're already eating. What do you think is the better strategy?

Ann Gentry: I think it's always good to eliminate, especially the things that are definitely not good for you like processed foods that are loaded with a lot of corn syrup and cheap white sugar. The sugar is on the forefront now. People are paying attention to it. A very powerful movie called *Fed Up* really laid it out with visual descriptions of how it is processing in our body in a very negative way. For some people I would say, "Hey, just give up the soft drinks. There's your starting point." Then, people say, "Well, what do I replace it with?"

You've got to get educated. You've got to understand in eliminating something, what am I replacing it with? I thought giving kids fruit juice that was organic and certainly had no additional additives of sugar or any other kind of additives was good, not finally realizing, "Oh, this is horrible." You're better off having the real fruit, a whole piece of fruit, than having X amount of apples or oranges that it takes to make a juice.

Sharon Weil: That's right. A lot of us moms did that.

Ann Gentry: Even when you look at veganism, people have eliminated animal products and animal byproducts from their diet. That is a noble thing to do. People are driven to that for ethical, environmental reasons that are really powerful tenets in their life. I see a lot of vegans out there and they've got a really poor diet. They're running around eating a lot of sugar, a lot of carbohydrates. I look at them, I go, "No, no, no. You might be better off having animal products to have more balance in your life if you're not going to make the commitment to buying those [plant] proteins which are important."

Little by little, step by step. I don't have to make change all at once, and I don't even have to know what I am doing in order to start. Simplifying my diet, my lifestyle, or the clutter in my house can be done incrementally, and best approached that way. All change requires time for me to make adjustments in my nervous system, in my thinking, my emotions, and in my ways of living. Incremental moves are usually easier to adjust to, and I am able to see more clearly what has just occurred and what needs to happen next. More radical shifts certainly can happen, and certainly do happen, they just require more radical adjustment as well, and can challenge ChangeAbility.

SUMMARY

So how can #4 Proceed Incrementally increase the ease and effectiveness of ChangeAbility?

If ChangeAbility is the facility of moving easily with change, then Proceed Incrementally is the *strategy* for how to navigate. Even being able to view the movement of change as existing in smaller increments helps make the navigation more manageable and achievable. Aligning with the rhythm of change can allow me to get on the groove and dance with the change rather than be thrown all about. Proceed Incrementally is the surest strategy for good ChangeAbility, navigating the constant and enormous tides of change in smaller waves.

◊   Change moves incrementally from moment to moment, from breath to breath.

◊   Change does not move in a straight line; sometimes the increments of change will move from side to side, or back and forth.

◊   The movement of change is driven by the rhythm of change whether it is fast or slow, smooth or syncopated.

◊   Breaking up the larger picture into smaller moments, events, or increments allows adaptation to change to be more manageable, and the initiation of change more achievable.

◊   When beginning change, start small and allow it to grow over time.

◊   Ripple out is an effective way to being with a small and strategic action and let it expand to include a larger and larger territory, or number of people.

◊   Bite-size actions are small, individual actions that are achievable actions.

◊   Proceed Incrementally requires patience at each step of the way because incremental movement can be slow. Patience is not waiting; it is a quality of waiting.

◊   Set small, achievable goals as part of a larger strategy for change. Achieving even a small goal brings satisfaction and encouragement to try for the next.

SPARK FIRE

HAVE HOPE

BRING AWAR

ALIGN WITH NATURE

LISTEN DEEPLY

PROCEED INCREMENTALL

FIND COMMUNITY

5 ALIGN WITH NATURE

Life, Cosmos, Mother Earth, wilderness, biology, winter, spring, summer, fall, fire, water, air, earth

"The goal of life is to make your heartbeat match the beat of the universe, to match your nature with Nature."

—Joseph Campbell

YOU ONLY HAVE TO LOOK AT the ocean's tide as it moves in and out, or the clouds as the wind pushes them across the sky to know that the natural world is nothing but change. Nature is in constant and continual transition and transmutation, completely interdependent and symbiotic. Ancient people articulated their belonging to the ever-changing evolution of life. Native peoples honor that they are inseparable from tree, deer, river, and wind. Humans, in modern life, have created industrial models and mental constructs that separate us from the wholeness of our belonging, which also separate us from belonging to ongoing change. When we #5 Align with Nature, we return to Nature, and to our own nature. We align with the nature of change, itself—our inherent and deepest resource for ChangeAbility.

"We participate with nature, with planetary influences, with cycles and seasons, times of day or night. It's recognizing that we are organic substance and we are surrounded by organic substance. Everything in our environment, everything in the heavens, everything below us that we can't see, all participates in harmony. We all dance together, and when we learn how everything in our environment is dancing, we can learn how to gracefully move into the transitions of our lives, into new chapters, and it helps us to have a more harmonious existence."

—Rachel Lang

I perceive the constructs of time and space in the natural world through seasons and cycles, the natural increments in the rhythm of change. At the most basic level, I am organic material living in resonance with an organic environment, so there is no difference between the internal and external. I belong to my surroundings that are made of up the same basic atoms, molecules, organic compounds, and design motifs. I can best feel my sense of belonging to this larger shared "field" when I am in the natural world, in rapport with the towering trees that breathe in exchange with me of O_2 and CO_2, or sitting next to moving water that is in resonance with the waters inside my own body, or among other animals and living creatures that share traits and similarities to me. This relationship is most apparent to me when I can Bring Awareness to include all this.

The way of nature is adaptation. Charles Darwin said that the survival of a species is based on its ability to adapt. Adaptation is a constant and evolving response to events of light and dark, hot and cold, moisture and dryness, access to nutrients and water, competition for resources, the threat of predators, and unexpected catastrophe. Animals can move about in search of sources of food or to flee hungry predators. Plants that are rooted to a place have to have more clever strategies to move themselves about, or they have to develop greater reach for their resources through crawling vines, plant volunteers, or the "fairy ring" spread of fungi on the forest floor. They develop strategies for their protection like thorns and poisonous fruit. A species' reproductive strategy defines its survival just as much as their strategies for finding food and protection will insure it. As humans, we can recognize our own similarities and differences as we find our place of belonging in the bio-world.

James Stark finds that we can relieve ourselves of enormous stress when we reframe our own nature in alignment with the natural world.

James Stark: The easiest way to do some changing is to sit in nature. It's basically sitting in the *verb* of life and appreciating, "Oh my God, right now I'm in the *noun* of life. I'm trying to hold on to this non-changing world and the energy that it takes to hold that is too much." Then there's the *verb* of it, and so sitting in nature I find that everything then becomes possible. You don't have the trees trembling in trepidation about what's going to happen tomorrow. I see the jackrabbit out there in the garden. Jeez, there are six foxes in the same space and he's not sitting there fretting. He's just present. Thank God he's not a human being or he'd have to be taking tranquilizers because there are six serial killers in the neighborhood right around him.

Amanda Foulger values the necessity of spending time in deep nature in order to connect with and recalibrate our natural rhythms.

Amanda Foulger: Traditionally, shamanic cultures spent time in nature, not just daily life, but time in nature to really be with the trees, or be with the waters, be on the mountain. It's not just to have a photo opportunity, but to attune to that deeper level of being that connects us all. That deeper immersion time in nature that is less compromised by human activity is critical for getting into those deeper rhythms. That is the sacred piece, and it doesn't matter so much what you call it or how you describe it as much as that you feel it and you sense it with your heart.

When I Align with Nature, the movement of change flows more easily. When I am aligned with my own *personal* nature, within the *particular* nature of my local surroundings, and within the largest gestures of seasons, cycles, and planetary movement, there is less resistance to change because I am going along with what already is, and I am assisted by its principles of being. This is the nature of tree. This is the behavior of hawk. This is the character of river. They cannot be another way. In aligning with the qualities of nature, my surroundings will support the direction and the quality of my change. My change flows like water, ignites like fire, or sails like currents of air. In a more forceful expression: my change surges like floodwaters, spreads quickly like wildfire, and blows me over like the strong wind. In the natural world there is symbiosis, there is competition, there is the predator and prey relationship, but these are all within the natural design of things. You don't see water refuse to flow, or a tree afraid to breathe—even in smoky winds. They will respond and successfully adapt—or not—but they do not have resistance, or what we humans would consider to be reluctance. Resistance to change is a human phenomenon. It's fueled by the belief that I am somehow separate from the natural world, and therefore separate from change. It creates the false idea that if I'm separate from change, I therefore can *stop* change or delay it. But nature runs its own course.

RENEWAL OF NATURE

> "Anything that's created requires a structure and anything that's destroyed creates something new."
>
> —Adam Wolpert

Nature holds the gift of renewal. Life and death turn the wheel of existence in the natural world. All individuals within a species are born, live, thrive, reproduce, fade, and die. As individuals, they give way for new generations of life to emerge. Some life forms can have lifecycles that last for up to two hundred years: geoduck clams, koi fish, and Galapagos tortoises. Some, like the mayflies, cycle through in only one day. Everyone is food for someone else. Most species—like humans, lions, sharks, and rabbits, just to name a few— feed upon the life of other animals, plants, or organisms. Some feed upon their death—like hyenas, vultures, maggots, and the fungi that decompose the fallen trees in the forest. The cycle of life and death is interdependent between species, and contributes to how they mutually thrive. It is the ultimate mechanism of balance. The choreography of life is one of colonies, pods, herds, flocks, villages, communities where the existence of the whole is most certainly contributed to by the individual, but the biological goal is long-term survival. That is only ever achieved through generations, for the benefit of the species.

Renewal. Life begets life. Pulses of life force recede and then return anew. Humans shed their skin cells every day; every cell in their body is replaced each seven years. The maple leaves turn colors, fall to the groud, and new leaves appear on the branches. The pond freezes in winter then thaws, and new life appears in the spring: frogs, fish, baby ducks. All life renews. Perhaps the individual frog or leaf does not return, but others like them do, to take up their place in the larger choreography of existence. I could say that each individual and their life is an incremental part of that choreography. The renewal of life, however, is based on being able to see the larger picture of how it all works together.

By far, my biggest resistance to change is my refusal to accept death as the natural and inevitable part of the life cycle. I'm sure I'm not alone in this. My keen sense of survival-at-all-costs tries desperately to keep death at bay. But it's my resistance to accepting the surety of death in all things: my body, my relationships, careers, or good times that keeps me stuck and unhappy in response to change. Dying is the gradual movement toward death, and so the fading of my youth, a relationship that is losing the love, opportunities lost, lingering illness, or the limitations that come with old age are all reminders that I am that much closer to death in this larger cycle of life. Only when I embrace that life contains death as well as life can I appreciate the preciousness of the magical mystery of how it all works together. Only then can I recognize all the ways that the renewal of life comes to me. Whether I use renewal as a metaphor or as a description of an actual biological process, the inspiration for renewal comes from nature itself.

PERMACULTURE—HOW DOES NATURE DO IT?

"Permaculture is a design science that's rooted in the observation of natural systems, asking the question "How does nature do it?"
—**Penny Livingston-Stark**

Perhaps a more accurate word to use in regard to Align with Nature would be the word "restoration." I used that word earlier in the book in connection with healing, saying that the navigations of change are Initiating, Inspiring, Adapting, and Restoration. Restoration means to bring back, whether it's to bring something back to its original state or to something close. The urgent questions of our time are: *Will we be able to restore the land, the waters, and the life forms from all the environmental assault being done by chemical pollution, fossil fuel extraction, and agribusiness practices? Can the earth restore itself?*

I do not claim to understand how the designs of nature work, how intricately all the natural systems of air, water, soil, plants, animals, and microbes work together. However, permaculture designer and educator **Penny Livingston-Stark** knows. She travels the world teaching others how to design farms, build structures, and create communities that incorporate the designs of nature into human design. All aspects of life intersect and are interdependent. Therefore, whole-systems thinking leads to whole-systems solutions, and is the most effective way to innovate workable answers for the deep challenges we face from climate change and the industrial and technological co-opting of the resources and rhythms of life. Penny believes that the solutions we need already exist, but we'll need to change the way we think of our world in order to put them into play.

Penny Livingston-Stark: Permaculture is a design science that's rooted in the observation of natural systems, asking the question, "How does nature do it?" Then we humbly try to understand nature's operating instructions and nature's principles and apply them to the design of human settlements. It was developed by a young Australian environmental design student named David Holmgren and a professor from Tasmania, Bill Mollison. Bill actually coined the term "permaculture" like "permanent culture." This was back in the seventies when there was no word for sustainability. The concept of permaculture goes beyond sustainability because it's not about being sustainable, it's about being restorative. It's about not being less bad or just maintaining status quo, it's actually building more fertility, and abundance, and verdant ecosystems in our wake through our activities than what was there prior. A permaculture garden is full of fruit, and flowers, and herbs, and berries, and microorganisms, and fungi in the soil. Life above and below the earth.

Sharon Weil: Working altogether.

Penny Livingston-Stark: Yes, and the other piece that's important to know is that it's not just about gardening and food. It's about economic systems, its about social structures, it's about energy systems, shelter. It's about all aspects of human activity. Everything is connected, and everything is affecting everything else. As scientists observing nature, instead of observing things in a reductionist manner in isolation, we're actually observing the interconnections of things and how different elements interact in a system. That system could be a social system, like an urban community of different cultural groups coming together in a city. It could be how water, soil, plants, fish, birds, and people interact.

Penny Livingston-Stark cofounded Regenerative Design Institute at Commonweal Garden with her husband, **James Stark**, as a model permaculture classroom and farm. James talks about invaluable education a garden can offer, and how "a garden in the world right now is the starting point of a journey back home."

James Stark: We've been doing this kind of work for about eighteen years, and it's about how to reconnect and eliminate the delusion that we're separate from the natural world. We *are* the natural world. This is an institute that provides pathways for people who are feeling the call to move into a different way of being with the earth, and aligning themselves ecologically with the green movement and all those different pathways.

We operate from a seventeen-acre garden that is a site for permaculture. We provide programs to assist people in those journeys of returning to that balance. People can learn how to grow food, and have natural building, and collect water off the roof—all those ecological design elements. What's unique about us is that we also provide pathways for the "inner gardening," because we see the journey of the great turning and if we're going to stay on the planet for a long period of time it is really an inside job. Ultimately, all the things that we see that are challenging in our world are really an outer reflection of the consciousness of seven billion people. We want to provide opportunities for people to cultivate rich, vibrant, resilient inner gardens as well.

We haven't been considering our communities as ecosystems. What would a healthy community look like that is totally attuned to the natural world, dissolving the delusion that we're somehow separate from the natural world? However your garden, or that forest outside your window, or that one tomato on the potted plant, it's all one organism.

Movement artist and educator **Fred Sugerman** takes his primary inspiration for knowledge and self-knowledge from his experiences in the wilderness. He spends time each year hiking in the mountains, being as close to the undisturbed natural world as he can. Fred knows that the forces of nature are the same forces at work within his body and his psyche, and that those forces create his sense of belonging to a much larger field of existence. He uses the natural forces as a guide for what he can discover about himself and other people, healing, and the movement of change.

Sharon Weil: You have said to me that above all, your work is about the relationship to the Earth, and that your greatest passion is the wilderness.

Fred Sugerman: I'm defining wilderness as places in nature where men and women have not had a large, if any, impact. Places in the mountains, or desert, or forest where there's been little or no intervention. To me, that's where I get all the knowledge I need. It's my sanctuary. It's my most authentic temple or church. Life and death are apparent. Health is apparent. I just look at a pile of rocks that slid down a granite mountain, and they're just lying there haphazardly, but there's so much perfection, and design, and beauty in the chaos of where they land.

To me, that says a lot about their movement and also the art. It appears like it doesn't have any logical sequence or order but there is some kind of intelligence at work that I believe runs through our own bodies as well as through the rocks, and through the trees, and through the plants that goes beyond anything that we could construct with the cognitive part of our brains. Therein lies the greatest challenge of our time: that for the last few hundred years there's been such dependence upon the rational mind, and upon the scientific model, and upon a linear way of constructing our world.

These forces of nature that are at work in the wilderness give us knowledge of what that means in relationship to our illnesses and diseases, and our states of mind and mental health. By studying our biology, by studying what our bodies are telling us in what they're feeling, and responding to that one moment to the next, there's something that can be discovered that nobody else can tell us about ourselves.

"If we surrendered
to earth's intelligence
we could rise up rooted, like trees."

—Rainer Maria Rilke

NATURE'S ELEMENTS

There are numerous ways that I can perceive and receive the natural world and divide it into categories for understanding. There are the three states of matter: solid, liquid, and gas. Biological classifications of life forms: life, domain, kingdom, phylum, class, order, family, genus, and species. We observe the four seasons: winter gives way to spring, which ripens into summer, harvests in the autumn, and prepares to quiet down to retreat into the stillness of winter, only to have the cycle renew again with the next coming of spring. I can observe the season through changes in the weather, the activities of animals, and the maturing of plants. Seeds sprout in the spring with vibrant yellow green. Fruit and vegetables begin to appear and ripen throughout the warm summer months. In the early autumn, the leaves turn colors, the food is harvested, and the remains are turned back into the soil. Trees lose their leaves, and the sap withdraws into the trunk and down into the roots to remain still and dormant through the winter's cold. Cues from the weather and the sun's light give a wake up call in the spring for life to return to its fullness. That is, unless you live in sunny Southern California like I do, where you have to look very carefully for the more subtle cues of the seasons' passing.

The Native American tribes honor the four directions. They offer gratitude and blessings to the east, south, west, and north, and the energies and spirits they represent.

Throughout the ancient world, cultures divided the physical world into four, sometimes five, elements reflecting the worlds' essential nature: fire, air, water, earth, and, for the Ancient Greeks, the addition of aether. The first four describe elements of matter and the fifth was the element that was beyond the physical world.

Astrologer and intuitive healer **Rachel Lang** talks about the four elements that are used in western Astrology. The qualities of fire, air, water and earth characterize qualities of personalities and dynamics based on the signs contained in an astrological chart. People born under the sign of Aries, Leo, and Sagittarius are fire signs. Gemini, Libra, and Aquarius are considered air signs. Cancer, Scorpio, and Pisces are water signs. Taurus, Virgo, and Capricorn are earth. In astrology, it is the unique blending of these elemental energies that correspond with the constellation of planets in my chart that reflect my unique personality, influences on my life, and the way I might meet my choices and challenges.

Rachel Lang: The concept of the four elements is earth, air, fire, and water. Each one of those elements represents a different energy that's a part of our lives. Fire is a real playful, active, energizing, very action-oriented energy. Earth tends to be more practically minded, very sensual. Earth signs love to have a sensual experience, so they're the ones who are going to connect with the ground. They need to touch things. Earth also connects us to our purposes and how we give back, and where in our lives is the most fertility. Air is our mental process. It's our intellect. It's also how we communicate with one another, so it's very instrumental in communication. Just ask any Gemini. Water connects us to our emotions, receptivity and the conductivity, because water's a conductor. So, that's the element that's symbolic of, the ways in which we connect telepathically or energetically. The ways that we connect that are unseen, but felt.

In Chinese philosophy and Chinese medicine there is the additional phase of wood. It is referred to as a phase rather than an element because each phase is seen as a dynamic aspect that transforms into the next. Wood, I am told, relates to spring, fresh shoots, and flexibility. Its movement is upward and outward, but not so much as fire's. It is like bamboo—pliable when healthy, and when undernourished, it becomes brittle.

> "Water does not resist. Water flows. When you plunge your hand into it, all you feel is a caress. Water is not a solid wall, it will not stop you. But water always goes where it wants to go, and nothing in the end can stand against it. Water is patient. Dripping water wears away a stone. Remember that, my child. Remember you are half water. If you can't go through an obstacle, go around it. Water does."
>
> —Margaret Atwood

ALIGNMENT

What exactly does it mean to Align with Nature? What does it mean to align with the seasons, with the elements, with the wilderness, or the cycles of life and death? And, how can that alignment help me to navigate change? Aligning with nature removes resistance to change, because the very nature of Nature is unimpeded change. Align with Nature doesn't just mean *observing* the natural world, Align with Nature invites me to find more ease by utilizing the characteristics of that which I'm trying to become.

Here's an example: sometimes I need to really go after a problem, or I need to motivate myself past my fears and reluctance to initiate a change. Let's say, I have to find a job quickly—like one of my daughters just did. It would be quite helpful for me to animate the qualities of fire, that quick, fierce, active and energized quality of being. So, I put a list together of prospects, I send out résumés to each one on the list. I don't overthink it, just get into action. If I'm nervous to make a phone call, I might literally dance around the room to get my energy up, get my heart pumping, get fired up.

Then of course I'll need to wait a minute to catch my breath before I pick up the phone to call—but what I did was animate fire.

Lets say I was excited. Let's say, I received ten replies to my job search and they all wanted to interview me this week. Two of them were very good offers, but they would require me to move to another city. One of them was at a great company but the pay was low. Another was for a job I've never done before, but something I've always wanted to try. I have to prepare a bit differently for each interview: dress up for some, down for others. My head is spinning with all the considerations, the logistics, and wardrobe change from meeting to meeting. I'm feeling anxious, and find myself talking too fast. I need some earth. I need to ground myself from the swirl of excitement that has gotten me too heady. I have too much of the element of air, plus there's some fire burning out of control. To bring in more earth, I locate my feet. I feel how my feet feel on the ground. If I can get near some grass I take off my shoes and feel my feet literally on the ground, and drop my awareness to the sensations of my connection with the earth. And breathe slowly. Or I stop and smell the roses, as they say. Earth represents the senses and the sensuality of living, so stopping to look at the flowers in a garden, to notice their fragrance and color, could be helpful to find earth. Or my favorite one, I eat some delicious food. I stop for lunch and eat something wonderful, savoring the flavors, not rushing through the meal. In all that, I grounded myself with earth.

Continuum founder Emilie Conrad was fond of saying that we can take on the properties of something by putting ourselves "inside the metaphor" through movement. The metaphor could be image in the natural world. Continuum's fluid-based movement works with the imagery and fluid sensations of water. So if I want to align with the flow and ease of water, I move like water. I move like a wave. I put the slow undulation that imitates a wave in my spine, in my arms, in the way I slowly turn my head. In so doing, I can feel what it feels like to be floating in water, only these sensations are inside of me and I am on dry land. Water can flow or be stagnant. It can have gentle current or churn turbulently. Water can change form from ice to liquid to vapor. Water, unless contained, will seep in through any and every crack. If I want to align with water, not only can I learn about water or surround myself with water, but I can actually move like water—dance the dance of water. That undulating wave can move me through any stagnation in my body, in my thoughts, or in my emotions. When I move through a stuck or stubborn resistance to change as if I were water, I find resistance can dissolve more easily.

The same is true if I want to take on the quality of a particular animal to assist my navigation with change: a fierce tiger, a wild beast, or a playful monkey. I can find a wilder, or more playful side of myself, and can animate these energies by literally inhabiting their qualities. I can move like a tiger on all fours, face in a snarl, or act like a monkey, hopping all around in curious play. This is why people like to wear costumes, so they can play out the nature of other creatures and characters, finding that alignment within themselves to be a pussycat, a tiger, a dragon or superman.

When I take on the shape of an element, or an animal, or a shape or motif in nature such as a spiral or a wave, I align with the movement of that energy and it assists me with its very qualities of being. It's the same as asking, how would fox solve this problem? How would fire solve it? Let me try it on and see.

Align with Nature speaks to timing and finding proper timing. Nature shows me about the fertilization, gestation, birth, and nurturing that I can apply to any project or activity in my life. It shows me how to look for the signs of changes, and how to wait. When I move with nature's rhythms, I recall that there are other ways to run my life besides the ticking clock, and my overly full appointment calendar. The organic indicators of timing can serve me in a more satisfying and successful way for my overall well-being.

I find it useful to align with the seasons when I am starting a project or a large action. For one thing, I might need to literally wait for the right weather to say, build a pool in my back yard, or repair the windows to my house, but I am speaking energetically here. How can I best assist the forward movement for my burgeoning ideas? I think of it as planting. When is the best time to let seeds germinate, when is the best time to plant, and when is the best time to harvest?

Some times of year are good for beginnings, some are not. I used this approach when launching my novel in the springtime to find assistance from the seasons in order to bring it success. When teaching The Ageless Body® classes, I found that January was a great time to begin a series of classes, when people had made their New Year's resolutions to get into shape, but before they had given up on them.

Every business has its own seasonal flow. The book business has one. The garment business has one. The film business has its own cycles based on TV pilots, film festivals, and movie release schedules. I've found there are actually only a few windows of a few months each year when real work can get done. Find what the proper cycle is for your business or project and see how closely you can match it to the seasons for that extra assistance from Mother Nature.

THE WORLD THROUGH THE SENSES

The world arrives to me through the portals of my sensations. I eat it, drink it, hear it, roll in it, sniff it, and take in its beauty or its danger with my eyes. All life-forms have the ability to sense their surroundings. If they don't have sense organs, they have chemical receptors—such as cells and microorganisms do. Most mammals have a highly developed sense of smell and a heighted sense of sound perception in order to locate themselves in their environments. Humans rely more on their sense of sight, though they respond to scent cues and sensation cues in ways they might not even be aware of. A very important aspect of Align with Nature is using my senses to perceive my surroundings, locate myself in relation to my environment, and participate with the world. Not to mention, to enjoy all that life has to offer!

Our human existence is reliant upon our relationship with plants. Whether it's through the plants we eat for nutrition, the plants we use for medicine, the plants that we use for shelter, the plants that alter our perceptions and provide vision, or the plants and flowers we use to surround ourselves with beauty—our lives are entwined with the lives of plants. The more I pay attention to the properties of plants—savoring the flavor of sweet fruits and savory spices, or understanding the interactions of medicinal plants with the various conditions and imbalances in my body—the more pleasurable and beneficial my alignment with nature will be. As Ann Gentry demonstrates in her plant-based restaurants, I can change my health and my body through the foods I choose to eat. So, I eat good food and use food as medicine, especially from natural sources. The more organic the source, the better. Food that is overly processed, sprayed with pesticides, and grown from GMO seeds is not the best alignment with nature, and over a short time, will do damage to the nature of your body and health.

FIND THE PATTERN

So, as I've been describing, one way to Align with Nature is to resonate with some aspect of the natural world by inhabiting its qualities; another way is by literally taking in its nutritional or medicinal value. Yet another way is to take the overview of a system, and look for a tendency or pattern. Nature is built upon common motifs and patterns—symmetry, spirals, waves, tessellations, and fractals. These patterns are reiterated over and over again in all plants, animals, and geological structures. There are millions of expressions of these motifs, and millions of interactions in the ways in which organisms and systems influence and shape one another, and yet, they can be recognized by their patterns.

Adam Wolpert looks for the patterns in nature, art, and in how people organize themselves. As a permaculturist and fine art painter, he has spent so much time watching and understanding the movement of change, evidenced by the patterns left behind. Adam knows that when you can recognize the patterns you can map out the journey.

Adam Wolpert: I have learned so much from watching water and nature. One of the things that always strikes me is how when you're looking at a whole system, you usually see a very small part of it, what might be called the surface of the system. If you're looking at a river and if you're rafting, you often go ahead and scout. You'll stand on top of a rock and look down into the valley. The first thing you see is all of this foam. If you stand there for a while and you study the river, you start to see these flows, these patterns. The patterns are really expressing the relationship the river has to that canyon, and the structure of the canyon.

Sharon Weil: The patterns also tell you where the rocks are?

Adam Wolpert: They tell you where the rocks are, and the rocks can help you predict where the water's going to go. The way water comes into relationship with its surrounding is often both passive and active at the same time. It conforms to its surroundings, but it also is energized and invigorated by its surroundings. That relational quality that water has, I think is so magical and powerful.

Sharon Weil: I want to share with the listeners that you were facilitating a group that I was involved in. When you began, you not only brought in a typed up moment to moment agenda, but you brought in this sketch of a river that was laying out the territory that we were going to need to cover over the day, and over the next several days. You drew in the rapids. You drew where we could possibly eddy out and take a breath. It was a very different way of expressing the journey that lay ahead of us. I thought it was brilliant. I fell in love with you right then and there.

Adam Wolpert: Yeah, that was really fun! Sometimes that's the most fun thing I do, when I put together these agendas. What really is powerful about that I think, is the idea of having a framework, having a map. Everybody knows when you go on a trip, having a map doesn't mean you know what's going to happen.

Penny Livingston-Stark doesn't work with water as a metaphor, she literally works with the most effective uses of water by utilizing natural design that includes water harvesting and storage. As a permaculture designer, Penny creates design solutions work in concert with other systems to channel the most efficient use of what nature already offers.

Penny Livingston-Stark: We're in a drought here in California and so all of a sudden everybody's getting concerned about water during a drought. They want to start planning for drought and that's a little bit too late. You have to start planning for drought before the rainy season so that you can actually put the systems in place to harvest water. Our farm here, even during this drought, all of our systems are full. We are not suffering from a drought here because we've been putting water-harvesting structures in our farm in various methods for the last eight years.

We have contour swales that infiltrate water into the soil so we don't have to irrigate our trees. We have these dinky-winky little trickles of springs. We put a lot of our water from this dinky-winky little spring into tanks so we have ten thousand gallons of tank storage, because even though that spring is a little trickle, it's 24/7. We have a solar pump that pumps water up to a tank, another five thousand gallons on a ridge that then gravity feeds down. Then we also have water that we collect off of a roof, about 2,800 gallons, so we have multiple sources of water, which is one of the principles of permaculture.

How many ways can you achieve your goal? Instead of putting all your eggs in one basket, you diversify and create multiple ways of, in

this case, getting the water we need to have our water security.

Another major area of concern for Penny is soil. The effects of factory farm practices for both growing food and raising livestock have depleted the topsoil and released large amounts of CO_2 into the atmosphere, exacerbating the dangerous impact of greenhouse gases on our environment, and endangering future of life on planet earth. But she knows of solutions that are available right now, some that are in trial stages, but clearly effective.

Penny Livingston-Stark: I'm very excited about this idea of soil carbon sequestration. We're so concerned about how many parts per million of CO_2 is in the air right now. What we're finding out is that the best way to take that CO_2 out of the air and put it back into the ground is through soil building and plant photosynthesis.

All that excess CO_2 in the air is not just from burning fossil fuels; it's from bad agriculture. Every time we dig a hole in the ground or disturb the soil, there's a poof of organic carbon that gets oxidized and turns into CO_2, carbon dioxide, and it evaporates into the air. I've heard statistics that there's been way more CO_2 that's gone into the atmosphere because of bad land use and bad agriculture than all of the fossil fuels ever burned. Even if we stopped burning fossil fuels today, there's still going to be a buildup of CO_2 from inertia and it's still not going to solve the problem until we start actually taking it back out of the air and putting it back in the soil where it belongs.

The most efficient way to do that is through plants. If you imagine you plant an acorn that turns into an oak tree, and that oak tree grows. As that plant is growing it's breathing in CO_2 and breathing out oxygen, and as it's breathing in CO_2 it's creating the building blocks to create the carbon that becomes the body and the roots of the tree. The other very powerful solution is in rangeland management where you have deep rooted pasture grasses, and there are a lot of caveats. Deep-rooted pasture grasses, not shallow-rooted ones like prairie grasses and native bunch grasses.

Then you graze cows or cattle in a manner that you concentrate them and intensify them. You don't give them any antibiotics so there are no biocides passing through the manure killing microbes. You actually increase their manure in a zone, and if you're lucky, which we've been observing, you get the return of the magic creature called the dung beetle. The dung beetle comes along, and because there are not any antibiotics in the manure, it will most likely be the one to dig a hole maybe two or three feet down all over the pastures. These dung beetles come and they dig holes, lay their eggs, and then their whole life is rolling dung balls and depositing them in these long, tubular holes that go down into the earth.

When you start mimicking the wild herds, you bring back the dung beetle, and then you start stimulating the grasses. When the grass grows, it's taking atmospheric CO_2, putting it into the roots, which will remain there virtually forever, until somebody comes along and digs it up. It will start to build up humus. Only 8.5 percent of the Earth's surface is arable land. It's land that we can actually do something with. It's not locked up in ice, it's not all craggy mountain ridge tops, but it's arable land. If we can increase the humus content on that 8.5 percent of the land by 1.6 percent, we could bring our CO_2 levels back to preindustrial levels.

Penny discussed other methods of building humus in places such as the Amazon basin. There are solutions, as she says. And she continually works toward promoting and instituting those changes on behalf of a restored environment.

Another remarkable field of pattern recognition I want to mention is that of biomimicry. Permaculture and biomimicry go hand in hand in their study of how nature does it. Biomimicry studies nature's best ideas and adapts them for human use, borrowing nature's solutions for manufacturing, building structures, harnessing energy, creating medicine, and producing food. In each case, nature provides the models, using what has worked and what has lasted for millions of year. Years ago, when I read *Biomimicry: Innovation Inspired by Science* by science writer and lecturer Janine Benyus, I was completely fascinated. It changed the way I saw the world, caused me to marvel at bio-intelligent design, and have hope for truly innovative solutions to our enormous challenges.

> "Biomimicry is basically taking a design challenge and then finding an ecosystem that's already solved that challenge, and literally trying to emulate what you learn."
>
> —**Janine Benyus**, *Biomimicry*

RHYTHMS OF NATURE AND DISRUPTION

Nature is our best teacher when it comes to navigating the dynamics of change. Nothing remains still in nature, not the wind, not the water, not the sun or the moon, nor any of the creatures on earth. We've already established that the natural world is comprised of a multiplicity of rhythms, complex rhythms that move in accord with one another, such as the phases of the moon, the pull of the tides, and the creatures in the crevices of rock running from the shore birds.

Entrainment is a universal physics phenomenon of resonance, appearing in chemistry, pharmacology, biology, medicine, psychology, sociology, astronomy, architecture, and more. First observed in the seventeenth century, it is defined as the tendency for two oscillating bodies to lock into phase so that they vibrate in harmony. It is also defined as a synchronization of two or more rhythmic cycles. The classic example shows individual pulsing heart muscle cells. When they are brought close together, they begin pulsing in synchrony. Another example of the entrainment effect is women who live in the same household often find that their menstrual cycles will coincide.

In the natural world, and in our relationship with the natural world, we can observe and experience many different forms of entrainment. When I speak of feeling resonance with water, feeling expansive among the trees in the forest, or feeling in resonance with another human being, I am speaking of entrainment. It's also how I feel when I am in love.

Shamanic healer **Amanda Foulger** works with rhythms in many ways. She has keen observations and experiences with entrainment.

> **Amanda Foulger**: Cycles and seasons—those are rhythms. Those are very, very big rhythms that are operating on the planetary, solar system, and galactic levels. Not just the Mayans, but other cultures had calendars that extended over very long periods of time. They understood that change was part of those calendric systems. If you get entrained, you get entrained to these rhythms. We also have very small rhythms that are daily rhythms, hourly rhythms, and breath rhythms. It's the entrainment of the brain, the entrainment of the heart, and coherence.

Amanda uses drumbeats and rattles, various types of rhythmic sound in her shamanic healing work, and she incorporates specific rhythms for the purpose of healing.

> **Amanda Fougler**: There's a huge field now of sound healing, and a lot of really interesting research that has been done. If you have a rhythm that is, say, four to eight beats a second, you start to alter brainwaves. When the brainwaves are altered then you get into different states of consciousness. This is something that very early people discovered. They didn't know anything about brainwaves particularly, but they understood, what happens is that it encourages people to come into coherence.

When you have a group of people who are using the same rhythm, you can definitely get into altered states of consciousness. If you know what you're doing with it and you are deliberately trying to do something with it…rather than just going to the grocery store and there's a pop tune on in the background. Believe me, all the marketers are aware of this stuff, too. They know if they keep music going, people get into these entrained states, but very unconscious ones, whereas if you are working with rhythm and sound to cultivate altered states for purposes of healing and of connecting with these other spiritual realms beyond the middle world, a lot of really wonderful things can happen.

It's a high science now. There's a lot of information out there that recognizes traditional cultures. They have different rhythms to deal with different spirits and with different kinds of things—very sophisticated stuff—but people didn't know that until relatively recent years, "Oh, something really happens when people sing and dance." People are moving in a shared state and particularly, they said, when you're getting into these four to eight beats a second, you start to definitely get the brainwaves changing. That opens the door to being able to make these connections with higher states of consciousness, for sure.

Before we had the Internet, before we had smartphones, or even television or radio, before our lives were captured and run by the pulse of the electronic signal, we were more attuned to the natural rhythms of our surroundings. Life is full of trade-offs. I love that I can talk with a friend overseas on Skype and see their face. I appreciate that I can accomplish more business in a day through email and that I can send large documents with a press of a button, but those technologies have changed the pace of my life. The world I live in has a different sense of time that might not go 24/7 but it's at least 18/6. There are still a few undisturbed hours in the night available for sleep, but I have to work harder and harder to protect them.

Michael Stocker is especially attuned to the rhythms, sounds and signals of the natural world. As a bio-acoustician he knows those sounds and their effects. He also knows about the damage caused when these natural rhythms and signals are disrupted. His advocacy work to protect sea mammals from man-made ocean noise has him keenly aware of how all our human rhythms are being changed, as well. I asked him, "Does change have its own rhythm?"

Michael Stocker: The changes that are coming up are going to be completely erratic. I think the rhythms are disrupted. I have a section in my book about the mechanization of our sound fields. Like this air conditioning that's humming in the background here, it's got a pitch to it. Then if my computer was on, the fan has its own pitch. There are always different pitches. During the industrial revolution you had these large, lumbering, spinning things and they all just went *chung, chung, chung*, and everybody was being torn asunder. They weren't tuning those things to people's heartbeats. When you start getting this lumbering jabberwocky of a rhythmic soundscape happening around you, it tears you apart

Now we've got a situation where everybody is using their earplugs. We're so biologically separated from each other. Any time of the day—it can be nighttime or daytime. When we were kids, at 6:00 p.m. people were at the dinner table. If you wanted to get in touch with somebody, call him up just before dinner. Now I get emails from people where they sent it at 3:00 a.m. What did we do to ourselves?

Michael was speaking to me about seeing evidence in the past twelve years of rapid change and erosion of habitat in so many ecosystems. That deeply saddens him. He expressed his concern that the rhythms of change, and the changes themselves have become unpredictable. What we are seeing now in the environment, we have never seen before.

Michael Stocker: What does that mean in terms of change? Again, we have the potential to get in this cascading effect, where you have, all a sudden, the hole is there and everything falls into it. Nobody would even calculate that the hole is there. It's just happened that this one rhythm is going like this, and another is going like that. It's created a situation where there is a non-resonance, then everything is getting rushed into it. It gets sloppy.

On the other side of that, you have the cicadas, the seventeen-year, and eleven-year, and thirteen-year cycles of these animals. What's beautiful about it is they assure that the species are going to survive because they never show up at the same time, except for like every two hundred and thirty-seven years. They're all there, and then they dispose again. They get on different cycles, and that creates a homeostasis in terms of their survival. If they ended up all showing up every year at the same time, all it would take is some catastrophe to happen and they would all be gone: a fire, or the deluge, or a freeze.

Sharon Weil: Part of nature's strategy for survival is to use rhythms.

Michael Stocker: Yeah, complex rhythms. They meet each other in places where they need to. What's happening now, is they get torn asunder.

Change will happen. Everything tries to reach homeostasis with its surroundings, but

when there are so many things changing, the predictability factor goes way down. That's why I like that phrase, "the new abnormal."

Sharon Weil: Right. Don't even think about normal. It's the new "abnormal."

Ultimately, we can entrain ourselves to the rhythms of the natural world through our most simple and basic relationship to all of life. Again, **Robert Litman** brings us back to our breath.

Robert Litman: Every sentient being on the planet breathes. We are connected as a community through this one atmosphere. That includes all the trees and all the plants. Everything is breathing. Everything is evenly as rooted and everything is in the space of the earth. When I pay attention to my own breathing, I'm paying attention to my own biological nature, which immediately brings me into the nature.

SUMMARY

How can principle for change #5 Align with Nature increase the ease and responsiveness of ChangeAbility? By aligning myself with nature I match myself with my surroundings and avail myself of all the successful strategies that nature has perfected for ongoing existence and flourishing. How would nature do it? That's my leading question—and the answers that come have been proven over thousands or millions of years.

◊   The nature of Nature is change.

◊   When I Align with Nature, I move in the same direction as the natural world around me, and thus decrease resistance.

◊   I receive and perceive the world through the portals of my senses: sight, sound, smell, taste, touch, and the felt sense of internal sensation.

◊   Life, death, and new life form the ongoing cycle of renewal in the natural world.

◊   **Resilience is key to ChangeAbility. The ability to respond, refresh, renew, and restore is essential to my incremental course correction and the ability to thrive.**

◊   **The natural world is built upon common motifs and patterns. Recognizing patterns in nature creates a map for locating yourself in change, and anticipating what is yet to come.**

◊   **Align with Nature helps me find proper timing for my change.**

◊   **Nature moves in rhythms. "Getting on the beat" of the rhythm of change carries me through change with less effort or struggle.**

◊   **By aligning with the rhythms of cycles and seasons, change be supported in its proper timing.**

◊   **Disruption of natural rhythms from speed, noise, technology, and other human constructs causes damages to animals' and plants' natural cycles in ways that are both seen and unseen.**

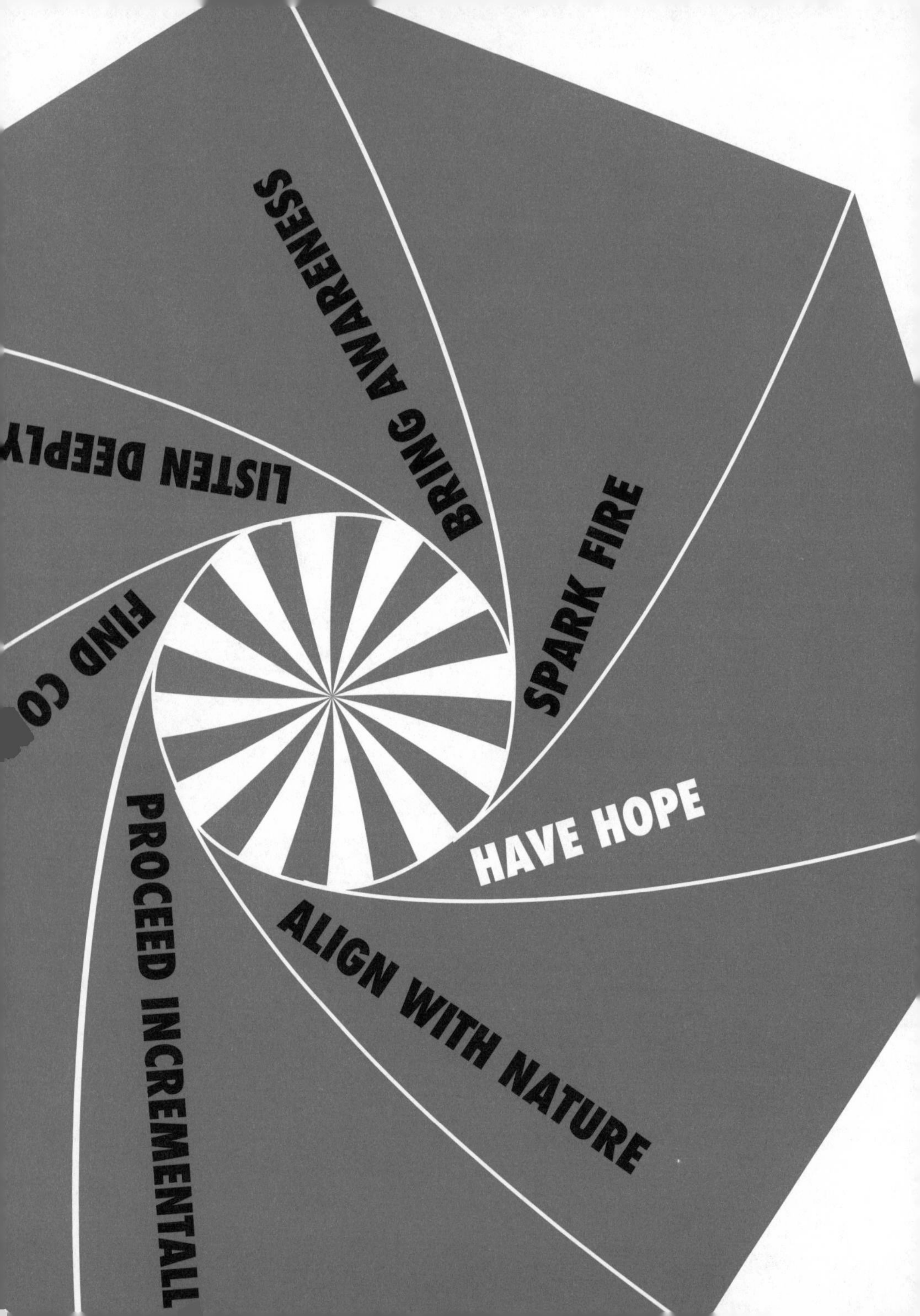
BRING AWARENESS
SPARK FIRE
HAVE HOPE
ALIGN WITH NATURE
PROCEED INCREMENTALL
FIND CO
LISTEN DEEPLY

6

HAVE HOPE

Belief, vision, dreaming, optimism, cherishing, desire, anticipation, expectation, longing, want, wishing, anticipation, aspiration

> "Hope is the thing with feathers, that perches in the soul, and sings the tune without words, and never stops."
>
> —**Emily Dickinson**

T HIS CHAPTER IS ACTUALLY ONE OF the more buoyant ones to write in relation to ChangeAbility. Hope is light. Hope has lift. Hope is what allows us to carry on, despite reason, and despite grim reality. Hope leads the way.

The human capacity for hope is enormous. It's what helps us dream into being what is possible but not yet formed. Hope springs eternal. It flies in the face of facts. When I hope against hope, when I have an expectation of fulfillment of a better outcome even when it seems a lost cause, hope is the spirit that cannot be crushed.

I was surprised to find that the word "hope" is in the top 1 percent of the lookups in the Merriam-Webster online dictionary. People are obviously interested in hope, and what it means. Interestingly, there were many more words for "hopeless" than for "hope" in the Synonym Finder. It seems there are many shades of disappointment and despair, but there's only one high note for hope. Hope has a recognizable and universal quality. Big hope, small hope—it's just a matter of volume, depending upon how much I might dare to hold hope. I always hope for the best.

When I have been articulating the Have Hope principle of this book to others as part of the Seven Principles for Change, I get a curious response from some who say that hope is not enough. They caution me that hope does not get the job done, that hope can lead to delusion, and replaces proper action with some "airy-fairy dreaming." They're right. Hope, in and of itself, doesn't get the job done. But hope is what will *inspire* me to try and try again, or to try an altogether different approach. Hope floats expansively, and anchors when in combination with the other principles for change. First, I determine the nature of my circumstance and rightful response to my need or problem through Bring Awareness and Listen Deeply. Then Have Hope helps me imagine what is possible—even if it's not apparently doable—and I Proceed Incrementally, strategically moving toward my dream, making course corrections along the way based on my failures as well as my successes. I renew my hope with each correction, especially when my actions, or the reactions of my world, missed the mark toward my hopes and dreams. All along, Spark Fire gives me the passion and the compelling reason to stay the course when I have to renew my hope, often over and over again. I Align with Nature to find ease in the proper timing, according to the cycles and season, and the observed nature of nature. I Find Community in people and things that support both my dreams and my actions toward them. Have Hope will be my guiding star. It's my long-range vision. My "North Star" as James Stark likes to say, it's what I set my compass to as I navigate toward my desired change. Hope is essential for ChangeAbility; it lifts me with inspiration all along the way.

President Barack Obama used the word "hope" as his campaign slogan for his first presidential campaign. As a country, we needed it, we wanted it, we voted it into office. He inspired us to have hope, and he gave voice to our dreams, even if he did not, nor could not, deliver all his campaign promises.

Hope is not the delivery of outcomes. It is the way we set what to reach for.

Even if it took far too many years of struggle for the abolishment of Apartheid, or for the independence of India, or for women's right to vote, or for African-Americans' right to vote, or for the passage of marriage equality, people never gave up hope. Even if it takes yet more years to bring our soldiers home from war, or raise the minimum wage in this country, or to move away from fossil fuels for our energy—hope is the guiding star. It reminds me of what is possible, what I truly desire, and what I will dedicate myself to try to achieve.

> "The very least you can do in your life is to figure out what you hope for. And the most you can do is live inside that hope."
> —Barbara Kingsolver

Hope is a helium balloon. It's a wish lantern sent out into the dark sky of night.

In the face of changing circumstances, trust and faith have sustained confidence and conviction. Hope is more tenuous—not as sure of herself, but she very much wants to be. But in all cases, I must realize my trust, faith, or hope through action.

Hope requires imagination. Or is it that imagination is inspired by hope? Imagination is the creative dance of possibility. What the imagination can conceive and reveal sets the stage for the creation of wondrous, positive, innovative objects and outcomes. However, as John Weeks pointed out to me in a side conversation, our imagination is powerful in *all* directions and can come up with some pretty dark and scary scenarios, and convince us just as much—especially against ourselves. The awful things I have told myself, I would never be so discouraging to another. I can imagine all kinds of reasons why the man I've been dating has stopped calling, or why I got fired off the movie I wrote, or what's going to happen to me if I travel alone in the Middle East. If I have that tendency, I can imagine the worst in all situations. Given that imagination works in all directions, if I can help it, why not cook up good stories to tell myself, rather than bad ones? Why not be hopeful? Chances are none of my stories are actually what is really going on any way, so I might as well tell myself a good one.

So then, if hope inspires imagination, and imagination inspires hope, regardless of the area of life, I want to be able to free my imagination for innovative solutions to come. **Rebecca Mark**'s process of writing through movement seeks to free the imagination from what it already knows.

> ## "What can we imagine that goes out of the narratives that we are so used to? We look at the same old story, the same old story, the same old story, and where can we go that breaks into the frontier of the imagination?"

As she will describe later in this chapter, new stories require new forms. You cannot tell a new story in the old way. It doesn't fit. The old form becomes a tight context that doesn't allow for new movement. Anything that is truly innovative has a new movement and can't fit its old forms. The new story of India's independence had to be won with a new form of non-violent mass protest and support. The new story of how we incarcerate prisoners will not come from the old forms, but from innovative programs of reflection, respect and transformation, like GRIP.

Dreams belong to hope. *What can I dream up? How far can I go?* Whether they are night dreams, daydreams, or hope and dreams, the dream I hold sets my vision for putting change in motion. Possibility, and therefore hope, is only limited by the limitations of the imagination. I can have times when something is "beyond my wildest dreams," something happens that was so much better than I could have ever dreamed up, like the path of my career, the perfect travel adventure, or the love of my life. As well, there are horrible scenarios that far exceed my imagination, like the destruction, torture, and killing being done by ISIS, or the calculated plans of the Nazis to exterminate millions. I can't even imagine some of the cruel nightmare scenarios I see in action-adventure movies, let alone in the news. Who thinks this up? Part of how I Bring Awareness to others is to get them to accept that events beyond their ability to imagine are *actually* taking place: in war, in politics, or in the environment. I need an open imagination in order to expand awareness, my own as well as others.

WAITING

> "And sure enough, even waiting will end…if you can just wait long
> enough."
>
> —William Faulkner

Hope requires waiting. Waiting requires patience. Patience is always easier when it is hopeful. In an earlier chapter I said that Proceed Incrementally will require patience, and that patience wasn't, itself, waiting but a quality of waiting. Have Hope definitely requires waiting, because inherent in hope is that whatever I am hoping for is not happening right now. It is off in a possible future, but it is not now. Even simple gestures like saying "I hope you have a good day" or "I hope you feel better" imply a time that is later than now. So If I hope, I will have to wait. Patience is a quality of waiting that makes my waiting more pleasant, more tolerable, and therefore easier to renew my hope as the waiting drags on. And by waiting, I don't mean you sit idly by—but you do need to let time pass.

> "I heard a preacher say recently that hope is a revolutionary patience;
> let me add that so is being a writer. Hope begins in the dark, the
> stubborn hope that if you just show up and try to do the right thing,
> the dawn will come. You wait and watch and work: you don't give up."
>
> —**Anne Lamott**, *Bird by Bird*

DISAPPOINTMENT

People caution me, "Don't get your hopes up," as if I don't know that there's the possibility that my hopes might not come true. When I have hope, I'm very aware of the alternative. Walking across a suspension bridge over crocodile infested waters, I *hope* I make it, knowing full well I could fall. Or, I *hope* I get that job, knowing full well I am up against ten other candidates and I might not. Here's where imagination can be my friend or foe: I can try to convince myself of either outcome. Some believe that imagining the worst somehow prepares them for disappointment. But does it? I'm not sure I am ever prepared for disappointment. Imagining the worst just puts me in the state of disappointment before I actually need to be. But if I am going to have hope I will have to learn to endure disappointment. It goes with the territory. Disappointment is not the worst thing in the world, especially if I can find hope again, somehow.

I was crazy in love with a man and had high hopes for us. I waited in that hope for a long time. Our timing was off. My hopes were dashed. It happens. I'm flippant in my description now, but I was devastated for a long time. I still have hope that I will find a man I can fully share love with in this lifetime. I've had to make a course correction on my hope, but my hope for love didn't die with the man.

I hoped against hope that my father wouldn't die, when he was suddenly intubated in the ICU from pneumonia and a number of complications. My hopes and my prayers did not bring him back. It was literally beyond my imagination at that time that he could die. As long as he was alive, so was my hope. But, now, I know I can survive, even thrive, beyond the thing that was unimaginable.

I can enter a situation with hope, with trepidation, or with dread. Some people who have mastered the art of detachment enter in neutral. A new job, a new school, a new relationship, a new campaign, my hope for the outcome is my "North Star" even if the hope is to just watch and see what happens.

So many people don't dare to have hope for fear that they will be disappointed. They say, "Why even try?" They feel themselves to be a fool when they held hope and that hope didn't come to pass. "False hopes," is a very embarrassing term. It says, "I'm crazy, I'm making things up, I'm silly and unrealistic." It implies that I had hope, but I had no reason to hope, as if the lack of success was due to my hoping rather than the outcome of the situation. Again, I can talk myself out of having hope. I can tell myself not to have false hope, but then, if there's no hope, I might not even try. Why bother? I've been there. I've missed creating job opportunities and social opportunities because I feared there wasn't much chance. I didn't want to have false hopes, or be seen that way. And I certainly didn't want to be disappointed.

We get kicked around in this life. Some disappointments seem impossible to bear, but even with those we find a way to continue on. Amazingly, people recover from war, financial ruin, lost loves, lost loved ones. We will be marked in this life. Even after we've healed, we will carry our scars—proudly, I hope, like Deena Metzger does. My resiliency keeps me returning for more life and more hope. Clinical psychologist and trauma specialist **Amber Gray** believes we can all restore.

> **Amber Gray**: I believe we're all born with an inherent resiliency. We also have inherent vulnerabilities. I often say that hopefully nobody's lived a life that is entirely made up of traumatic experiences. Lots of people have a lot of them, but I've never met anybody who didn't have some segment of their life that had some beauty, some joy, some connection. We place the traumatic process, or the traumatic memory, in its right place in the timeline of an entire life. That's also part of the restorative process.

Hope is far easier at the beginning than at the end. By the end, or by the middle, I've had to renew hope over and over again. Even if nothing has happened to dissuade my hope, the waiting, alone, can drain hope away. *Will this ever happen?* When I've given up hope that this will ever happen, I despair. Despair is the opposite of hope. Despair is when all hope is gone.

> "The whole thing is quite hopeless, so it's no good worrying about tomorrow. It probably won't come."
> —**J. R. R. Tolkien**, *The Lord of the Rings*

A WISH AND A PRAYER

I make my wish on a wishbone, in a long tunnel, when I throw a coin in a fountain, on "the first star I see tonight." I would say that a wish is a single unit of hope. It's a single request for something I dearly hope for. It always has confused me why I'm supposed to keep these wishes to myself, as if wishes are granted by magic, and not facilitated by the assistance of others. I'm told that if I share my birthday wish as I blow out the candles, it might not come true. If I'm a child wishing for a new bicycle and no one knows, I'm less likely to receive it than if my parents knew and could therefore buy it for me as a gift. If my wish is for an end to war, then the others in the room can share that wish with me. Holding hope seems like a longer run than a single wish. A wish is a gesture, it is a request from whatever powers that be for me to be joined with that which I desire, be it an ice cream, a return to my homeland, or world peace.

Prayer facilitates hope. Prayer is an active participation in focusing on a desired outcome. It is a request, usually of a spiritual nature, to some sense of higher power or order of the universe. Prayer can be for myself, but more often it is on behalf of someone else. The prayer could be for a loved one who is sick or troubled, or for an entire group of people like the survivors of Hurricane Katrina or the earthquake in Nepal. Prayer can also be on behalf of the earth, and the animals and the plants. A prayer that the inherent wisdom of the natural world will prevail. Prayer adds potency and the desire for protection. Many people believe in the power of prayer and have experienced the sensations of well-being when they know people are praying for them. The beneficial effects of prayer on patient outcomes have been demonstrated in scientific studies. Patients who receive the prayers of others heal more quickly and show greater signs of well-being.

Many people work in the field of hope: spiritual leaders, health care practitioners, teachers. Their jobs are to instill hope in others, carry it with others, and to lift people's spirits and light the way. For **Tom Verner** and **Janet Fredericks** of Magicians Without Borders, their intent is to bring hope to some of the most forgotten corners of the world—orphanages and refugee camps in war torn and impoverished countries. Some of the residents have been living there for upwards of twenty years, most of the children have been born into these camps, or left at the orphan homes quite young. Tom is a retired psychologist; Janet is a fine arts painter who draws inspiration from nature and from world travel. Tom has been performing magic for over thirty years. Janet assists the shows and entertains the audiences as the colorful mime, LaFleur. I asked them about how they began their magical journeys around the world.

Tom Verner: Let me say what inspired us to start this. I was traveling to a meeting in Eastern Europe in 2001. Through an amazing set of circumstances, I ended up in the refugee camps in Kosovo. The very first camp I went into, I was introduced to this little girl. She was only six years old. Her name was Fatima. I was told she was going to be my guide that day. I was told that she knew everybody in the camp and everybody knew Fatima. She would help me. She was one of those really bright little kids.

I spoke no Romani, no Serbo-Croatian. She spoke no English. Yet, we really seemed to communicate. It came time to leave. I was talking to some Roma women. Fatima was standing beside me. I said goodbye to the women. I turned to say goodbye to Fatima. She was gone. I said to the Roma women, "Where's

Fatima?" They said, "We thought she was with you." I felt badly that I wasn't going to get to say goodbye to her. I take my magic props over to the car. I look in. There's Fatima, hiding on the floor of the backseat of the car…wanting to run away with the circus. She was a good Roma kid. She took her best shot. It didn't work, but she was smiling, waving us down the road.

We came to a little town called Shutka. It really wasn't a refugee camp, but my UN driver said it was swollen with refugees. He said, "Life is terrible in Shutka. They need some magic in Shutka. Let's do a show for the people of Shutka." We go in. We set up our stuff in the town square. Within a few minutes, there were like 350 people.

The show went well. People dispersed except for one old, wild-looking, Roma woman with a big head wrap, gold teeth, mirrors all over her dress, and a small group of Roma men standing to my left. The woman, she comes up to me and she drops a coin into my hand. Somehow I knew it wasn't a tip. She points to it. She had seen me multiply flowers and sponge balls and all kinds of things. She points to the money and says, "Make more money." I laugh, but she was completely serious.

I take the coin. I put it in my hand. I squeeze it. I open my hand and there's a big chunk of what looks like gold. I offer it to her. She's mildly amused but she says, "No, no. Money. More money." I pull the gold back in my hand and I squeeze it. I open it. There is a fifty dinar Macedonian gold coin, about ten times what she had given me. It's still only eight cents, but she was totally thrilled. I drop it in her hand. She walks away smiling.

Instantly, those two Roma men say, "Make us visas to America." I laugh. I looked at them. They were also completely serious. They had just seen money multiply ten-fold; surely, I could produce a visa out of the air. I told them I didn't, unfortunately, know that trick.

The end of the day came. I'm sitting in this little place in Skopje, Macedonia, and I'm thinking, "This is the first time I've ever been in a refugee camp." LaFleur and I have been in hundreds of refugee camps now, but that was the first time. I didn't realize that the seed of Magicians Without Borders was planted that day.

Two things struck me. First thing I realized was nobody spoke English, I didn't speak their language—but we all spoke magic. I realized the magic I'd been doing for thirty-some years was a universal language. It was amazing. The other thing was, I thought of this Jewish refugee from Hungary, who came to America in the late nineteeth century with his rabbi father, mother, brother, and sister. His name was Erik Weisz. We now know him as Harry Houdini. Erik, Harry Houdini, once said, "Sometimes when I do magic, especially for poor people, it not only amazes and amuses but it sometimes awakens hope that the impossible is possible." I said, "That's what I saw today."

Janet Fredericks: I think there's mystery all around us. It's very mysterious to see somebody make things disappear and then reappear, even if you know it's a trick. That's even better sometimes, that the ball can return or the silk scarf returns. Where was it? How is it that I didn't see where that went to? If he can make it happen, maybe there's hope that some greater power can make something happen.

Tom Verner: Fatima saw magic. She thought maybe I can get out of this camp. Those men from Skopje saw magic. They said, "Maybe we can go to America and realize our hopes and dreams."

Magic is a language. It can inspire hope that the impossible is possible.

THE HARD WORK OF HOPE

For most people, other than magicians, hope does not arrive through magic. Hopeful outcomes arrive through focused action, perseverance, and the confluence of fortuitous factors. **Paul Rogat Loeb** compiled the anthology *The Impossible Will Take a Little While: Perseverance and Hope in Troubled Times*. It is a very hopeful book, filled with tales of trials, errors, disappointment, and triumphs of many activists and leaders we all admire. Paul feels that in order to take action, we have to have a sense of what is possible, and have the sense that our actions do matter. He says the reason most people don't act more for change is because they think their actions don't matter.

And yet, the one so many have taken inspiration from is Václav Havel, the writer, philosopher, dissident, and statesman who became the first elected president of the Czech Republic. Havel held hope, against so much hopelessness, for democracy and Czech independence during Soviet rule, and yet he continued on.

Paul Loeb: Václav Havel, the former Czech president and the leader of their democracy movement, used this phrase, "Hope is not the same thing as optimism. It's not prognostication." It's not saying this is going to turn out as I want. It's this deep-rooted sense that something is possible—which is very different from saying the world is going to end up the way we want it to. I look at that and it's interesting because *The Impossible Will Take a Little While* is an anthology, I had to go through and edit because right there are twenty different essays that were quoting Havel and it's like okay, yeah, I agree. This makes lots of sense, except everybody quoted him five times.

I know one of your earlier guests, you've mentioned, is my good friend, John Weeks, who did this activism on complementary and alternative medicine. The Havel quote is extremely important in his life because sometimes the current goes with you, and sometimes it isn't. You've got to be able to be acting in both cases. You can't just act in easy times. To me, the hope is what carries us, and it's just the sense that our actions matter even in the situations where it seems like were facing setbacks and defeats.

> "Hope is definitely not the same thing as optimism. It is not the conviction that something will turn out well, but the certainty that something makes sense, regardless of how it turns out."
> —**Václav Havel**, former President of the Czech Republic

John Weeks confirms that he has great regard for Havel and for the possibilities of hope.

> **John Weeks**: I've shared with you before that my motto comes from Václav Havel who says that hope is not the same thing as optimism. Hope is not doing something because you believe good will necessarily come of, because in this world working with the medical system, it's hard to be hopeful a lot of the time. Hope, actually, is doing something because you know it's the right thing to do. And what I take from that is that hope is actually a verb. When we're engaged in seeking to make change, then we can have hope that change is possible. It's when we let go of engagement that it is likely to drop in on us.

For men like Havel, and Paul Loeb and John Weeks, and frankly all my guests, hope is a verb. It's an action word. They know that you hold hope out as your ideal and then you work like hell to make it happen. I was in Northern California recently, attending an event in honor of James Stark and this quote by David Orr was mentioned at least three different times. "Hope is a verb with its sleeves rolled up." I believe that says it all. Hope is an expansive dream, but it has to be grounded in hard work.

> "Hope is a verb with its sleeves rolled up."
> —**David Orr**, eco-philosopher and professor

John Weeks reflected to me why he's been able to maintain a hopeful outlook and make important strides working in what some consider to be an overwhelmingly hopeless arena—that of the health care industry.

John Weeks: Hope takes a village. I don't know of a person who works as a solo operator or believes that that's what their job is. To me hope is something that takes place with community.

Where it comes from for me, I think, is from the luck of birth. I came from a family that was an activist family. My parents were involved in things. We grew up believing that was a part of life. They were working as change agents in their ways. The interesting question is: how do you stimulate hope, or the action around hope, in somebody who didn't have the good fortune to have that background? I guess it may be similar to asking, "Can everybody be a creative? Can everybody be an artist? Can everybody be an X, or do you have to be born with the gift?" More than by birth, one is nurtured into activism or engagement.

I was raised into the gift of hope.

Certainly through context you can potentiate hope. That's part of why I like the Václav Havel line so much, it is different than optimism. Optimism is, I think the girl that I just passed in the hallway likes me. It can be this wild arc of the excitement of possibility that's not necessarily very grounded. I think optimism can be this ungrounded kind of idea. What I love in the Havel's line is that hope is a verb.

I really do believe that hope is a by-product of engagement. If you're not engaged, that's where you become the classic arm chair critic because you're sitting back, you're watching the thing, and it does not take much imagination to have a negative take on the universe that we live in and the course of our environment, our relationship between peoples, what's happening with the economy, what's happening with the divisions… It changes with engagement and that's not optimism.

It's really not that I need to be sustained by the belief that the world is going to get better, because I don't know that it will. It's just my world is better when I'm engaged and I'm doing something like this.

There are many times when even my hard work is not going to bring about my desire. Not even all my wishes and prayers will bring about what I hope for. And yet, I continue to work toward my hope. Why?

> "Do not depend on the hope of results. You may have to face the fact that your work will be apparently worthless and even achieve no result at all, if not perhaps results opposite to what you expect. As you get used to this idea, you start more and more to concentrate not on the results, but on the value, the rightness, the truth of the work itself. You gradually struggle less and less for an idea and more and more for specific people. In the end, it is the reality of personal relationship that saves everything."
>
> —**Thomas Merton,** writer and mystic

Jacques Verduin does it for the gesture. He works on behalf of hope because he knows it's the right thing to do. Jacques speaks about his frustrations with the criminal justice system and why he persists, anyway.

Jacques Verduin: Working within the criminal justice system is very taxing because the department is very bureaucratic and it has no management culture. It's unbelievable. No management culture for fifty-something thousand employees. Things are very dysfunctional and everybody knows it, and you've got to work within that. It very frequently happens that you go to work and the place is closed down. They knew ahead of time and they just haven't bothered to tell anybody. There are hundreds of people coming to their groups and they drove there for nothing. That happens on a monthly basis. So either you give up, or you learn to deal with if for the gesture.

Sharon Weil: Speak more about that.

Jacques Verduin: Well, Merton has a beautiful quote on that. You have to be really clear why you do it. If you do it for the results, you sort of screw it because you see people come back [to prison] sometimes. If you take that personally, then you're in the wrong business and you're going to burn out. At some point, it's not that you have to be substantiated by results or people's approval, you do it because you understand that at this point you cannot not do it.

That's what we call learning to do it "for the gesture." You have just taken the stance, and you actually don't know if you're going to be effective or not. You make peace with that because you know it needs to be done, and a lot of things needing to be done involve your showing up no matter what. It's actually very freeing. I didn't start out with this. I had to discover this the hard way.

REFRAMING

> "The difference between hope and despair is a different way of telling stories from the same facts."
>
> —Alain de Botton

One of the effective ways that I can renew hope, or refresh hope, is to reframe my situation, or reframe how I think about my circumstances. Just like how choosing whether I tell myself a good story or a bad story about whether or not I got the job will affect my approach to my next job interview. Changing how I think about a particular task at hand, or a problem I am in, or the nature of a relationship will help me renew my hope. Early-twentieth-century playwright Luigi Pirandello said it in the title of his well-known play, *Right You Are! (If you think you are!)* It's all in how you look at it.

Professional mover and organizer **Amy McEachern** helps her clients give away unwanted possessions they can't seem to let go of by helping them reframe how those items will be used.

Amy McEachern: I help people purge out the stuff that they don't want, or that doesn't reflect who they are anymore, and that's hard for them sometimes. They're like, "Well, this is a perfectly good thing and I don't want to just throw it out," and I have to explain to them, "We're not just throwing it out. We're offering it to people who this type of thing is more relevant for them, now. For instance, women who are trying to come off drugs or get their kids back and they need to set up an apartment full of pots and pans."

Then it shifts, it just changes the relationship between my client and their stuff. Now it becomes something that they're actually contributing out into the world to help other people, as opposed to, "I'm just throwing this perfectly good thing away." Usually that's coming from the voice of a critical parent back there, saying, "Well, honey, you paid good money for that…" Reframe what the process is about, and then they're running around looking for things to help these women that are trying to set up apartments.

Amy also helps clients reframe their emotions and fears around making big life moves.

Amy McEachern: I had an injury as an infant and it caused these night terrors—these horrible, terrifying dreams—and I have sort of battled that my whole life. But what it gave me was an empathy for people who are afraid. People are typically afraid when they're moving because they're going from one place to another in themselves, in the world, whatever. I think people are more afraid of their own feelings around it than they actually are of the new place and the new thing. They know, "I'm not necessarily in physical danger in this new house, but what if I'm not going to like it here? What if I hate it? What if I make that decision and then I'm going to be blamed for something?" Then it gets into this whole sort of swirling. I tell them, "We don't have to be afraid. Let's call it excitement, you know?" I really think that most people are just afraid of being alone in some sort of process and so I try to be the one that walks in and says, "Look, I got this. This is going to be fun. We're going to have a good time here so let's get excited about your new place, and let's get your stuff there, and let's set it up, and make it really cool." Then people relax. "Oh, okay. I forgot that fear is only one of the emotions." It gets up front in the way of everything else if you let it. I just try to put people at ease and help them be excited about their move even if it's for a reason that's painful, like a divorce. Again, it's about reframing.

John Weeks has found that his holistic approach to his own personal health care has reframed his approach to thinking in all problem-solving arenas. John postulates that to be true for all people, and that if someone has a simple "fix it with a pill" approach to their own personal health issues, they will carry that thinking into all other aspects of their lives. In that way, the holistic framework of multiple, interactive causes with multiple, interactive solutions can and has changed people's thinking in general, and has brought about more creative, hopeful solutions in all of life.

John Weeks: I think that the most fundamental lesson that people learn about problem-solving is how they learn to solve the problems of their own health, their own body, their own selves, and how we are taught to do that. We're taught that if you have a problem, there's a simple solution. Take a pill, suppress it, suppress the feeling, try to act as though it's not there—that's a type of problem-solving mind. If we are taught to understand my problem is a function of potentially a whole variety of things and that it's something that I can move on internally, then I'm an agent and was not just taking something from the outside.

My postulate is that the more people who have learned to do this in the context of their own personal health care practice, the more people are sitting in board meetings, in family systems, in team meetings, at school and something comes up, where they'll go in understanding it will be a problem-solving process that's holistic.

That has a different relationship to change and changeability than taking something to suppress the thing, because the holistic thinking, when it's applied well, it's all about engaging the person in an active change. It's a very individualized process, but it's a habit of mind and it's become my habit of mind.

I was disposed toward the value set when I got in, but living with naturopathic integrative thinking, whole-systems thinking, for all these years, I don't have any other way to look at a problem set. It's there when I'm reading the newspaper. It's there when you look at international affairs. It's there whatever the situation. That's the framing, right? I think ultimately, that's one of the great long-term, unquantifiable, gifts of the holistic health and medicine movement is that it's changing multitudes of people's ways of problem-solving—and their families, and their corporations, and their schools. That's a nice spread of fact and that's hopeful.

Amy McEachern's entire helpful career came from a wish and a prayer. She had a hope that she focused on every day for a year, and then was surprised to see how the answer to her prayers actually manifested. Again, it came not from magic, but from awareness and the ability to reframe her own fear into action.

Amy McEachern: I was fighting horrible, horrible nightmares. I was literally emotionally paralyzed at one point, in the early nineties, and I went and meditated every day for a year with a friend and she kept saying, "Set your intention, set your intention, set your intention." We'd meditate on it and my intention was, "Dear God, please, help me not be afraid to make a move. Help me not be afraid to make a move. Help me not be afraid to make a move." I did it for a year. I repeated this mantra, and I repeated it, and repeated it, and then *boom!* The earthquake happened in 1994 in Los Angeles and we got rattled around like rats in a cage, and it was scary.

I was living in your guesthouse and we just pulled it all together and we put stuff back on shelves and somehow in all of putting our little places back together, you said, "Amy, you're like an idiot savant with this and you need to help other people organize and transition." I was like, "Ahh, whatever." So, then you hooked me up with some friend of yours and off we went. And then I just got inundated, overwhelmed, started hiring friends to help me, and I accidentally, suddenly, had an actual company.

Probably five years into it, I had seventeen women working for me and it was this fabulous "hand-holders of the moving industry" kind of thing, and I realized, "Oh my God, I prayed for a year 'Help me not be afraid to make a move' and now I have a moving company? Are you freaking kidding me?" I didn't quite mean it so literally. I wasn't trying to be that literal.

But here's the thing. The answer to that request to the universe, to the higher whatever, that request was answered in the fact that every single day I was walking into people's homes who were standing up and walking into the unknown, and were afraid and were doing it anyway. I got to watch them do it, I got to watch them be okay and that is how I got less afraid to make my own moves in life. Talk about the answer coming in through a back door, you know? I could not have orchestrated that any better. I got referred to somebody else that referred me to here, that referred me to there, that referred me to there, and referred me to eventually the woman that I moved who became my wife. Do you know what I mean?

HOLDING OUT HOPE

Bio-acoustician and naturalist **Michael Stocker** works in some pretty hope-challenged situations—hope-challenged for the oceans and for the animals that live in them. Hope is something that he has to renew constantly, and even when he doesn't have much hope, he continues to work against the increased industrial intrusion into the environment. Michael was talking with me about the oil spill that took place off of the coast of Santa Barbara in May of 2015, spilling over a hundred thousand gallons of oil into the Pacific Ocean, damaging sea birds, sea lions, elephant seals, and destroying habitat along the coast. Michael is currently working to oppose oil and gas exploration off the Atlantic coast because there is so much evidence that these practices are detrimental to the environment.

Michael Stocker: This is a replay. In 1969 we had that oil spill in Santa Barbara, and people didn't like seeing the animals suffering that way. Then the Cuyahoga

River was on fire that year, and Lake Erie was pronounced absolutely dead, as well as the Stringfellow Acid Pits down our way. There's a whole bunch of things that came up in '69, and people finally said, "You know what? We're done with industry getting their way. There's no job this is providing which is good enough that we can live in this poison." I'm hoping that we're on the edge of that again. We could be.

Sharon Weil: Because of what just happened in Santa Barbara?

Michael Stocker: Santa Barbara is an interesting harbinger. It's still getting play, which is good. This Atlantic stuff I've been working on this past year, the old guys are just so convinced they're doing the world a favor and everybody, I mean, 70 percent of the public out there is saying, "You're not doing us a favor." They old guys are saying, "We can give you jobs, we can invest in infrastructure here." The public is saying, "Well, actually, we kind of like it the way it is. We have a nice tourist industry, we have commercial and recreational fishing, and that's fine for us. We don't need to have huge industry."

These industry guys, they just have this cowboy mentality, "We'll save you." I don't want to be saved that way. I don't know what's going to happen because we are on the edge, but they were going to have seismic survey air guns for oil and gas in the water by July. Just to clarify, the Bureau of Ocean Energy Management has decided to open up the Atlantic seaboard for oil and gas prospecting. It's a long, complex story, but there are a lot of us saying, "You know, we don't need to pull any more oil and gas out. We know this stuff's killing us. Let's not do it. Let's not even look for it, because if we look for it, and they find it, they're going to get it—so let's not even look." The people who do the surveys, this could be one of the biggest heyday contracts in the world. Six big companies, but ten companies that are basically proposing surveys. That means they're surveying a lot of areas ten times over. You're magnifying the impact ten times, just so they can have their private information, even though it's our information. It's our commons. The ocean is our commons.

He admits, he gets discouraged. It's hard to hold hope when so much industry is moving so quickly to such harmful effect.

Michael Stocker: These are the things that are testing my ability to continue to have faith. I know the power of creation in nature is so vast, and it is so generous, and it's so humbling, so how can I not have faith in the sun coming up? But my faith in my participation, my faith in somehow being able to affect the positive difference, sometimes gets a little eroded, so I do get discouraged. Conversations sometimes do end up like, "Oh, great. Why did we go there?" Now we all feel invisible.

And, I asked **Janet Fredericks** and **Tom Verner** how they cope with the harsh and dire circumstances they encounter on their journeys to orphanages and refugee camps. I asked them, "How can you bear the heartbreak while you are carrying the messages of hope?"

Janet Fredericks: We go into these places to bring some fun and laughter. Most children still are in touch with that part of themselves. When the kids are laughing and having a good time, we're having a good time. They can forget for a while.

Tom Verner: There really is a lot of sadness. I think one of the things that early on we would talk about with each other was about these folks being isolated in these camps for so many years. These young people, you can just see it in their eyes, they're so bright and talented. Some of the kids we've met in these camps, they're shut off from life, from possibilities. It's day-after-day in the refugee camps. They have so little.

Something that happened in one of the very first camps, which we wouldn't have realized if we hadn't talked to some of the folks afterwards—this man said, "You know? We laugh. We sometimes have a good time in our little separate huts, among our families. But today we laughed, for the first time I can ever remember, as a community." It was really an amazing thing. He said, "You brought us together as a community. We laughed together." That was a wonderful thing that we take for granted. You know?

Janet Fredericks: We do see some pretty difficult things at some of these places, sometimes being in an orphanage and realizing that these children have no parents. They don't really have anybody to hold them. They're, yes, sort of families, but it really makes you think about how much we do have here in this country, how privileged we are. We bring back a sadness with us, sometimes. We find ourselves unexpectedly crying or being agitated for some reason. Then, we realize. "Yeah, we've come back from seeing some pretty amazing stuff." Of course, we have to process it somehow.

Tom Verner: We spend a lot of time when we come back. Last Friday, I spent a couple of hours talking with a group of middle-school kids about refugees. Janet is really good at this, when we talk to middle schoolers or high schoolers about inspiring them to find whatever it is they love. Whether it's soccer, or math, or art, or whatever it is, that they can use that love to make the world a better place by tutoring, or volunteering, or going to hospitals, or traveling with us. Some of them have now traveled with us. I think there are lots of things people can do. Sometimes, they are afraid that these places are so dangerous. Sometimes, they are, but I think it's important to try to do whatever you can, wherever you can do it.

Deena Metzger, author, teacher, and healer, tells a story about how even in grief there is hope. She says we must feel our grief completely, but we can't let it paralyze us. You can let the community help carry your grief whether it's personal grief, or collective grief over what we can't seem to effect, like environmental ruin. "The other part of grief," Deena says, "is that grief has to sit with possibility and hope that you can do something."

Deena Metzger: I was at Hanford Nuclear Reservation in Washington State at the Columbia River. The most polluted toxic site in the United States, one of the ten most polluted toxic sites in the world. It's the place where we created plutonium, and we have not been able to face that we don't know how to clean it up, and so the river is polluted and people are dying of cancer, and the Yakama people whose land was taken to make this are suffering, on and on and on. While I was there, I read an article in *Scientific American* that spoke about the situation and said we don't know how to fix this. They spoke about it in such a language that as I was reading it I became more and more and more depressed because the implication was that only science could clear this, and science didn't know how. The government was lying, and so it was a done deal—we were all doomed.

I had met with some Yakama elders and I did not believe that science was the only way, or that the way science was approaching it was the only way, or that the way the government was going was the way it would always go, and I saw that we were being paralyzed by being told that we had no power.

Sharon Weil: Sure.

Deena Metzger: That's what happened to Native Americans. White people came across this country with their guns, and their poison blankets, and native people felt there was nothing they could do about it. But it is possible that there are other ways that we don't know, and that the spiritual consciousness of other peoples might be a wedge. We don't know. Holding one's grief is essential. Being willing to be absolutely heartbroken—because that's where the heart comes alive—and holding hope and not being undone by what anyone tells you.

Change has to do with magic, and something new coming in. We don't know, some people will call it spirit, some people will call it intuition, some will call it imagination—so who knows what we'll call it, but you have to believe that

that's possible, and you have to believe that you might be part of that—that it could land on you. Not because you're some great brilliant person, but just because it might.

Deena Metzger: So you know my essential attitude in the world is "why not?"

Sharon Weil: I know, I love that.

Deena Metzger: Should we do this? Why not? That's where change comes from.

Sharon Weil: That's right.

Deena Metzger: Give it a shot. Certainly your life is more interesting when you try it. Even if you fail, you can't be a complete failure because in order to do anything you've done so many things. You never know where those are going to go. Random conversation, it's some word you said that went out somewhere.

Sharon Weil: That's so true. We never know how it's affecting people.

Deena Metzger: Or the earth, or the trees, or who's listening.

FREEING THE IMAGINATION

For permaculture designer **Penny Livingston-Stark**, the ultimate reframing for hope would be to write a new story altogether, about who we are on this planet, and how we form a shared intelligence with all other life forms. Perhaps if we saw ourselves differently, in a different creation and evolution story, we would find our deeper connection, and act accordingly.

Penny Livingston-Stark: In many ways I see that we're suffering more of a crisis in consciousness—a spiritual crisis—than anything else. You can go back to so many threads throughout human history and human development that have led us to where we are today. To unravel that would be like trying to untangle a rubber band ball. Almost impossible, it's so inter-tangled. What we need to do, and what many people are talking about doing, is write a new story for who we are as a species on this planet and recognize in a humble way that we have a lot to learn, and that we have a form of intelligence—but it may not necessarily even be the highest form of intelligence.

Writing new stories requires tremendous imagination. Writing hopeful stories depends upon our ability to imagine beyond our present circumstance. We tend to be shaped by the stories we hear, and we repeat old stories over and over again. The old stories can tell us "this is who we are" or "this is where we come from," like the Bible, or the story of Thanksgiving, or stories our grandparents tell us from their childhoods. Or they can be cautionary tales, like Aesop's fables, or the Greek myth of Psyche and Eros, crime dramas, or what our grandparents tell us not to do. Or they can be genre stories, where the plot is basically the same with the same outcome.

The stories of hope that can lift us out of tight places of unmoving change have to be new stories and have new forms, according to writer and professor **Rebecca Mark**. After extensively studying all the classic literary forms of story, Rebecca confirms that the story of something new can't be made of the same substance it is trying to depart from. It just won't fly. I asked her, "Do you feel that new stories require new forms?

> **Rebecca Mark**: Yes. Absolutely. Sometimes the new forms aren't absolutely evident, like somebody's using an old structure, but what they're doing with that structure is so different. Yeah, I don't think you can actually tell something new without changing the container in which you're telling it. In how I work my process, I think I am inventing something new, but I do think it comes from careful awareness of literary traditions. I'm not working in a vacuum. Having read thousands and thousands of pages of literature, the inference is in my ear and my touchstone too.
>
> The moment we talk about shifting the modality of what we're doing, the story itself demands it—so it's simultaneous. What we are saying demands a change or transformation in how we're saying it, and how we're saying it is going to transform what we're saying. They happen simultaneously. While we tend to think of the thought process as some abstract thing, I think of it as directly connected to the impulse that literally just gushed from the imagination: from the brain stem, through the hand, down to the paper so that that gesture—once it's been reconnected—instead of being severed, is reconnected.

What can come forward is change.
It will change the way that you write.
It will change the way that you can think, and it
will change the way that you can
be imaginative.

If I were going to advertise Words and Waves, I would say it was a kick-start for your imagination, or it was a way to literally feed, and nurture, and build your imagination so that it was constantly being nourished in the most positive way. It's super important because—you and I have talked about this before—when the imagination is not nurtured is when we can be controlled by dictatorship. That's when somebody else is doing the imagining. When the number of possibilities has been reduced to two or three, rather than to multiple possibilities. The multiplicity of that awareness will create a kind of freedom. It creates the freedom of imagination, and when the imagination is free, then there's no possibility of dictatorships and control.

Michael Stocker finds his renewal for hope in the renewal of the earth itself. Despite frustration, struggle, and disappointing setbacks, he believes in the magnificence of the ongoing life on this planet. This is where he finds hope.

Michael Stocker: The power of nature is going to be there. There's always going to be life on this planet. Or in the billions of years it will take life to extinguish, a lot of magnificent and wonderful things would have happened. What gives me hope about stepping outside and smelling the daphne is I have to take more of those moments. I feel right now the sense of desperation of trying to preserve stuff, and I really need to get out in nature a little more, go to the beach, or go to mountains, or hang out at a hot spring because that gives me hope.

Magicians Without Borders always leave their audiences with the inspirational message of return, restoration and hope.

Tom Verner: Early on I realized how magic shows are filled with metaphors of hope. You take a piece of rope. You cut it. Clearly, you cut it in half. Then, you put it in your hand and it's all healed and back together again. This is the psychologist in me, I think. On some level, that gets communicated—that the broken can be healed.

Often the way we end the show, I have a long, thin, piece of tissue paper. I talk about their lives. "Imagine this is your life. It was a good life. You had friends, family, work and school. Then, the war came. Or the hurricane came. Or tsunami came and your life fell apart. You lost your friends, family, and work." As I say each of those things, I tear another piece of paper off of the whole piece. I end up with a handful of tattered lives and pieces. I say, "Maybe with hope, courage, imagination and love, your life will come back together again." I try, and it doesn't work.

They really, really want it to come back together. It's really amazing to see these folks looking at my hand as if it really matters. Then, I'll sometimes say, "Oh! I forgot something." I say, "No matter where we go, it seems like the spiritual teachings say our suffering can be like bread. It can make us stronger and more beautiful sometimes." I start eating the pieces of paper.

They all start saying magic words. Out of my mouth, LaFleur will pull a forty-five foot rainbow streamer. All the pieces have come back together again into this beautiful rainbow streamer. People in the camps stand on their feet. They're screaming. After one of the shows we did, this one man who worked for the UN said to us, "You could just feel a wave of hope go through the audience." We try to end each show with that particular bit of magic.

SUMMARY

So, how can principle for change #6 Have Hope inspire the ease and responsiveness of ChangeAbility? Hope gives me the lift and the encouragement to reach for my heart's desire. Hope will give me the glide to navigate the tricky passages in the movement of change. Hope leads the way. When I am hopeful, I feel the possibilities of what can be. One of the basic requirements of ChangeAbility, the ability to make effective and favorable change, is that I Have Hope that favorable outcomes and desired change will happen.

◊ **Hope dreams into being what is possible but not yet formed.**

◊ **Hope is the guiding star; it reminds me of what is possible, what I truly desire, and what I will dedicate myself to try to achieve.**

◊ **Imagination belongs to hope, it's the creative dance of possibility.**

◊   Hope is light; it's etheric and may not be easy to hold on to. Therefore, hope can be difficult to sustain and will need to be renewed with each course correction.

◊   Hope holds the vision, but strategy and action are needed to enact the changes held high by hope. For many, hope is a verb.

◊   If I'm going to have hope, I'm going to have to learn to endure disappointment.

◊   A wish is a single unit of hope. It's a single request for something I dearly desire.

◊   Reframing my thinking renews hope.

◊   Hope requires waiting. Waiting requires patience.

LISTEN DEEPLY

FIND COMMUNIT

BRING AWARENESS

PROCEED L

SPARK FIRE

ALIGN WITH NATURE

HAVE HOPE

SPARK FIRE

Passion, courage, daring, love, life force, Eros, attraction, enthusiasm, zeal, heat, light, energy, vitality, ignite, galvanize

"Rebels and lovers are ignited by the same courageous heart."
—**Sharon Weil**, *Donny and Ursula Save the World*

THIS CHAPTER FOR PRINCIPLE #7 SPARK Fire ought to be the very first one because Spark Fire is where ChangeAbility ignites. Every journey may begin with Bring Awareness, but Spark Fire is what compels me to travel. And Spark Fire is what fuels my desire to stay the course over the rocky road of convoluted change navigations. Passion, courage, zeal, lust, whatever it is that fires me up and gets me going—that's what is needed to carry me through change. Just as actors, when approaching a scene to perform will say, "What's my motivation?" I might ask, "Why am I making this change? Why would I even want to? How can I ever pull it off?!" Spark Fire is my motivation for change. It's also the exclamation mark!

I struggled with what to title this particular principle for change because it had to include courage, passion, power, love, energy, and attraction: the qualities that make for a great swashbuckling movie trailer. In order to respond to change or to initiate it, I absolutely must have a compelling reason. I must have a strong reason why I'm doing this, and why I'm doing this now. When it comes to making change, there are lots of reasons to not want to, and tremendous resistance when I do.

Something ignites me, something draws me in—that's fire. Something sustains me, it keeps me moving forward—that's fire on simmer. Fire dances, it jumps, it spreads, it quickens. It takes on many forms: it can be a roaring blaze, or smoldering embers. It can be heat or light. Throughout human history we have placed fire at the center. We have gathered around the campfire: to tell our stories, to cook together, and to find warmth. Fire is the heart and the hearth of our belonging.

By Spark Fire I mean spark interest. Spark purpose. Spark pleasure. Spark the life force within you in all its expressions. Let it be exciting, let it be juicy, let it galvanize your entire being with your own particular sense of aliveness.

We've all known passionate people in our lives, the ones who get really enthusiastic about their favorite movie, or travel spot, or their wine collection. Or the fiercely devoted way they express their love for their children, or their lover, or their dogs. Or the ones who can get so intense about the causes and injustices they feel strongly about, the wrongs they want to right, or simply *must*. My friend, Fernando, is passionate about camping in the outback of Yosemite. Being there fills him with a quality of aliveness that he finds nowhere else on earth. He will clear his work schedule to make sure he gets there at least three or four times each summer. Another friend, Georgianne, comes the most alive when she is belly dancing. Her moves are gorgeous and playful, and the look on her face when she is dancing conveys sheer delight. Her enthusiasm is absolutely contagious and makes you want to get up and dance with her. Yet another of my friends is compelled to tell stories through documentary films. He always has at least three major projects going at a time, each one fascinating and vitally important to not only to the people in the film, but also to a larger public that can carry the message out into action.

Each of the podcast guests featured in this book has a passion that has directed and sustained their life's work. Each one has had to struggle with obstacles and resistance. Each one has had to show courage and hutzpah in order to let their passion lead. Having a strong Spark Fire seems to be the only way.

"Let all of life be an unfettered howl."

—Vladimir Nabokov

COMPELLING REASON

I don't do *anything* toward change without a compelling reason. I certainly can't sustain any efforts toward change without a compelling reason that keeps reminding me of my purpose. *Why bother? Why make a change unless I have to, or really, really want to?* What compels me to change has to be important, strong, and contain lots of fire; otherwise, I just might not.

In the hierarchy of needs, my survival needs will come first. My motivations toward securing food, water, shelter, and safety will take precedence and demand immediate responsive action depending upon just how hungry, thirsty, or in danger I am. If I have children, loved ones, or pets under my care, my impulse to protect them and provide for them might even take first priority before my own needs. Even if there may be many strategies available to me to secure resources for my basic needs, the urge to resolve these needs will compel me toward action. The urgency of satisfying these needs will benefit from my animating fire in some form: energized activity, fierceness, and courage. I might even have to fight for my life, or for what I need for survival. This fight could be a literal battle or an economic one: competition with others, overcoming the weather conditions, or even fitting into the context of the social order so I can secure what I need and survive.

But, beyond the primacy of my compelling reasons for survival, I would say that the biggest reason I do what I do, and the reason you do what you do, is on behalf of love. Love of another, love of nature, love of people, love of country, love of beauty, love of spirit, love of words, love of food, love of body, love of the process with creating art. Even if I'm fighting, I'm fighting on behalf of what I love.

"The true soldier fights not because he hates what is in front of him, but because he loves what is behind him."
—G. K. Chesterton

You only have to go visit the grey whales with Michael Stocker in the bays of Baja California to understand the appreciation and love he has for these majestic animals and why, therefore, he is willing to devote his life to protecting them. Just to walk along the shore with him as he identifies all the different forms of sea life and their interactions is to know his understanding of the interconnectivity of the ecosystem and why he is so passionate to preserve the intricate balance. His love is his compelling reason, and it sustains him when he has to come up against the actions of the military, the shipping industry, and oil and gas exploration that will damage the habitat of the ocean.

If you were to understand Beth Rosales' connection and gratitude to the community of Filipino immigrants that welcomed her and her family when they first moved to California and how they took care of one another as she was growing up, you would understand why she has such compassion for other immigrant and underserved communities. Her gratitude and her love for people is her passionate, compelling reason for dedicating her life to the service to others.

Amanda Foulger is compelled by her own sense of connection to help others find connection to their inner spirits and the outer worlds. She speaks about how without that compelling reason, without the fire of inspiration, we would not be motivated to face the large global changes facing us today.

Amanda Foulger: You speak about fire. I think about that as inspiration; that's what inspires us. When we're inspired we will change, we will do what we need to do. When we're not, then we don't have what it takes to deal with change on a big level. I think that's what we're facing now. The changes are not teeny ones—they're really big ones. The gravity of what we're dealing with comes home when we get to those moments of truth and recognize… We have those little moments in our personal lives, and then we've got these bigger ones that we've got to deal with, collectively. How the heck are we going to get together collectively to deal with some of those changes?

ATTRACTION

Global political change, personal change, social change, climate change, none of it is simple, and none of it is easy. All of it disrupts my current comfort and the familiarity of my current discomfort. So to get *to* change, and to get *through* change, I'm going to need the fire of a very good reason—and that very good reason is going to be something I'm drawn to. I'm talking about attraction. Whatever it is I'm drawn to is because it makes me feel most alive. I'm attracted because of my interest, its beauty, or because my raging hormones are running the show. Within attraction, there is an Eros—a life force that ignites me to a greater sensation of aliveness—that will lead me to take action on behalf of change. I'm compelled toward more aliveness.

Sometimes my compelling reason comes from my fear. It's from the fear that I will lose what I cherish if I don't take action. The more I love, the more I fear its loss. If fear shuts me down, locks down my body, and clamps down my emotions in a type of paralysis, Spark Fire is what is needed to burn through my fears on behalf of what I care about and what I truly love. The heat will melt the freeze. It's that moment in every action movie climax where the hero or heroine finally gets fired up to go "kick ass" and "take that hill" against the worst of enemies or the most treacherous of obstacles.

DISCIPLINE

I want to bring up here the idea of discipline. You might ask, "What is that word doing in a chapter that's all about flames and Eros and passionate impulse?" I want to reframe the idea of discipline. Discipline is working steadily on behalf of what you love or what you desire, rather than some sort of tedious punishment. The word "discipline" comes from the same root as "disciple," which means pupil or follower. To be disciplined means to be a disciple, and that you are in service to what you are learning, or what you want to dedicate yourself to: I want to lose weight, I want stronger abs in ten days, I want to play the piano, I want to become a soccer star, I want to advance in my career, earn a larger income, save up for a new car. If I want to improve my lot somehow, improve my skill, make a big change, or if I want to get from any here to there, over time, I will need focus and I will need discipline.

Discipline is the incremental, daily strategy for practicing on behalf of what I love or desire in order to reach my goal.

Discipline is not self-denial, rather it is prioritizing on behalf of what I care about most in the larger picture. Discipline is often hard work. However, when I am tired, a bit lazy, or want to give in to a spontaneous impulse that is not consistent with my discipline, then my compelling reason on behalf of my passion, or love, or interest, or goal will carry me through. I may have to remind myself of this *daily* as part of my daily practice, but still, it is the compelling reason that will remain my purpose and goal. My greater health, the seamlessly beautiful music I can play, the winning goal I will score, or the car that will take me where I want to go: these are the reasons I remain in my practice, and in my discipline.

Writing this book required lots of discipline; I was at my desk all day, every day until it was done. But I was energized each day by my interest and curiosity in the subject matter, and the project delighted me with its own sort of intellectual Eros so much so that it carried me through the patches when I couldn't quite find the words or the flow, or when I got tired of sitting for so long in the same chair. Spark Fire carried me through.

For each of my podcast guests, their compelling reason for being involved in the change work that they are, their manifestation of the fire, is their passion. And their passion is what has led each of them to delve deeply into their respective fields for twenty, thirty, forty years, at least. Their discipline has helped them to "stick to it" and achieve all that they have. I imagine that they would each describe their approach to discipline differently, but I guarantee, it is part of their success.

PASSION

"Color is my daylong obsession, joy, and torment."

—Claude Monet

Passion is heat, no question. Passion is urgent, intense, hungry, irresistible. Passionate people are interesting people. They are animated and exciting people. They are often poetic and artistic people, and sometimes they can be a little too much. Who can resist the fires of the passionate lover? Even the passionate lover cannot resist being consumed by the fires of their own passion—to the point of obsession. It's a fine line that crosses passion over into obsession—it's a matter of volume and exclusivity of focus. But without passion, life is pale and a lot less fun. Passion is a driver. Without the passion, I would not be driven to create the beauty in my life, nor take the risks required to create it. My life would seem much more random and arbitrary.

For some people, identifying their passion is obvious and apparent from the day they were born. For others, their passion and what truly inspires their life eludes them. People suffer from not knowing what to do with their lives, or what would give their lives purpose, aliveness, or compelling reason. It's not just the pressing question of "what do I want for my major in college?" but "how can my life serve me and others toward utilizing my greatest gifts?"

Intuitive healer and astrologer **Rachel Lang**, works with many clients who seek her counsel because they are seeking a fuller life and a greater purpose. They are looking for how they can change their lives to fulfill a passion, and how their income and careers can align with that passionate purpose.

> **Rachel Lang**: A lot of people know what they're passionate about and have a difficult time transferring that into "how do I make money?" There are two different answers. First of all, how do you get in touch with that passion and let it lead you? I think that our survival instincts come into play. When we're afraid that we're not going to be able to support ourselves or we're going to lose our friends or our family, then we close those doors.

Rather than looking at your passion as how you're going to support yourself financially—just go into it. Just explore it without expectation.

> What you'll find is it starts with the seed of excitement, and euphoria, and possibility, and that stirs within. The more you engage with that feeling, the bigger it gets. All of a sudden you start connecting to people who are of a like mind, or who are attached to similar interests. Then your world starts expanding. The more your world starts to expand, the more people come into it to facilitate the process of breaking down those fears. It requires an openness, and it requires a letting go—a surrender of the expected outcome.

The passionate filmmaker **Corinne Bourdeau** talks about how her own passions led her to change her career path entirely. From the publisher of *Los Angeles* magazine, to eventually owning her own marketing firm that specializes in social change films, it was her passion that motivated her change, and continued to give her the courage during the uncertain times.

> **Corrine Bourdeau**: Well, it's interesting. It wasn't a straight path. Like so many people, it was a zigzag. What's the Joseph Campbell quote? "You climb up the ladder, and you find out it's against the wrong wall"? I kind of did that. I was publisher of *LA* magazine, a bit of a glamorous job, and that quote came to mind.

I was in my thirties at that time, and it was unfortunately, during 9/11. I had one of those "is this all there is? I really want to be doing more!" moments.

I had been passionate about film, and it was a leap of faith. I'd be lying if I said it wasn't scary because I left this very stable job to start my company. The very first film I worked on was also a risk. It was called *The Celestine Prophecy*, which was based on the best-selling book. It wasn't really a social change film; it was a spiritual film, but I felt spirituality impacts social change. It was a real leap of faith that I did this, but *The Celestine Prophecy* ended up being a great project, I was lucky. It was a great first project; it's how I started my company.

As many in the film business know, when you start one film, it leads to another; people tend to go around in tribes. So, I bounced around to other films, and then one of those films actually led to *The Cove*. *The Cove* was my life. I was so passionate about that film. From there on in, I finally knew what I wanted to do when I grow up, and the ladder was finally against the right wall, so to speak.

Sharon Weil: That's right, because when you are in your passion, you are inspired and that makes you feel alive. When you're in it, things happen! You make things happen, and then more things happen.

Corrine Bourdeau: We're from LA so we can get a little whooey-zooey on this… Energetically, when you're in your passion, or your Eros, that energetic is attracting more of the same. That's a little bit of what they say in *The Secret*. They were like, "Oh, you visualize a bike, and then it shows up," but I don't think that's what it's about. I think when you're in that passion, and in that Eros, and sending out energetically what it is you love to do, more of it comes.

Sharon Weil: You're also spending the time in that quality of Eros, or in that quality of passion. It's not just about future projection, or trying to "I want" in the future, it's as you said, "For these ten minutes, I am actually in the sensation of what I love."

Corrine Bourdeau: And that's so important, that's why I tell people, "Just do it ten or fifteen minutes of every day."

"Passion is something that you don't find; it's something you live into."
—Rachel Lang

In **Rachel Lang**'s experience, we don't have to spark our passions, because they are already residing there within us. Our passions are a part of our unique makeup. What we need to do is uncover our passions and let them flourish. If not, we can suffer personal consequences when we don't live into our passions.

> **Rachel Lang**: It's not even about sparking it as much as it is that the fire is burning already and you can either resist it—try to push it down—or let it out. We've talked in the past about following your pleasure, but it's not just pleasure, it's not just what feels good to me in this moment. Because a lot of times when you're following your passion, you come up with all of your resistance. When you live into your passion, it's not necessarily that life's going to be easy—because in some ways it gets harder, and it gets scarier.
>
> A lot of times when that happens and you feel compelled anyway, then you step into courage in ways that we've seen so many of our leaders do. Martin Luther King Jr., Joan of Arc, all of these leaders for whom following their passion meant a pursuit of justice, a pursuit of something higher. It's not even beyond myself, but something so deeply within myself that it connects to everyone else, and it connects to the whole. When that happens, it's almost like there's a little internal Big Bang and something is created that has a life of its own.
>
> Oftentimes what happens is that there is an event in a person's life that establishes the breaking point—the moment—and I see this a lot of times looking at astrological transits. You can see "oh, this is a moment of courage; there's something that's going to be happening here." Often, someone will come into that person's life and reflect or mirror back for that person either a fear, or a belief, or a reminder like "hey, aren't you supposed to be doing this?" What usually sparks is a kind of an intensity of emotion, a sensation…
>
> For example, I have a client that always wanted to be an actor and she resisted it, resisted it, resisted it. Every time she went to see a play, she would find herself getting really angry at the performers on stage; that anger caused her to resist going to see theater, and resist acting, and she had this anger against actors. But ultimately, the anger, the frustration, that spark of sensation, was an indicator. It was like a sign, like an "aha" moment, like "hey, this is a moment of guidance." The fire of passion lifts up when we have emotions, and when our bodies signal that it's time. We all feel that internal clock, like something's shifting, something's changing. We can feel the stirrings of it and we make choices every single day when those sensations occur. "Am I going to go into this, or am I going to shut it down?"

At some point, following your passion will require courage, when you come up against obstacles and negative reactions, and as Rachel mentioned—when you come up against your own resistance and fear. Then you will galvanize your forces because you care so much.

Claire Hope Cummings has lived a lifetime of courageously following her passion for people and their relationship to the land, and her passion for engaging the passions of others. As an environmental lawyer, Claire represented Native American people in their struggles to preserve the lands of their origin. One of the groups she worked with was at Mount Shasta, California. She no longer works as an attorney, but she is still dedicated to the same people and the same concerns for the land. The two words she would use to describe herself are "passion" and "integrity." I wholeheartedly agree.

Claire Hope Cummings: That's what I do now, I work primarily with land-based traditional people, but I have for forty years.

The people that first invited me up there were called Save Mount Shasta. "Yeah! We're going to save Mount Shasta!" Well, forty years later, I don't know about saving Mount Shasta, but I do know that Mount Shasta saved me, that I have learned so much through that mountain and through the people for whom that mountain is their place of origin. I'm no longer the same person I was when I went up there.

Passion and integrity. Making the commitment to have integrity about engaging with change, to me, is the key because you can't just go in there and stay one step or five steps removed and say, "I'm just going to fiddle with it." That's that technological model that we know doesn't work.

You can't stand off. You can't be indirect. You have to actually be involved, and you have to be committed, and you have to hang in there when it's really, really, really, really, really hard. And when everybody turns against you, and when you don't like it, and you don't have any money, and you get stuck, and everything goes wrong, you stay in.

I used to give these talks at the Public Interest Law Conference and these young lawyers would come up and say, "Oh, how do you do what you do?" I'd start talking about it, and they'd go, "Yeah, but how do you get paid for it?" End of the conversation. It's true for organizations: if you put the grant first, you'll never get the job done. Not to say that money doesn't matter—but being changed, allowing yourself to be changed by the work you do, is part of what you're doing, so choose carefully. Choose carefully with whom you associate and how you engage with it.

When I follow my passion it is a joy, because my actions are most aligned with my heart—and that energizes me. But following my passion is also a risk—and risk is scary. If I jump off the cliff, I might fall. If I fall in love, I might get heartbroken. If I dedicate myself to stopping the Keystone XL Pipeline and it still goes through, I will be terribly disappointed and my heart, my passion, and my motivation might not recover. I could turn cynical or apathetic.

My passions may well lead me, but they can also push me, drag me, and hurl me into places that are unknown and dangerous at different levels. This is where Have Hope is helpful. Hope is the balloon I can hold on to keep me from falling too far or too hard. If I remain tethered to hope, if I can be accompanied by hope, then I can move past the fears my passions might bring to me, or at least lighten my load.

VITALITY

One of the exciting aspects of fire is its energizing quality. My vitality is made up of the surges and simmers of life force energy that can be responsive to what is called for in different situations. Spark Fire's enthusiastic arousal activates my vitality. When I talk about my "energy," I mean my own personal sense of vitality. Within the spectrum that goes from available readiness for activity all the way to fatigue: I talk about having "high energy," "low energy," or "no energy."

The nature of Spark Fire is to heat it up! It's the elemental nature of fire itself. So depending upon how much I move my body, play with my breath, get excited, get angry, dance, sing, run fast, or hop all around, that will activate my personal energy, by generating more body heat. Building heat is how I gain momentum. As a dancer, I know I have a better performance when my muscles are warmed up. Or, as an athlete, I know that my bike moves faster and the ride is easier when I build up the speed and momentum. The same is true metaphorically. When I activate, animate, and increase my vitality, or when I vitalize *activities* such as accelerating a marketing campaign for my book, or calling a bunch of my friends to a party in order to be more social, or gathering thousands together for a march, I have more sustained power and effectiveness out there in the world. More activity will start to happen in response to my activation.

My dear friend Ann Sheree, a deeply dedicated practitioner of yoga, meditation, and felt presence, often talks to me about vitality. When I'm about to invest myself in some activity that might be time consuming, she will ask me, "Is that the best use of your vitality?" It's another way of saying, "Is that really your priority?" I like it phrased in regard to the use of personal energy. Whether or not there is endless availability of energy in the universe, as a human in a body that is over fifty years old, there is a limit to my time and energy on any given day.

When I talk of the use of my vitality, I'm not just talking about my physical energetic availability, but also about how I want to be *spending* my time. I have to ask myself if this is a good use of my time when I go around town shopping at four stores to find just the right party favor for my daughter's party. Could I be happy with the favors I found at the first store and then use the time I saved in a way that is more essentially important to me? Or shopping online could save me even more time and travel.

But how I use my vitality and time will and *should* depend upon my priorities. I love going to the Sunday farmer's market in my neighborhood, even though I have to get up very early in the morning to go, and it takes more time to shop there. I love the array of fresh produce—it helps us eat more healthily at home, and it supports local farmers. So, it is the best use of my vitality because it serves my priorities. If I ask myself the question, "Is this really the best way for me to be spending my time and energy?" often my answer will be "no." Of course, if I'm asking at all, it means I already have a question. However, if I were immersed in the priorities of my passion, the answer would most likely be yes.

At no time was the question about the use of vitality more clear than when I had young children. Because children, especially young ones, have their own needs and schedule demands of feeding, and napping, and needing to be engaged and supervised that take up most of the day. Anything else you might want to do has to fit into the limited time windows between these activities. You learn very quickly to prioritize and to multitask, but you do see very clearly where your vitality goes, where it needs to go, and where it simply can't go.

If you don't have children, you could replace that centerpiece example with a demanding job, or athletic training, or a relationship. Where do you want your vitality to go in the moment and the hours of your day? Toward your passion and toward what gives you the most pleasure. When I'm in sensations of pleasure, I'm vitalized. I'm happy. I'm feeling no resistance—which in and of itself is vitalizing, because my energy is not tied up in that tug.

When I'm seeking to change how I use my vitality toward something more closely aligned with my passion and pleasure, that is when I'll need to heat my passion up, in order to motivate myself. Like Corinne Bourdeau says, I can start with just ten minutes a day. And best if it's ten minutes of good vitality, and not at the very end of the day when I am already exhausted from having used up most of my vitality, and ready to shut off the lights. When my vitality is activated, I'm already in a more pleasurable state of flow and excitement. Leaning toward pleasure is always a helpful state.

PLEASURE

"Pleasure in the job puts perfection in the work."

—Aristotle

When I smile, it changes my whole physiology. When I act on behalf of someone I love, it makes me happy. When I'm in the sensations of pleasure, when something feels good, my body softens and I relax. The sensations of pleasure come through all the portals of my senses: pretty music, delicious food, fragrant smells, beautiful vistas, or the feel of silk against my skin. Animating Spark Fire isn't just about animating my passion, it's about animating what feels good to me and letting that lead my interest.

It is a radical idea to be led by the pleasure principle, rather than to be led by the avoidance of pain. There are so many cultural taboos around pleasure and sexuality that translate to taboos about simply pursuing things that feel good.

Even activists can be intensely impassioned for a cause, but not allow pleasure in their pursuit. This can be compounded if their motivation comes from fear and the need to fight: I am fighting cancer, fighting the Keystone Pipeline, fighting the takeover by the Tea Party—or the Tea Party is fighting the damn liberals. The grave seriousness of the issues can override any possibility for something that feels good. Unless I get pleasure out of the fight itself, its more likely that my fight is being fueled by fear and not by pleasure. If those fights were on behalf of pleasure, then they would be framed differently: I am working on behalf of life, I am working for the balance of the ecology, or I am promoting freedom because I love how freedom feels. Reframing my intent in relation to the pursuit of pleasure on behalf of what I love is a radical and enjoyable shift.

Camille Maurine teaches women how to begin to discover the power of their innate feminine embodiment by first contacting the sensations of what feels good. Camille authored the book *Meditation Secrets for Women* with her husband, Dr. Lorin Roche. She also teaches courses worldwide using these principles. She tells us that when we open to what feels good it's a very different and much more pleasurable orientation.

Camille Maurine: Apropos of pleasure, a subtitle of *Meditation Secrets for Women*, is *Discovering Your Passion, Pleasure, and Inner Peace*—so it's very helpful to actually start with things that are pleasurable. To look around inside the world of sensation and the senses, how they operate in the outer world can also lead us into sensing our deeper sensorium in the inner world—beginning to come home to our own sensuality that way.

Everybody has something that is pleasurable, but it may go unrecognized.

They're very simple things like how the breath expresses itself. Every exhalation that we're releasing out is an expression, it's part of that dance. So sometimes working with the breath is a good doorway. Playing with the breath, playing with the changing of the mouth. Having fun. Starting to open new territory. It's about the path of intimacy and the path of engagement.

As Camille and Lorin articulate in their book, a woman's practice is by necessity different from traditional meditation practices that were designed so many years ago, not only just for men, but for monks. A woman's meditation and embodiment practice is based on feeling intimate engagement with her own sensory world.

Camille Maurine: As women, we are so empathic and tuned in to the world around us— taking care of everything and everybody—that there are things that we actually require in our inner practices that can support our woman's way of being: all of our energies, all of our biological rhythms, our hormonal rhythms, our emotional fluidity, the intensity actually of being alive.

The intensity of loving—whether it's our kitty-cat, our child, our lover, or our friends who may be taking their last breath on this planet—to be engaged and intimate is intense. So much moves through us. The twelve secrets in *Meditation Secrets for Women* are to give us ways of meeting ourselves on every level—no matter what is going on—and embracing whatever it is that comes up: thoughts, feelings, sensations, energies, surges of what we call Eros—the life force.

How can I allow, embrace, celebrate, and creatively move with all these energies that are life and love moving through me?

In working with many thousands of women, by now I know those energies can move and transform. They give some gift of energy, and inspiration, and connection, and again, intimacy, with life itself—and with nature, and with the cosmos in which we are living and moving and having our being.

Camille and I spoke about Eros in the way we both understand and work with it. Eros is the life force. It is an attractive principle of aliveness that has a variety of expressions. Most often people associate Eros with sexual energy, and only with sexual energy. To us, Eros has so many other expressions, for the surging life force animates everything, including all of Nature.

Sharon Weil: You've mentioned a few times the life force, the Eros, as being part of passion or being part of enlivening. There's nobody that I would like to talk about Eros more than with you because we both understand it in a very similar way. In my book *Donny and Ursula Save the World*, the whole playful premise of the book is that it's Eros that motivates all human behavior and that, really, it's the pursuit of pleasure that drives us. In the case of the book, it's playfully talking about sex and lust as being the motivators for all these characters' actions, but really, you and I know that Eros is something much more generalized and much,

much larger. It is the life force. It's the enlivening principle that takes on many different expressions, sex being only one of them. Other expressions are passion, beauty, fierceness; all of these things that are enlivened by it.

Camille Maurine: Eros can be seen as that primary relatedness and communion with life, with each other, and as you said, with the beauty of nature. We can look at a gorgeous sunset and there's that awe and wonder, and that gasp. It's a natural state, like a spontaneous meditative state right there where we're touched. We're moved through our senses. And in that moment, we are completely engaged with that experience.

Again, for my own journey, to keep inviting that quality into my embodied experience is a practice—to keep dilating my kinesthetic awareness to be able to feel, and embrace, and enjoy that primary movement within me. It's a practice, because as we all know, most of us have been socialized, and conditioned, or perhaps there's been abuse or something that has shut down those circuits. So that's where that great tenderness comes in, in the great healing touch of our own compassion for that little one inside of us. We just want to keep being able to soften to that touch of life that is always right here. That current of movement, and breath, and life force that is always right here informing us, literally informing us all the time. We don't have to make ourselves do anything. It's more about a recognizing, celebrating, and being willing to gently, organically open to that flow more and more.

Sharon Weil: You're describing the metaphor of flow in talking about this life force. There's also the metaphor of charge, like electrical charge. An activation principle that activates us and actually brings a fire in, right?

Camille Maurine: The heart is often characterized as a fire, a flame—like the flame of the heart—and I think that's what they're talking about, that fire of our own. It is fiery, and it can feel aggressive, and it can feel like we're afraid that we're going to go out of control. But I absolutely agree, it's that surge, that charge, that intensity, that I had to get used to, actually—and we keep getting used to more and more of it.

It shows up in sexuality for sure, and it also shows up in our creativity, and it shows up in simply inhabiting ourselves and having the right to exist and claim this breath and this body. This is my body. This is my breath. This is my life. That can burn through a lot of illusions, a lot of false constrictions, what I call "the shrink wrap." You know, where you can barely breathe inside of the old habits. In claiming that it can be enormously liberating.

I think about Passion and Eros as being the fire that can burn through fear.

Rachel Lang also spoke about the creative, enlivening power of Eros. Rachel has felt that aliveness when she was immersed in the study of Astrology. That feeling quality gave her abundant energy for the pursuit of her studies, even in the midst of other work obligations.

Rachel Lang: The power of Eros is that enlivening, creative force, that passion, that inspires us to do things, to confront our fears, to come up against our fears. I think that Eros doesn't just have to be a sexual impulse. It can be an unknown, unseen force that propels you forward. That's kind of how my journey has been. It's been propelled forward by this passion. Astrology was the one thing that I could study until three o'clock in the morning and not be tired. I couldn't wait to read more. I have hundreds of books about it. I couldn't wait to study, to get classes. I guess you could say that I had sort of an "Eros awakening" that led me into this path. Just like Ursula in your book, she had political and legal restraints, but she kept moving forward. She kept feeling this pull to be brave. Love was part of that—and her passion for the mushrooms, and for seeds, and for the environment was all part of that. That creative force has always been pulling me. I did choose at times to ignore it and things in my life started falling apart. I started getting sick. I started having relationship troubles. Then, when I followed it, doors would open. That doesn't mean that it was easy, it just means that I felt more alive.

Harvey Ruderian, biodynamic cranial sacral practitioner and structural bodyworker, finds connection with his clients, and with others, through what he is also calling "the power of the erotic"—a deep energetic connection that is at the heart of healing.

Sharon Weil: One of my passions and revelations about this life is that the body is such a precious and multifaceted event, and that many people seek spirituality, they seek transcendence by trying to go up and out of the body into more etheric realms. What I know—what you know—what we work with is that by going into the body, into the tissue, into the breath of what this human body is also takes you way out into this place of deep, deep connection with everything.

Harvey Ruderian: This is actual pure tantric healing, really, because it's that piece that's the sensual, not the sexual. I say sensual meaning it's all of the senses, integrating and allowing the power of the erotic, because what is the erotic, what is that organ energy but the power of the earth energy coming through and meeting the divine—allowing the two to come together as one Eros, the divine Eros.

That piece is the alchemy around which you meet somebody at that deep place, heart to heart, the heart of listening. That is another piece of what happens when I sit with my hands on someone and literally feel them, and I'm feeling that change take place. They go, "Oh, my gosh. My pelvis just let go. My shoulder let go through the whole body."

The sensations of Eros are the sensations of Spark Fire. I want to lean in toward the flame. I'm attracted, interested, engaged with people and things that are full of vital life force. That fullness inspires me to not only flow with the movement of change, but to dance with it, and be very playful.

PLAY

There is little that is more pleasurable than play. Or freeing. Or creative. The free and inventive exploration of play has a fire-like quality to it. It dances around. It often elicits laughter in the players. Surges of life force, surges of spontaneity are folded into the game plan. The ability to play is a form of inquiry, asking of your play partners, "What next? What after that? Now what?" So much discovery, learning and change can come through play. I've watched children learning to socialize first through parallel play, then through more interactive play. I've watched dogs, cats, and sea lions play as a way to establish social order, learn to feed, and learn how to cooperate.

Jackie Welch Schlicher is all about play. A master at improvisation performance, she is highly attuned to the cues and nuances of play. She values the discovery aspect of play in all the art forms she participates with. She still considers herself new to ceramics and refers to herself as a "puppy potter." She calls herself that, rather than a "baby potter," because of the playfulness of pups.

Jackie Welch Schlicher: I'm a puppy. That's kind of where I am. I do love to watch children who are in that play, creatively, of being so connected to whatever is right in front of them. They may even have a smile on their face as they're trying to figure out which crayons to use, which paintbrush to pick up. It's that place of curiosity and exploration, and a willingness to just cook something in front of yourself to make that bottle, make that house, make that blue doll—whatever the thing is. Just be willing to put yourself out there because that's what the world is for, to put ourselves out there to connect with others.

COURAGE

> "Life shrinks or expands in proportion to one's courage."
>
> —Anaïs Nin

The word "courage" comes from the Latin root *cor*, which means heart. To have courage means to have heart, for that's where courage is centered. Don't you feel your heart pounding when it's time to take a brave action? Don't you feel your heart warm when your brave act is well received? Physical courage and moral courage belong to Spark Fire, for the demands of passion, as well as the demands of change, require it. Change often comes with fear. Courage is not the absence of fear, but taking action in spite of it. Courage is to be brave in the face of fear and to take action in the face of change. Sometimes the courage is simply to face what the change is, the willingness to see the change and to accept it. Whether it's changing schools when you are a kid, or changing jobs, changing towns, changing mates, changing destructive habits, changing the way you view something, or changing the policies of the government, they all require that we overcome our fears and act anyway. Whatever fire I need to animate in order to overcome my fears, that fire can give my heart the courage to allow myself the changes.

> "I learned that courage was not the absence of fear, but the triumph over it. The brave man is not he who does not feel afraid, but he who conquers that fear."
>
> —Nelson Mandela

Then there are those who have the courage of their convictions. People who will make personal sacrifices and face known danger in order to stand for what they know is right. I admire war heroes, firefighters, emergency first responders, people whose job it is to face danger in order to protect others. I marvel at social movement leaders who face tremendous opposition and risk. I applaud the whistleblowers who show enormous courage to expose the illegal or dangerous actions of industry and even the government: Karen

Silkwood, Erin Brockovich, Daniel Ellsberg, Edward Snowden, and so many others who knowingly have risked their lives and their way of life in order to expose the truth of what they know.

It was my admiration for the bravery of activists that set me on my journey to write *Donny and Ursula Save the World*, and then to interview some of my own personal heroes on the *Passing 4 Normal Podcast*. I wanted to learn from them how they were able to do what they have done. How could they be so brave?

Deena Metzger says she wasn't always so brave and outspoken. As a young teacher, she had not yet found the voice that she now uses on behalf of so many others. She told me the story of standing up at the rally that was in protest of her dismissal from her teaching position at a community college for reading one of her own poems in class that was considered inappropriate. This was the beginning of her life of speaking up and speaking out.

Deena Metzger: I did have a difficult time, as I think you know, when I was fired in 1969 from a tenured teaching position in a community college for teaching a poem that I had written. Then, I was courageous when I decided that I would go to court and fight for academic freedom and for the rightness of the lesson that I had given. I remember the moment when I walked up to the podium. There was a big rally in the gymnasium on my behalf. There were two thousand people there, and I had been a very, very shy teacher. Very shy.

Sharon Weil: Hard to imagine, but okay.

Deena Metzger: When I walked into the classroom for the first time, I said to myself, "Deena, you'd better write your name on the board right now, because if you don't do it now you will never have the courage to do it." My hands were shaking. When this occurred after my third year of teaching, and I was tenured, and there was the rally, and it was my turn to speak, and as I walked to the podium I said to myself, "Whatever happens now will change your life. If this goes well, your life will be changed, and if it doesn't, it'll be another path." Fortunately, or unfortunately, it was very successful, and my life changed. Then it was clear. Maybe all of us have the opportunity to come onto the Earth to be born in order to make a change, in order to bring benefit. I think we all have that opportunity. For whatever reason it was, and remains, an obsession for me. I really love this planet, and I love all the creatures, and so I live on their behalf because there's no difference between living on their behalf and living on my behalf. That's the important thing.

I say, find your voice. Don't listen to how it's supposed to be. What's your voice? What is the story you must tell? What's the story that's been given to you? What are the ways that you know you must speak this and have the courage to enact your soul in the world?

For **Claire Hope Cummings**, standing with the courage of her convictions meant deeply researching the science and growing technology of the genetic modification of seeds. Her important book on GMO technology, *Uncertain Peril: Genetic Engineering and the Future of Seeds*, not only exposed readers to the dangers of genetically manipulated food combined with the overuse of pesticides and herbicides, but she herself had to face the grave horrors of how deep and wide the biotechnology has already spread.

Claire Hope Cummings: A lot of people so believe that technology is going to solve their problems. That's what's driving this GMO thing, that's what driving a lot of these worse uses of fossil fuels and industry—it's that industrial model of a better life. They believe in it and, in their minds, they know that they'll be saved. It's sort of like the rapture, right? They're enraptured with technology. Yet, I don't think it's proven itself out if you take the bigger picture of civilization. Those that have relied on technology drove themselves into the ground, and the ones that were like traditional people managed, and are still around. They're still right around us, still trying to preserve their ways.

Before I wrote my book on GMOs, I had to deal with the ravages of biotechnology on the natural world. I mean, it's a horror and I was hoping at the time we could stop the patenting of life and stop the manipulation of life, and it's gone beyond anything. The worst horror I can imagine is already here, the synthetic biology, the geo-engineering, and the plantation of GMO trees spreading pollen—GM pollen for thousands of miles. I mean, the horrors are here. So do I feel that? You bet.

So one day, I have a friend, part of my support system, and I was going on and on and ready to quit. I say, "Let's just go party. It's over, forget it." She said, "You know, Claire, if you had somebody you really loved and they were dying, you'd sit by their bed and hold their hand, and offer palliative care and do what you could. You would not go party." That's the right response.

Things are really dire, right? But that not only means its not time to give up; it's time to sign up.

Permaculture designer, **Penny Livingston-Stark** courageously challenges the ravaging of the natural world, as Claire refers to it. Penny calls upon our courage to implement the natural solutions we already have. She calls upon our courage to change.

Penny Livingston-Stark: The solutions, like I said are there.

Sharon Weil: The solutions are there and it sounds like what you're saying is that the biggest solution is to be connected to nature, and to find our place in nature as it works with all the other creatures, and beings, and plants.

Penny Livingston-Stark: Which also leads us to being connected to ourselves, and being connected to our families, and to our neighbors, and to other human beings, and to be respectful of all of creation. To honor ourselves the same way we honor everything else we love. It's an inner landscape that we also have to cultivate in order to shift our relationship to our world. It's odd but this appears to be the reason why we're not actually shifting and healing the planet, because without the bio-systems that are on this Earth with clean water, clean air, biodiversity, with that interconnection we've been talking about, it'll be very difficult for us to survive. Our resiliency is completely dependent on the resiliency of the Earth. If we compromise that resiliency, we're compromising our own resiliency.

Time for us to wake up and see what's going on, really have the courage to look around and have the courage to change.

Sharon Weil: The courage to quit.

Penny Livingston-Stark: It's a courageous act and it's an act of trust. We have to also trust in the Earth, and in each other.

SUMMARY

So how can principle for change #7 Spark Fire increase the ease and responsiveness of ChangeAbility? Spark Fire brings motivation and compelling reason to my navigation of change, and Spark Fire sustains my efforts, by sustaining my purpose. The quickening heat of fire has many expressions: love, Eros, vitality, courage, and play. The bright light of fire can bring illumination so that I can proceed more clearly and with eyes open. Both the heat and the light of fire are attractive and draw me close for warmth and interest. Who is not fascinated by the dancing flames of fire? Fire shape-shifts rapidly, and quickens the movement of change.

◊   Fire cranks up the heat through passion, love, vitality, Eros, and courage.

◊   I will need a compelling reason in order to go on the challenging and unknown journey of change.

◊   When I take action toward change, it is on behalf of whom or what I love. Even when I have to fight against something, it's because of what I value and hold dear.

◊   Passion has many expressions, and will pull my interest towards what I love.

◊   Pursing passion will involve risk, but when I am aligned with my passion, I feel energized and alive.

◊   Passion is the fire that can burn through fear and resistance.

◊   Whether my vitality is high or low, understanding the best use of my vitality will help me conserve and direct my efforts, allowing me to be more effective and energized.

◊   Discipline comes from the same word as disciple and means to be in service. My discipline is my dedication to what I want to achieve, and is larger than the annoying task at hand.

◊   Pleasure feels better than pain. Make the pursuit of pleasure your guide.

◊   Nothing is more pleasureable than play. Play helps me delightfully dance through change.

◊   Courage is the fire of the heart. Love inspires courage; acting on behalf of what I love requires courage.

◊   Courage is not the absence of fear, but the willingness to act in spite of it.

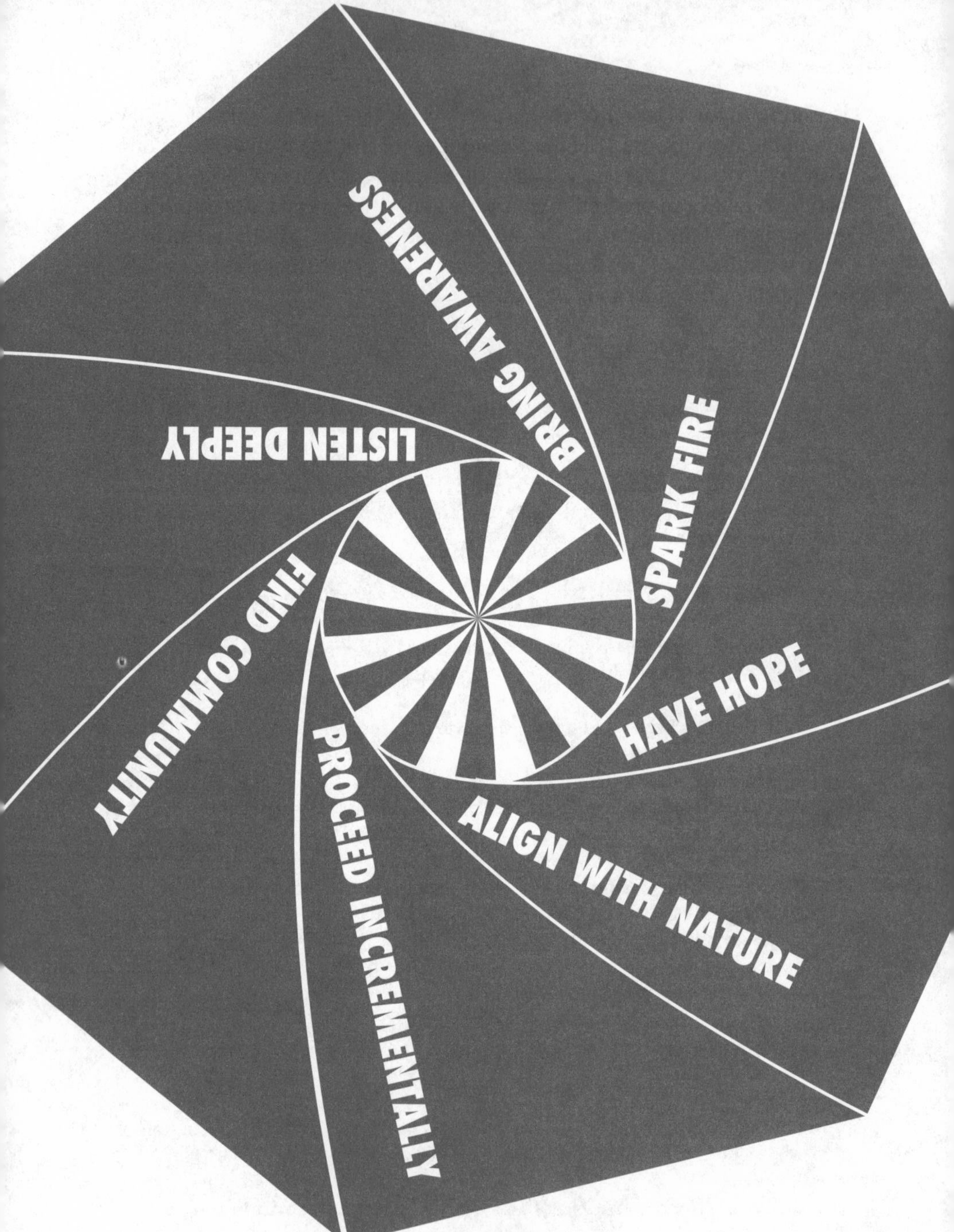

BRING AWARENESS
SPARK FIRE
HAVE HOPE
ALIGN WITH NATURE
PROCEED INCREMENTALLY
FIND COMMUNITY
LISTEN DEEPLY

PUTTING THE CONSTELLATION OF CHANGE TOGETHER

S O, MY FRIENDS, THERE YOU HAVE it, ChangeAbility, the template for navigating the full spectrum of change—in one book. From the most personal and intimate to the most complex and public social matters, it seems we are always responding to change after change after change. Sometimes we respond with great facility, sometimes not so facile—avoiding, denying, and pushing change away. It is my sincere hope that my guests and I have helped you slow down and isolate the different navigations, directions, and principles for change so that you can better understand the changes you are in, and then respond to them with more flexibility, fluidity, resourcefulness, good humor, and a sense of hopeful possibility. If not, please go back and read the book again!

In fact, if you are the sort who likes to read the end of the book first (and just did) then you can glean all the book's nuggets of truth right here in this final summary chapter. You'll have saved yourself the time of reading through the entire book, time that you can now apply to considering the nature of change in your own life and how you now want to respond. Of course, you will have missed out on all the luscious experience-earned wisdom from the innovative and diverse change-makers featured here, so you'll want to go back to the beginning, too. Regardless, this summary will give you a more condensed version of our discussions and conclusions about the nature of change, and how best to meet it.

Each reader will come away with something that is personally relevant to him or her. Whether it's a book, a film, a class lecture or a conversation with a friend, we take away the essential concepts or images that we most relate to and that have impacted us the most. The rest of the content might fall away over time, but there will always be a few things that we remember, and that will remain influential. So I am listing the main ideas of the book here so that you can pick and choose which ones you want to take away with you and treasure.

Keeping in mind that ChangeAbility is an interconnected interplay of four navigations, four directions, and seven principles, here is what we've said:

THE NATURE OF CHANGE

CHANGE
- ChangeAbility is the ability to effectively navigate change.
- Change is happening all the time. (We are never not changing.)
- I am either experiencing the flow of the movement of change, or my resistance to it.
- Change is disruptive and disorienting, whether the change is welcome or not.
- Navigating change is the new stability.
- Navigating change can be complex, messy, stressful, and therefore I can use all the help I can get.
- It is very helpful to locate the nature of the change I am in.

THE NAVIGATIONS AND DIRECTIONS OF CHANGE
- I DON'T KNOW! (Anything.)
- Given that I don't know anything, when I am making up stories about the future, why not make it a good story instead of a scary one?
- The Four Navigations of Change are Initiating, Inspiring, Adapting, and Restoration. (Restoration is the Fourth Navigation.)
- Change occurs on a continuum and does not move in a straight line. Change evolves and unfolds, meanders and spirals, and like all nature, moves in waves.
- The movement of change moves incrementally from breath to breath and moment to moment, allowing for course correction along the way.
- We utilize the constructs of time and space, and therefore experience the directions of change as: internal/external and fast/slow.

THE PRINCIPLES FOR CHANGE

- The Seven Principles for Change Are: Bring Awareness, Listen Deeply, Find Community, Proceed Incrementally, Align with Nature, Have Hope, and Spark Fire.
- The Seven Principles for Change are interactive and interdependent, but you can look at them separately and use them for support in times of change.

WHAT STOPS CHANGE?

- Attachment to how things are right now is what delays personal or social change.
- Resistance, anxiety and fear impede the movement of change—and can drag it to a halt.
- All fear is the fear of death. (Any ending can be experienced as a death.)
- Life, death, and renewal make up the cycle of existence. Only by embracing the inevitability of death can I flow more easily in the movement of new life.
- Loss is an inevitable part of change.
- Sometimes you have to have a good cry and let waves of grief wash over you. Grieving loss is essential for opening to the next movements of possibility.
- A large part of navigating change is managing disappointment.
- We cannot protect ourselves from disappointment and still live a fully engaged life.
- Make mistakes. Failure gives me feedback for course correction, and guides me what not to do next time.
- A daily practice like meditation, exercise, spiritual contemplation, or studying nature is a way of gaining a larger perspective and helps move emotion and fixation.
- Individual change takes place within a context. That context can either be fixed or flexible, but it contributes or inhibits one's ability to make a change. The context surrounding the change needs to have enough room for the play of change to occur, and it cannot be so tight as to choke off emerging change.
- A context that is too tight becomes a closed system and loops upon itself, gradually losing coherence and overall health.

- Community is a context.
- The thoughts, feelings, and beliefs I hold create a context for what change will be possible.

HEALING

- Healing restores to wholeness that which has been injured or fragmented.
- Healing is essential for lasting change.
- Isolation is at the heart of all disease, therefore healing requires community and the support of others.
- Whenever my survival circuits are engaged with the need for food, shelter, safety, belonging, or reproduction, they will take priority.
- Trauma is defined as "too much, too fast." Shock is a natural body response to sudden or traumatic change.

MOVING WITH CHANGE

BRING AWARENESS

- Every journey towards change begins with awareness.
- Awareness, like change, is all that we are.
- Awareness can be cultivated internally, or directed outwardly toward others.
- We often gain awareness through a baseline comparison of now and next.
- Information, by itself, is not enough to motivate change.
- Direct first-order experience is the most effective way to know what you know.

LISTEN DEEPLY

- Everything in my environment is offering me feedback, if I will only listen.
- The practice of deep listening is the practice of inquiry, without assumption or judgment.
- Recognizing patterns is a good way to assess the terrain of any given situation or problem, and an effective way to navigate change.
- An important part of ChangeAbility navigation is the recognition of the need for small course corrections on the path of change. Listening deeply is how I determine which corrections to make.

FIND COMMUNITY

- Get help for everything you do! Find support and companionship in all areas of life.
- Socially we are pack or herd animals with an innate need for belonging.
- Separation from community creates isolation. Isolation is the source of most physical, emotional, and spiritual disease.
- There are many ways to gather community and form community.
- Collaboration, working together for mutual benefit, is a good use of community.
- Celebrate differences. Look for creative ways to resolve conflict. The best methods involve inquiry and listening, rather than operating from assumptions.

PROCEED INCREMENTALLY

- Change moves incrementally from breath to breath and moment to moment. When I break up the larger picture into smaller moments, events, or increments, change navigation becomes more manageable.
- We navigate change through course correction, evaluating each step as we go through awareness and deep listening—like stepping across rocks in a stream. By using each increment as a baseline, I can evaluate where I have been and where I want to be next.
- Proceed Incrementally represents the most effective strategy for navigating change because it allows for informed course correction.
- Ripple out is an effective movement for incremental change. It's how something can begin small and grow larger, affecting a larger and larger territory or number of people.
- The movement of change is driven by any number of rhythms.
- Patience is necessary for incremental change.
- Patience is not waiting; it is a quality of waiting.

ALIGN WITH NATURE

- An important aspect of ChangeAbility is resilience. The ability to respond, refresh, renew, and restore is essential to my incremental course correction, and my ability to thrive.
- The nature of Nature is change.
- Nature holds the gift of renewal.

- When I align with how nature does it, I am imitating survival and cooperation strategies that, in some cases, have existed for millions of years.
- When I align with the natural rhythms of cycles, seasons, or with the natural elements, my body and mind are more at ease and feel supported. Change can feel in its proper timing.

HAVE HOPE

- Hope dreams into being what is possible but not yet formed.
- Imagination belongs to hope.
- Hope holds the vision, but strategy and action are needed to enact the changes held high by hope.
- Hope is light; it's etheric and may not be easy to hold on to. Therefore, hope can be difficult to sustain and will need to be renewed with each course correction.
- Reframing is a strategy of hope. If I can see my situation differently, I can respond in new ways that often renew hope.
- Hope requires waiting. Waiting requires patience. Sorry.

SPARK FIRE

- Fire cranks up the heat through passion, love, vitality, Eros and courage.
- I will need a compelling reason to go on the challenging and unknown journey of change.
- When I act, I act on behalf of who or what I love. Even when I have to fight against something, it is because of what I value and love.
- When I have discipline towards a goal, it is because of my dedication to what I want or care about, which is larger than the annoying task at hand.
- Pleasure feels better than pain. Make the pursuit of pleasure your guide, rather than the avoidance of pain. Nothing is more pleasurable than play.
- Courage is the fire of the heart. Love inspires courage; acting on behalf of what I love requires courage.
- Courage is not the absence of fear, but the willingness to act in spite of it.

BRING AWARENESS underlies all the seven principles.

LISTEN DEEPLY informs all the seven principles.

FIND COMMUNITY supports all the seven principles.

PROCEED INCREMENTALLY strategically builds all the seven principles toward realization.

ALIGN WITH NATURE creates proper relationship and timing for all the seven principles.

HAVE HOPE lifts and inspires all the seven principles.

SPARK FIRE compels and animates all the seven principles for change.

In putting all the Seven Principles for Change together, I'd like to go back to my example of the woman who needed to change her diet and her health profile in order to improve a deteriorating health condition that was moving her toward diabetes. If I were to walk her through the Seven Principles for Change to see how she could get the most understanding and support for her needed changes, it would go like this:

Her journey began when her doctor brought her to a new awareness by giving her the prediabetes diagnosis based on her weight and blood tests. She was impacted by the information. She then went home and raised her own awareness by doing more research, reading information on various medical websites, and checking out books from the library. However, just the information alone—as startling as it was—didn't necessarily motivate her to take the necessary actions of changing her diet, and her lifestyle. For that she would need a compelling reason. That compelling reason was her young children, and her husband. She wanted to remain healthy, active, and vital for her family. Or perhaps she had older family members that already had diabetes. And let's say, one of them did not take care of themselves and suffered medical consequences of painful neuropathy in his feet, and eventually had to have a foot amputated from lack of circulation. This was enough to scare her, but her fear was not what motivated her, it was the love for her family, and her care for them that ultimately would be what motivated her.

When her friends decided to join her on her diet and exercise plan as a way to support her new decisions, they provided a context for positive change. Their support and care helped her hold to her discipline, which was on behalf of feeling better and having greater health. On those days when she was tired and didn't feel like going out to exercise, she'd need to animate more fire, she'd need to get herself actively motivated, reminding herself of her larger goal—and her friends could help. Once she was moving and exercising, it all seemed easier.

She set her goals incrementally. Lose twenty pounds over the next six months. After that, she would assess her situation and lose another twenty pounds. After she lost the initial twenty pounds she would stop smoking. She would have to listen deeply along the way to see whether it would be better for her to stop smoking all at once, taper off, whether or not she would join a program to stop smoking, or try and do it herself.

She also found that taking a meditation class helped her with all her goals. Learning to sense the quality of her breath made her more aware of all the other processes of her body. She was able to feel herself from the inside, and not just from the outside. Her breath work also helped her relax when she was anxious or when she felt overwhelmed by too much change demand going on at one time. In the past, the times when she felt anxious or overwhelmed were the times when she would reach for a cigarette. Being able to listen deeply and understand this connection helped her, eventually, when she was quitting her smoking habit. When she slowed rhythms down through the breath awareness and meditation, she also became more sensitive to sound, taste, touch. She became more aware of the world around her, and enjoyed a stronger relationship with the outdoors. All these were ways she aligned herself with nature to support her for this change.

Once she lost her weight, stopped smoking, and became more active, she felt so much better, overall, that she wanted to share her new awareness with others. She decided that she wanted to make health a more central piece of her life, and so she studied to become a nutritional counselor. She wasn't able to go to school full-time because of her family responsibilities, but she took classes while her children were at school, and eventually graduated and dedicated her life to helping others change theirs. She adapted to her declining health condition by initiating action, incrementally, and eventually went on to inspire change in others. She started by restoring her own health and well-being.

Or let's take the example that Beth Rosales provided for the grassroots change in Richmond, California, in response to the fires at the Chevron refinery there. What the grassroots organizers wanted to do was to create a system of bringing awareness to residents when there was a fire so that they would close up their homes and remain inside away from the toxic effects of the chemical smoke and fumes. Some people first had to have the awareness, and then share the awareness throughout the community via phone trees where people were called and alerted.

In Beth's story, she said there were three different fires with three different strategies for communicating with residents. Each time was an improvement upon the last because they listened to what was needed—what had worked and what had not worked—and made a course correction each time. Each time, there was the hope that more neighbors would be notified and protected. Each time there was the hope that more fires like these would not occur. The compelling reason for the community action was clear: older adults and young children, especially, were at risk for their health and their lives. The strategies involved community members acting on behalf of the community. Beth said firefighters, churches, and activist organizations came together to solve the problem of notification. She also said that many in this community were immigrants who did not speak English so it was important to understand the particular needs of this community in order to serve their needs.

This listening and course-correction approach was an example of proceeding incrementally. Whether incremental action was the intention or not, it was the way the changes unfolded, and it resulted in actions that were effective in protecting the neighbors from direct expose to the toxic smoke.

Toxic smoke from a gasoline refinery is not exactly aligned with nature. So anything on behalf of protecting health will be in alignment with nature. When we can find cleaner sources of energy than burning fossil fuels that will also align us with nature.

What are the examples of the changes in your own life, right now? How can you apply these seven principles to help you find better resources and solutions for the responses to the needed change? If you are in a change that seems to be stuck, first identify the nature of the change you are in, then reflect upon these seven principles. See which ones are present, and which ones could be more present. Bring those in—even if what you bring in is more patience. Once you look at your changing scene, it might just be that you can fully acknowledge that change is indeed happening, only that it's very slow, incremental, and requires more patience. Undoubtedly it also needs more community! I find that true across the board.

As I have begun to share the ideas about ChangeAbility with my own community of friends it is inspiring them to reflect upon their own challenges to change and the ways in which they meet those challenges and opportunities. It immediately sparks discussion as they offer more reflection to me about where they are fixed and where they are fluid in their lives, and what they would like more help with. Above all, I have been told that this is a hopeful and helpful book. I know that is because I am reframing how to think about change, and from reframing, comes hope.

Over the course of writing this book, over the time of digging deeply into understanding the nature of change, I now know so much more than when I began. The process of articulating the nuances of the movement of change, and then to test out my conclusions everywhere I looked, deepened my understanding and confirmed my awareness. Working with the guests' interviews and excerpts caused me to internalize each of their worldviews in order to be able to frame their comments and present them to you. In so doing, I had to learn each of their languages—biology, psychology, spirituality, ecology, prison speak, clay—so that I could better present them to you. The tapestry that is represented in the book is woven through me. I am forever smarter and forever grateful.

In closing, I want to say, don't be afraid of change.

Don't be afraid that things are changing, because indeed they always are.

Be elated about the change itself, yes. Be displeased, sure. Mourn what you have lost. But don't be afraid or surprised that things are changing, it is the way it is.

Change will bring us to the edge of the unknown.

We may thrive; we may die. The cycle of life brings renewal after death. Endings are but transitions to something yet unformed and unseen. Everything in life gives way to something else, eventually.

We live in a time of inescapable, snowballing, complex change. When change comes too fast and overwhelms you: slow it down, and break it down into smaller parts. If change is moving too slowly and discourages you: crank up the heat of passion, or effort, or just love what you love while you have to be patient for its arrival—even if it never comes. Become more flexible in this understanding, and you will become a more willing participant with the movement of change. The open flow of movement feels better than the bound struggle of resistance. Pleasure feels better than pain. Our laughter opens our hearts to new possibilities, and these possibilities become the seeds of hope. Our passions spark them to life and compel us to work on their behalf. Always. It is our true nature and the truth of our human spirit to have hope and work for what we love.

Please, have the courage to face change. Have the playfulness to court it into form. Work for the change you want to see in the world and in the mirror. You have all the assistance you need once you start reaching for it.

Do it now. Don't be afraid. Once you become a ChangeAbility artist, you'll see what I mean.

ChangeAbility = The New Stability

PART THREE

GUEST BIOGRAPHIES

Corinne Bourdeau

360degreecomm.net

Corinne Bourdeau is a social change media producer and marketing director. She is the president and founder of 360 Degree Communications, a boutique entertainment agency specializing in inspirational films and media dedicated to enriching the human spirit. She specializes in publicity, grassroots promotion, and distribution for independent films with a strong focus on environment and social justice. She has brought her innovative expertise to the marketing campaigns of leading films including the Academy Award winners *The Cove* and *Boyhood*, the Sundance Award wining film *Fuel*, indie hit *Bottle Shock*, and the audience pleaser *Buck*. She holds a master's degree in depth psychology and mythology with a focus on cinema and mythology. She is also the author of the forthcoming book, *The Passionate Filmmaker.*

Claire Hope Cummings

clairehopecummings.com
wisdomofplace.org

Claire Hope Cummings MA, JD is an award-winning author, broadcast and print journalist, and environmental lawyer. She is the author of *Uncertain Peril: Genetic Engineering and the Future of Seeds*, which won the American Book Award and the book of the year award from the Society for Economic Botany. Claire has been active in the local food and farming movement in the

San Francisco Bay Area. She brings over three decades of broad experience in agriculture to her work. She has farmed in California and in Vietnam, where she had an organic farm in the Mekong Delta. As a lawyer, Claire has represented and advised environmental and native groups on environmental and cultural preservation throughout the US, helping to found land trusts, representing native groups against development on their lands, and protecting sacred sites. For four years she was an attorney for the United States Department of Agriculture's Office of General Counsel. As a journalist, Claire's stories focus on the environmental and political implications of how we eat, and how food and farming reconnects us to each other and to the places where we live, and the extraordinary knowledge of land based peoples. Claire was food and farming editor for Pacifica Network's flagship public radio station for six years, hosting a weekly radio broadcast. She reported for other public radio networks and PBS television, and produced award-winning radio broadcasts. She writes stories for national environmental magazines, newspapers, and online publications such as *Epicurean*, *Grist*, and *Beacon Broadside*.

Amanda Foulger
amandafoulger.com

Amanda Foulger is a practitioner of shamanism, an ancient system for healing, well-being, guidance, and growth. As a faculty member of the Foundation for Shamanic Studies, she has taught shamanic workshops in California and Colorado for the past thirty years. She has made presentations on core contemporary shamanism for organizations such as the Los Angeles Jung Institute, Yo San University of Oriental Medicine, and the San Fernando Valley Interfaith Council. Additionally, she has participated in special conferences and educational programs at UCLA, the Esalen Institute Work Scholars Program, Churches of Religious Science and Unitarian congregations, and The Mensa Society. She works privately with clients, receiving referrals from psychotherapists, ministers, and healthcare practitioners, and creates personal and group ceremonies and rites of passage.

Ann Gentry

realfood.com

Ann Gentry has spent the past twenty-five years raising the standard of plant-based cooking. As the founder and operating owner of the popular Real Food Daily restaurants in Los Angeles, she has innovated a vegan, organic cuisine that is sophisticated, delicious, and healthy. She became interested in plant-based cuisine in New York City during the eighties. Fusing the essential elements of Eastern macrobiotics with her own American culinary style, she gave birth to her distinct "gourmet whole food cuisine." Ann's recipes have appeared in countless magazines, as well as in her popular cookbooks *Vegan Family Meals* and the *Real Food Daily Cookbook*, and on her cooking show *Naturally Delicious with Ann Gentry*. Ann is the executive chef to *Vegetarian Times* magazine, and appears as guest chef at health centers and expos across the country. She has also taught at the North American Vegetarian Society, Central Market in Texas, and at the World Arts & Cultures program at UCLA.

Amber Gray

restorativeresources.net
traumaresourcesinternational.org

Amber Gray is a licensed psychotherapist, mental health professional, and movement therapist and teacher, working clinically with survivors of organized violence, torture, war, and combat related trauma, ritual abuse, domestic violence, and community violence for over twenty years. She has worked in program development and management with survivors of human rights abuses for almost thirty years. She has training in Somatic Psychology, Dance Movement Therapy, Contemplative Practice, Authentic Movement, Ecopsychology, Somatic Experiencing, EMDR, Trauma-Focused CBT, Parent-Child Psychotherapy, Mindfulness-based Therapies, Yoga, Life Impressions Bodywork, Cranial-Sacral Therapy, and is an Authorized Continuum Movement teacher. Amber provides training worldwide to professionals and paraprofessionals who work with survivors of extreme interpersonal and social trauma and who wish to integrate somatic movement, mindfulness, and creative arts–based therapies into their work. She also works with governmental and nongovernmental organizations around the world, responding to disasters and complex humanitarian emergencies to develop and sustain staff care programs for their teams.

Rachel Lang

rachelclang.com

Rachel Lang has had the gift of intuitive insight since childhood, and for over a decade has been offering intuitive astrology readings, meditation groups, and individual energy healing sessions to an international client base consisting of individuals, small businesses, and corporations. She studied astrology with internationally recognized astrologers and received certification from the American Federation of Astrologers. She is a member of the International Society for Astrological Research, writes regular articles and horoscopes for *The Live Box Magazine*, hosts the weekly astrology radio show *Blissen Up*, teaches workshops, and speaks internationally on spiritual and astrological topics. Rachel is also a marketing consultant, combining astrology with her brilliant marketing skills to create branding and guidance. She holds an MA in Theology, focusing on gender, religion, and justice. Rachel is passionate about social justice and environmental causes.

Robert Litman

thebreatheablebody.com

Robert Litman has guided clients and students for twenty-eight years in the use of movement, breath, and sound as tools for personal growth, restoring healthy breathing rhythms, structural alignment, and efficient body mechanics. He founded The Breathable Body in 2003. He codeveloped the Wellsprings Practitioner Program with Emilie Conrad, founder of Continuum Movement, and taught with her for eighteen years, until her death. He has made many contributions to Continuum's practices, particularly in the sciences, incorporating respiratory physiology, neuroanatomy, and cellular biology. Robert has been a faculty member and head of the Departments of Anatomy and Physiology and Movement Education at the Desert Institute of the Healing Arts Massage School. He teaches the Buteyko Breathing Technique and is as an organizing member, registered educator, and trainer of the Buteyko Breathing Educators Association. He was a preceptor at the

University Of Arizona School Of Integrative Medicine teaching the Buteyko Breathing Technique to visiting doctors for Doctor Andrew Weil for five years. Robert has an advanced certification in the Duggan-French Approach— Somatic Pattern Recognition, which has provided him with hands-on skills to help guide clients' movement and breath education awareness processes. Robert now makes his home on Vashon Island, WA, and offers private sessions, classes, and workshops in movement and breathing worldwide.

Penny Livingston-Stark

regenerativedesign.org

Penny Livingston-Stark is an internationally revered permaculture teacher, designer, and speaker. For twenty-five years she has taught and worked in land management, regenerative design, permaculture development, ecologically sound construction, and design—including natural and nontoxic building—rainwater collection, edible and medicinal plants, diverse field perennial farms, habitat development, watershed restoration, and cohousing communities. She holds a MS in Eco-Social Regeneration and a Diploma in Permaculture Design. In collaboration with Commonweal, a center for health, arts, environment, and justice, Penny comanages Commonweal Garden, a seventeen-acre certified organic farm where she cofounded the Regenerative Design Institute (RDI), a powerful hub of advanced permaculture and leadership training in-depth exploration of regenerative design, cultural mentoring, community building, and nature connection. Penny cocreated the Ecological Design Program and its curriculum at the San Francisco Institute of Architecture, cofounded the West Marin Grower's Group, the West Marin Farmer's Market, and the Community Land Trust Association of Marin. She is a founding member of the Natural Building Colloquium, a national consortium of professional natural house builders. In collaboration with an array of permaculture teachers and Native American instructors, she now leads intensive Peacemaking and Permaculture trainings, and programs for urban youth to connect with the natural world as an experiential platform from which they can act as peacemakers and foster interconnection within their own communities.

Paul Rogat Loeb
paulloeb.org

Paul Rogat Loeb is a renowned writer, speaker, and activist. He has spent forty years researching citizen responsibility and empowerment, asking what makes some people choose lives of social commitment while others abstain. Paul is the author of *Soul Of A Citizen*, which aims to inspire citizen activists, and the anthology of activist achievements *The Impossible Will Take A Little While*. It was named "number three political book of 2004" by the History Channel and the American Book Association, and won the Nautilus Book Award for the Best Social Change Book of the Year. In 2008, Paul founded and coordinated the Campus Election Engagement Project, a national nonpartisan effort that helped five hundred colleges and universities enroll three million students to engage in the election. Loeb also participated in the Department of Education's 2011 roundtable on higher education and civic engagement. He blogs regularly at *Huffington Post*, has written countless articles for major publications, has lectured at hundreds of colleges, universities, and national and international conferences, and has conducted over one thousand TV and radio interviews inspiring the courage to follow your heart and take necessary action on behalf of necessary change.

Camille Maurine
camillemaurine.com

Camille Maurine is a meditation and movement mentor, performing artist and teacher, and the coauthor, along with her husband, Dr. Lorin Roche, of *Meditation Secrets for Women: Discovering Your Passion, Pleasure, and Inner Peace* and *Meditation 24/7*. A dancer versed in the performing and healing arts, she is the creator of kinAesthetics and Moving Theater, a transformative creative process. Camille Maurine's unique approach to inner exploration and creativity integrates the fields of meditation, yoga, dance, and theater. Camille studied improvisational theater at Second City in Chicago. She has trained in modern dance and performed professionally in Chicago, New York, and Santa Fe—also learning a rich array of ethnic dance forms, including classical Indian, Middle Eastern, African, Japanese, and Flamenco. She attended St. Xavier College, DePauw University, and NYU

School of the Arts. Her experience includes four decades of yoga, twelve years as a practitioner of Essential Integration body therapy, and Continuum movement since 1983, as well as Transcendental Meditation, Zen, Tibetan Buddhism, Jungian depth psychology, and dreamwork. She gives talks, performances, and seminars at such places as Esalen Institute, C. G. Jung Institutes, and international conferences on psychology, art, somatics, and spirituality. She offers global teleseminars and teacher trainings in feminine spiritual empowerment and embodiment and travels the world giving workshops and retreats in meditation, movement, and expression.

Rebecca Mark

rebecca@tulane.edu

Rebecca Mark is a writer, poet, and teacher. She is an associate professor of English at Tulane University, and cofounder of Words & Waves, a whole body approach to writing. Rebecca teaches how to move seamlessly from words to movement to drawing and back again, as a way of generating deep creativity and giving birth to the unexpected. Her primary practice is the fluid movement work Continuum, through which the voice and words emerge. She has been teaching this work for nearly thirty years with Continuum founder Emilie Conrad. As a scholar, Rebecca's research addresses Southern writing and cultural representations of trauma. Her books include *The Dragon's Blood: Feminist Intertexuality in Eudora Welty's Fiction* and *Ersatz America: Hidden Traces, Graphic Texts, and the Mending of Democracy*. She was a founding director of the Newton College Institute in 2006, a founding member of the Deep South Regional Humanities Center, and a recipient of the Mississippi Public Humanities Award as well as many others. Most recently, she was awarded the Suzanne and Stephen Weiss Presidential Fellow Award for Excellence in Undergraduate Teaching, Tulane University 2015. She is currently working on a second book on Eudora Welty titled *A Private Address: The Radical Welty*, and a book of original poetry and art work, *Owl Eyes*.

Amy McEachern
creativemoving.com

Amy McEachern is a professional mover and organizer. She has a unique gift for understanding spatial relationships, logic, and the human condition. For over two decades, she has been helping hundreds of people navigate not only their relocations, but the life transitions that so often go along with them. She is the founder and owner of Creative Moving and Organizing—formerly Creative Order—a premier Organizing and Move Coordinating Company which grew to an all-women crew of seventeen packers/organizers and a client base that included some of the biggest players in Hollywood. Her company became known as the "Hand-holders of the Moving Industry." She is part psychologist, part tactician, and part comedienne as she walks clients through every part of moving from one home to another. Amy is a perfect example of how to make a living doing what you love. She combines service that rivals internationally renowned day spas, support and comfort previously provided only by a best friend, and efficiency that would make a military general proud.

Deena Metzger
deenametzger.net

Deena Metzger is a poet, novelist, essayist, storyteller, teacher, healer, and medicine woman who has taught and counseled for over forty years, in the process of which she has developed therapies which creatively address life threatening diseases; spiritual and emotional crises; and community, political, and environmental disintegration. Deena has spent a lifetime investigating story as a form of knowing and healing. She conducts training groups on the spiritual, creative, political, and ethical aspects of healing and peacemaking—individual, community, and global—drawing deeply on alliance with spirit, indigenous teachings, and the many wisdom traditions. One focus is on uniting Western medical ways with indigenous medicine traditions. With writer/healer Michael Ortiz Hill she has introduced the concept of Daré, meaning Council, to North America. The Topanga Daré relies on Council, alliance with Spirit and the natural world, ancestor work, indigenous and wisdom traditions and teachings, music healing, dream telling, divination, kinship, and storytelling to achieve personal transformation, community healing, and social change.

She is the author of many books, including most recently, the novels *La Negra y Blanca* (2012 PEN Oakland Josephine Miles Award for Excellence in Literature), *Feral*; *Ruin and Beauty: New and Selected Poems*; *From Grief Into Vision: A Council*; *Doors: A Fiction for Jazz Horn*; *Entering the Ghost River: Meditations on the Theory and Practice of Healing*; *The Other Hand; What Dinah Thought*; *Tree: Essays and Pieces*; *The Woman Who Slept With Men to Take the War Out of Them*; and *Writing For Your Life*.

Beth Rosales

bethrosales1@gmail.com

Beth Rosales is a Senior Philanthropic Advisor and has worked in philanthropy for more than thirty-five years in various capacities ranging from grant manager to programs officer to CEO at progressive foundations including Vanguard Public Foundation, Funding Exchange, Tides, Women's Foundation of California, Marguerite Casey Foundation, and The Lia Fund. Over the years, Beth has made it a priority to move money toward strengthening social justice movements across the nation. She is widely known for her deep dedication, and highly regarded for her wealth of experience, contacts, and understanding in the area of progressive social change philanthropy. She also has served on the board of Asian Health Services, a community clinic that serves low-income families in Oakland.

Harvey Ruderian

harveyruderian@gmail.com

Harvey Ruderian is a master of structural bodywork and biodynamic cranial sacral bodywork. Using his hands and awareness, he guides his clients into balance and release from deep-set holding patterns cause by structural compensation, stress, illness, belief, and simply the way they live their lives and how they move their bodies. In 1970, Harvey dropped out of law school and began pursuing a personal healing odyssey that redefined his world perspective. After experiencing a series of transformational awakenings, Harvey enrolled in massage school and began his lifelong professional journey as a student and practitioner of the healing arts. One of the early Rolfers and Aston Patterning Practitioners, Harvey has trained with, and then taught with, all these bodywork pioneers: Ida Rolf, Judith Aston, John Upledger, Hugh Milne, and Jean Pierre-Barral. Harvey has integrated the deep psychological work of the human potential movement into his work with his hands. Harvey lives in Malibu with his wife, pets, and fruit trees and has a full private practice in Santa Monica, California.

James Stark

regenerativedesign.org

James Stark, MA, FES, is the codirector of the Regenerative Design Institute at Commonweal (RDI). He cofounded and currently codirects the Ecology of Leadership and the Ecology of Awakening programs. James has committed his life to exploring how we—ourselves, our communities, and our species— might move into harmony with the natural world. As a community organizer in Marin County, James cofounded the following organizations: West Marin Growers group; KWMR radio, a public voice for West Marin residents; and CLAM, a community land trust association. He has served on many boards and advisory committees regarding permaculture and waste. Like the natural systems and patterns that guide permaculture, his work now is focused on helping others to lead from the inside out and source their lives from deep nature connection. James holds a master's degree in Spiritual Psychology from the University of Santa Monica. He has presented at conferences around the world.

Michael Stocker

ocr.org

Michael Stocker is an acoustician, naturalist, and musician. He has written and spoken about ocean bioacoustics internationally since 1992, presenting as the subject matter expert in national and regional hearings, national and international television, radio and news publications, museums, schools and universities, and court testimonies and legal briefs defending the environment against dangers of human-generated ocean noise. He is the founding director of Ocean Conservation Research (OCR), a scientific research and policy development organization focused on understanding the impacts of and finding solutions to the growing problem of underwater noise pollution. His work with OCR included many written responses to US Navy Environmental Impact Statements and ocean noise–focused text in many pieces of national ocean protection legislation including Barbara Boxer's National Ocean Protection Act and the California Ocean Action Plan. This work garnered Michael the 2006 Excellence in Board Leadership award from the Marin County Center for Nonprofit and Volunteer Leadership. Michael is the author of the book *Hear Where We Are: Sound, Ecology, and Sense of Place,* a popular science book that explores the effects that sound and sound perception have on our sense of self, community, and surroundings.

Fred Sugerman

medicinedance.wordpress.com

Fred Sugerman is a movement artist, educator, professional actor, and workshop facilitator. Through his company, Medicine Dance, in Los Angeles, California, he offers classes, workshops, theatrical events, and private work in the art of mindfulness and movement exploration, offering a body-based inquiry into living fully and surviving gracefully. Originally a professional dancer and actor, with Los Angeles and New York credits in theater, film, and television, Fred's background includes extensive training in improvisation, emotional release, sense memory, natural sound and voice production, classical and modern dance, Alexander Technique, the Dance Alive system, and various forms of relaxation. His expertise lies in creating a space of safety and permission that fosters presence in movement. His mission is to help people affect real change by allowing full-body change within themselves— which includes the mind, spirit, and the heart.

Jacques Verduin

insight-out.org

Jacques Verduin, MA Somatic Psychology, is the founder and director of Insight-Out, a nonprofit organization whose mission is to turn violence and suffering into opportunities for healing and learning for prisoners and challenged youth. Jacques has been a leader and innovator in the field of rehabilitation for prisoners since 1997, and an expert on violence prevention, emotional intelligence, restorative justice, and mindfulness. Jacques created and runs Guiding Rage Into Power (GRIP), a deeply transformational program for inmates. He founded and directed the Insight Prison Project, which under his leadership produced the VOEG program and spun off the Prison Mindfulness Initiative, the Prison Yoga Project, the Insight Garden Project, among other efforts—all of which are actively replicating. He is a consultant to the US State Department, and he travels internationally to train professionals. Jacques has received several prestigious awards for community leadership, as well as signed commendations from government officials. He holds trainings and presentations internationally, teaching the connections between the specific predicament of incarceration and the general suffering of the human condition. His perspective draws from working in-depth with victims and offenders, rival gangs, and racial factions, and articulates a methodology that helps transcend the "us and them" fallacy.

Tom Verner & Janet Fredericks

magicianswithoutborders.com
janetfredericksstudio.com

Since 2002, Magicians Without Borders has traveled to over thirty countries using magic to entertain, educate, and empower. By UN estimates they have entertained over 500,000 of the most forgotten people in the world—mostly refugees and orphans living in desperate, difficult, and often war-torn parts of the world. They are also educating children in El Salvador, India, and Colombia to become magicians, empowering these youth to develop self-confidence, self-esteem, discipline, focus, and a sense of personal power. They also perform in Veterans Administration hospitals around the United States, and train Warrior Wizards to perform magic for veterans and their families.

Tom Verner is the Founder of Magicians Without Borders, a psychology professor of thirty-five years, and an avid lover of magic. Tom left teaching to carry out this dream of Magicians Without Borders.

Janet Fredericks is the cofounder of Magicians Without Borders and performs as the quiet assistant, LeFluer. Janet has been a Vermont fine artist for over twenty years. She is a Vermont Council on the Arts and New England Foundation for the Arts Fellowship recipient. Janet exhibits internationally and is in many corporate and private collections. Her current work expresses her interest in her natural environment. With wonderment at nature's intelligence, interconnectedness and complexities, Fredericks' drawings and paintings are at once maps and conversations, tracings of experience of a deeper communion that begins with her reverent awareness of her native surroundings.

John Weeks

theintegratorblog.com

John Weeks is a writer, organizer, executive, and consultant in the field of integrative health and medicine. In 2014, he received a Lifetime Achievement Living Tribute Award from three prominent consortia in the field for his three decades of work. Known as "The Integrator," John has helped organize the most significant multidisciplinary collaborative forum among disciplines and stakeholders nationally and in Canada, linking leaders of integrative healthcare organizations and businesses on key policy, economic, and academic issues. Among his work was cofounding and servicing for eight years as executive director of the Academic Consortium for Complementary and Alternative Health Care, the mission of which is to integrate complementary and alternative medicine professions with mainstream medical training, practice, and policy. He is the publisher and editor of *The Integrator Blog News & Reports*, linking leaders of these organizations and business on key policy, economic, and academic issues. He has written hundreds of columns, research papers, and articles on integrative health topics. As a consultant in this arena, John has worked with multiple hospitals, professional organizations, insurers, and government and quasi-governmental agencies at the local, state, national, and international level. He is particularly proud of his service on two of the four working groups that led to the WHO 2014-2023 Traditional Medicine Strategy. He has been granted honorary doctorates by four institutions. John is based principally in Seattle, Washington.

Jackie Welch Schlicher
visionsmanifest.com

Jackie Welch Schlicher is a performance artist—an actor, singer, writer, director, voice-over talent—as well as a ceramicist and life coach. She believes in the power of creativity, the gift of humor, and the joy of living passionately and fully. She has worked for thirty years in theater as a professional actor and director, as well as for film and television. Jackie is known for her sharp depth and dry comedic improvisational theater skills. Since 2000, Jackie has brought her years of experience in the creative arts to help others to cultivate their own creativity as a personal development coach and owner of Visions Manifest Coaching. She has a BA in Psychology from Duke University, is a certified neurolinguistic programming coach, is ACC Certified, is a Member of the International Coach Federation, and served as the 2010 Board President of Tennessee Coaches Alliance. Currently, her passion is ceramics. She shows and shares her ceramics through her studio, Wildhair Pottery.

Adam Wolpert
adamwolpert.com
oaec.org

Adam Wolpert is a painter, teacher, facilitator, and permaculturist. He cofounded the Occidental Arts & Ecology Center in Occidental, California, bringing together permaculture, art, and whole systems thinking. In addition to its wide array of vital permaculture programs and courses, founding members of OAEC live in an intentional community that serves as a model for integrated living: life, work, and land. He has lived in communities for over thirty years and, since 1996, has cofacilitated OAEC's Starting and Sustaining Intentional Communities course. He leads workshops in group process and facilitation and has worked as a facilitator and organizational consultant with nonprofits, communities, and foundations since 1999. As a painter, Adam draws his inspiration from his understanding of relationships in nature and his own relationship to nature. He investigates movement, balance, and cycle, and a subtle distinction between representational and abstract art. Adam completed an MFA at UC San Diego, and trained in classical realism at Studio Cecil-Graves in Florence, Italy. He has had major gallery representation since 1988, including many solo exhibitions and group shows throughout California. He also teaches art to adults and has published and presented on the subject of Art and Ecology.

DONNY AND URSULA SAVE THE WORLD: AN EXCERPT

Rebels and lovers are united by the same courageous heart.

Chapter 4: Ursula Has an Idea

URSULA SAT UPRIGHT IN BED THAT next morning and knew, like she had never known, that she must save our food.

It was as clear to her as the water in Kitty Boy's dish how she would do it.

The party last night had gone late; and Ursula was drinking champagne, of all things, toasting some little secret she was keeping to herself. To her surprise, Donny had showed up, too. Well, it shouldn't have come as too much of a surprise since this was where she'd first met him. She felt awkward seeing him, at first. She felt revealed. This new little secret of hers would remain behind tight lips, that's for sure. But the champagne loosened her conversation with him about other things.

He tried to hold back the surly, sarcastic tone that seemed to always be his fallback with the women he had formerly known. It was his best protection against whatever they might throw at him. Instead, he drank a lot, which was no surprise for him, but the surprise was that even with the recent days of renewed food debauchery he had indulged in since he last saw her, all that cleansing had wrecked his capacity for alcohol.

He was higher than a kite, and she was only one more drink away from passing out. Of the two of them, he was used to driving under all kinds of influences, so he drove her home. He offered to stay the night on the couch in the living room and drive her to her car in the morning. Sweet.

"Donny," she whispered as she shook him awake in the early morning. He was still on the couch, burrowed into the fluffy down quilt and pillows she'd laid out for him. "How much money do you have? We have to go to the store."

"I only need coffee," he muttered. He turned with a moan, and buried his head deeper beneath the covers. She saw he was not going anywhere.

"Then give me your keys."

"In my pants," Donny said, starting to come to. "Give me a minute, I'll go with you."

"Never mind." She grabbed his keys from his pocket, threw on a t-shirt and some jeans, tied a scarf in her crazy hair, and slammed the door behind her.

•

THE CLERK AT THE Whole Foods was preparing to open. Ursula pressed her face to the glass door. She pointed at her watch and made a pleading face at the guy. He tried to ignore her. At 8:02 when he finally opened, she hissed, "two minutes late," grabbed a cart, and pushed right past him. This being early fall, she went right to the gardening section where the revolving rack still held packets of vegetable and flower seeds. She took all the ones labeled organic, putting back the brussels sprouts because she didn't really like brussels sprouts—then reconsidered for the sake of others, and took them anyway.

She then went through the produce section and bought anything that was a pod surrounding a pea, or a bean that could be sprouted and planted.

In the parking lot, she opened the trunk and was overcome by the odor of sweaty socks and a half eaten liverwurst sandwich that Donny had hastily tossed in while he was cleaning his car before Ursula rode with him. She put her groceries on the back seat.

That entire morning, Ursula went from health food store to health food store, from hardware store to garden supply shop, buying up all the seeds she could find. She put all the charges on her VISA card.

•

HERE'S A QUESTION. How do we know when it's time to act? What inner alarm clock goes off inside, and how many times do we press the snooze button and roll over before we actually open our eyes? At least three, that's the average. That's also how many attempts it takes to stop smoking, according to statistics, though in Donny's case, more.

M. Earth has set it so animals get their alarms from the natural world. A change in the weather or the position of the sun tells them it's time to mate, lay eggs, and build nests. The appearance or disappearance of a food source can start the chain reaction to expand or reduce the population.

Perhaps it was the change in the food source that triggered Ursula to finally take action. This was not her first impulse, but it was her first step into activism. Perhaps one awakening leads to another and follows its own chain. There ought to be a warning label.

•

BY 10:00 A.M. DONNY was curious. By noon he was hungry and getting pissed off. Where was that coffee? By 3:00 he was convinced she had stolen his car and had been planning this for weeks. And by nightfall, when she returned with 1,024 packets of seeds and miscellaneous beans in their shells, Donny was relieved.

She would explain later. Right now she needed his help bringing all the bags inside. Every inch of the car, including the smelly trunk, which she had completely emptied of its previous contents, was filled with bags of seeds.

She planted a big kiss on his lips. It took him by surprise, and he loved surprises. And like that, he was hooked, once again. It's amazing what a man will do for a woman with only the smallest encouragement. And that's good, because the next thing he did for this woman was…

Chapter 18: Earth: It Helps to Take the Overview

M. Earth's response to all this was less of a rise than you might think. She's seen it all before. Oh, maybe not this, where an entire species of "intelligent" life plots to annihilate itself—but she's seen so many come and go. She can't get attached. Otherwise she'd be crying all the damned time.

M. Earth has learned to take in the Big Picture with the necessary indifference that comes from too many disappointments. The closest we humans can get to the Big Picture is to get on Google Earth from a satellite, and even then we can't really comprehend the multiplicity of interplay that takes place in a given moment. But M. Earth always has her finger on the pulse... the pulse of creation, the pulse of destruction, and the pulse of extinction.

Yeah, that one. Where entire life forms and landforms disappear. Gone, done. Sorry, fella, your turn is over. It's partly her way of clearing the decks from time to time; partly this sort of mixing it up she likes to do. But there's a recognizable rhythm to these pulses of extinction—at intervals of say, 3 million years or so—if anyone were around long enough to take notes.

Ursula used to have a globe that showed the Earth as it once was: Pangaea.

At one time, about the time the first seeds appeared, all we had was Pangaea—one enormous continent surrounded by one single ocean. It was the conglomeration of all the continents of the northern and southern hemispheres together before they separated and drifted out into the continents we now stand on today. That took a while. About 100 million years.

To M. Earth, that's just like waiting for the bus.

If you saw it drawn out, as the continents split off from each other and drifted apart, they looked like bodies that had been spooning each other, holding that memory like sleeping lovers do when they separate into their day.

The continental plates are still moving. They shift at the rate toenails grow. That could seem long or short to you, depending on how often you need a pedicure.

Right now, new continents are forming that don't yet appear on one of Ursula's globes. The Northern Pacific Gyre, for instance. A landmass of garbage and plastic debris the size of Texas floating out there in the Pacific, collected together in one spot by the swirling current. It's exciting. Only problem is the whole damned thing is toxic, and can't support a speck of life. At least not yet. Give it time. M. Earth is very clever.

She'll come up with enough biodiversity to take hold and populate that plastic land through symbiotic relationships and odd pairings. Perhaps some of the species that are disappearing from our more conventional continents might have a better shot on the plastic.

One difference between humans and M. Earth is that we have such a short attention span, and can't stand to wait. In the Late Devonian Period, a wiping out of species took place over 1-15 million years. In the Late Petroleum Period, we're trying to go for it in one giant POP. It's what the AgriNu folks are betting on. The Ultimate Ejaculation.

M. Earth, like all good mothers, has infinite patience for the childish behavior of her offspring. She says… "I can wait." She's shown she can.

Here's the thing though—it's just not a big deal for her. Regardless of what the humans do, M. Earth Herself will be just fine. There's always some form of life that will adapt and thrive under any given condition, lying in wait for their turn at bat. They may not even know they've been played yet. And she understands, as a default, she can simply back up a bit to a far earlier time—say like 365 million years earlier—start the whole damned thing over again, and give some rookie a try.

Chapter 43: Road Trip

Not meaning any disrespect to Mother Earth—her wisdom or her rhythms—but if there were any chance Ursula could play some small part in moving things along, well then, she would. Even a speck can plant a few seeds, if they're small enough.

She now had a huge stockpile of organic seeds at home. She could get them started, but… she'd just have to leave it up to the plants to take over from there, and spread themselves. She'd seen it was possible. The occasions when she would pass by her earlier guerilla gardens, haphazardly planted near her office, she took pride in how yet more new plants were growing up among the weeds.

Donny went along with all this. It was a way to make her happy. He saw that by some miracle he, once again, had a foot in the door. Given a second chance, he would not blow it! He decided he'd rather dig dirt than drink the green drinks, but he'd rather make hot monkey love than either of those. Duh. Of course, they were just friends. Of course… but that could change.

Ursula knew Donny was fond of road trips, so she let him drive. The two of them headed out each night, in a different direction, from her place in West Hollywood. Sometimes a quick round trip, sometimes they would go so far as to stay overnight in a cheap motel. As friends. Planting by the roadside, or in a park, or in some cases, someone's front yard, these seeds would soon produce chemical free, modification free, wholesome, healthy food.

And by doing this, Donny and Ursula had become rebels.

DEFINED TERMS

ChangeAbility: the ability to effectively navigate change with ease.

Navigating Change: how I meet and move with any and all change. This includes my responses, motivations, strategies, feedback, and course corrections.

Moving with Change: understanding that change is a constant movement, this is how we align with the ongoing, evolving movement of change for greater ChangeAbility.

Initiating Change: creating something new.

Inspiring Change: causing yourself or others to want to make change, meet change, or to endure the challenges that change can bring.

Adapting to Change: recognizing that a change is occurring and finding flexible and appropriate response in order to accommodate change, in order to thrive.

Resistance: any obstacle, either internal or external, that impedes the flow of the movement of change.

Healing: restoring the organism—any organism—to wholeness. Seeking to repair, restore, or renew that which has been fractured, separated, or injured.

Restoration: returning to wholeness.

The Seven Principles for Change: the seven principles that are necessary for all change, whether it is initiated, inspired, or adapted change. These principles are interdependent and are present in all change scenarios.

Bring Awareness: any change navigation begins with the awareness of the nature of the change I am in, or the particular nature of the need for change.

Listen Deeply: gathering information and feedback from my environment without judgment or assumption. Using genuine inquiry as a way to develop creative, effective response for change navigation.

Find Community: finding support for change in all its many forms: friends, allies, experts, like-minded connectors. Creating supportive contexts that allows change to occur.

Proceed Incrementally: breaking down any larger change or task into smaller achievable increments that allow for course correction as you move with change.

Align with Nature: utilizing the cycles, rhythms, and characteristics of nature in order to facilitate change that contains more ease and less resistance. How does nature do it?

Have Hope: the dream of possibility that change can happen.

Spark Fire: sustains hope and provides the compelling reason why I am willing to navigate this change. Includes: love, passion, Eros, vitality, courage, pleasure, and play.

Change-maker: someone who is recognized as initiating change, usually on a large, innovative, and sustained scale.

Change-rider: like a skilled surfer, one who is adept at riding the waves of change as they come.

Awakener: a teacher, leader, speaker, or life-example. One who brings awareness and lifts others to inspire them towards desired or necessary change.

ACKNOWLEDGMENTS

THOUGH READERS OFTEN ASSUME THAT A book is written as a singular and solitary process by the author, it actually requires a community of talented and dedicated allies—especially a book that weaves in a community of voices, and is preaching Find Community. I have been well guided and supported by a number of amazing individuals in developing the ideas and the presentation of this book to you.

First and foremost, I want to thank Emma Destrubé for contributing to every aspect of this book: organizing material, reading, commenting, and creating marketing materials and social media. Her constant encouragement and her perspective have been essential to the formation of the book. She and I share a common field of concern and understanding that is reflected on these pages. She is an amazing artist in her own right, and I look forward to being able to return the favor on her creative endeavors.

Immense appreciation goes to Tyson Cornell of Rare Bird Books—a most nurturing and creative collaborator and publisher—for inspiring the idea for this book, as well as inspiring and producing the *Passing 4 Normal Podcast*. With his guidance, expertise, and innovative spirit, he is opening my work in new, exciting, and successful directions. I thank Alice Marsh-Elmer for her thoughtful, artful, innovative design navigations, and to the keen and cool team at Rare Bird Books whose efforts will be ongoing well beyond this writing. I have excitement and appreciation for Lisa Weinert of Archer Lit for this book journey we have begun. And thanks to Heather Huzovic, Julia Callahan, Winona Leon, and the entire team at Rare Bird and Archer for their assistance in bringing this book to fruition.

Rachel Lang was the marketing mastermind behind the *Donny and Ursula Save the World* journey. Her contributions to that "movement" were clever, enlightened, and they enhanced every aspect of the way that book reached out to its audience. The podcast and this book are direct carryovers from our efforts together. She is now putting her touch on *ChangeAbility*, and I am so delightfully grateful for all she contributes through her own understanding and expertise with the movement of change.

Heartfelt thanks to my posse of writer-support and life-support: Ann Sheree Greenbaum, Loree Gold, Mary Jane Roberts, Clarke Gallivan, Lesley MacKinnon, and Fernando Mata. Additionally, I thank Patricia Childs for her sensitive insight, editorial eye, and for always having my back as the last eyes on the manuscript. Thank you also to Reyna Monterroso for helping to free my time to attend the immersions that the writing process requires, and to my daughter, Sophie Aaron, for her patience and understanding while I disappear into internal worlds.

And, of course, my deep appreciation extends to all the guests on the podcast for their time, permission, and support in allowing me to use their experience with the movement of change in order to assist you with yours. This book is an intricate weaving of voices, interests, and understanding. I have created a community from the innovators in this book, or more accurately, in my knowing each of these people and deeply considering their wise and well-earned point of views, they have created a community *inside of me*—forming me, and allowing me to form the ideas conveyed on these pages. It is an honor to know them and to support the work they do in the world through this book. I am forever changed by each of them.

And finally, my deep gratitude goes to Emilie Conrad, no longer dancing in this world. Her vision and insight about the inherent mutability of form informs all of my thinking. I would not have known how to write this book, let alone have known how to navigate change, without her guidance and her love.

ABOUT THE AUTHOR

SHARON WEIL HAS LONG BEEN ENGAGED in the conversation about courage and change as an author, activist, award-winning filmmaker, and somatic educator. She is the author of *Donny and Ursula Save the World*, a political, romantic-mishap adventure, and the host of the podcast *Passing 4 Normal: Conversations with Authors, Artists, Activists, and Awakeners about Seeding Change in the World.*

Visit her at sharonweilauthor.com